A Study of Scarletts

A Study of Scarletts

Scarlett O'Hara and Her Literary Daughters

Margaret Donovan Bauer

The University of South Carolina Press

Published by the University of South Carolina Press
Columbia, South Carolina 29208

www.sc.edu/uscpress

Manufactured in the United States of America

23 22 21 19 18 17 16 15 14 10 9 8 7 6 5 4 3 2 1

Library of Congress Cataloging-in-Publication Data

Bauer, Margaret Donovan, 1963–
A study of Scarletts : Scarlett O'Hara and her literary daughters / Margaret Donovan Bauer.
pages cm.
Includes bibliographical references and index.
ISBN 978-1-61117-373-4 (hardbound : alk. paper) — ISBN 978-1-61117-374-1 (ebook)
1. Mitchell, Margaret, 1900–1949. Gone with the wind. 2. Frazier, Charles, 1950– Cold Mountain. 3. Glasgow, Ellen Anderson Gholson, 1873–1945 Barren ground. 4. Morrison, Toni. Sula. 5. Meads, Kat, 1951– Invented life of Kitty Duncan (Benedict Roberts Duncan) 6. O'Hara, Scarlett (Fictitious character) 7. Women in literature. 8. Social role in literature. 9. Man-woman relationships in literature. 10. Female friendship in literature. I. Title. II. Title: Scarlett O'Hara and her literary daughters.
PS3525.I972G677 2014
813'.52—dc23

2014004294

This book was printed on recycled paper with 30 percent postconsumer waste content.

This book is for the fabulous Starlight women.

"What should I wish for? Don't say a boyfriend. . . . If you say a boyfriend then the world will shrink so small that only toads will be satisfied to live and dream here."

Marianne Gingher, *"Teen Angel" and Other Stories of Wayward Love*

Contents

Acknowledgments

An early version of chapter three was published (with the same title) in *Ellen Glasgow: New Perspectives* (Knoxville: University of Tennessee Press, 1995) and is reprinted here with permission. More material in that chapter is also drawn from an article I created out of material cut from that essay and published as "Echoes of *Barren Ground* in *Gone with the Wind:* A P[re]. S[cript]." in the *Ellen Glasgow Newsletter* 29 (1992).

Several East Carolina University students served as my research assistants during this book's development, and I thank the ECU Department of English for graduate research assistantships for Debbie Shoop, Maggie Rogers, and Cheryl Scott to work on this project; the ECU Honors Program (now College) for assigning Ashley Arens as an undergraduate intern for this project; and ECU's Office of Undergraduate Research for awarding Rachel Ward a research grant to help me prepare the final manuscript. And of course, I thank all of these former students for their contributions.

My colleague and friend Randall Martoccia also provided useful feedback on the *Cold Mountain* chapter, and I thank him for taking so much time with it. I appreciate too the time I spent with writers Charles Frazier and Kat Meads talking to them about their books.

I thank the readers of the original manuscript submitted to the University of South Carolina Press, who recognized the value of this book and whose revision suggestions were invaluable—particularly the big-picture questions that helped me to figure out what it all means. Thanks, too, to the University of South Carolina Press editors, particularly Jim Denton, and copyeditors. I also appreciate the fine work of my indexer, Bob Tompkins. And I thank Martha Cook, who stepped in for my late mentor to read the "semifinal" manuscript.

I remember here and am forever grateful to Dorothy M. Scura, my mentor, who made me read *Gone with the Wind.* I acknowledge too the support I have always received from my father, Carl W. Bauer, who did not set limits on his daughters' ambitions, and from my mother, Jane Colvin Desonier, who loves me for who I am. I appreciate Andrew Morehead, who does not fear strong women, for his patience and good humor during the many hours I work. And to those fabulous Starlight women, thank you for being here and for your friendship, love, and acceptance. I am truly blessed.

List of Abbreviations

BG *Barren Ground,* by Ellen Glasgow
CM *Cold Mountain,* by Charles Frazier
GW *Gone with the Wind,* by Margaret Mitchell
KD *The Invented Life of Kitty Duncan (Benedict Roberts Duncan),* by Kat Meads
S *Sula,* by Toni Morrison

Introduction

> "Like the interpretation of dreams, the interpretation of an aesthetic object is motivated not by a wish to know the artist's intention . . . but by the desire to create knowledge on one's own behalf and on behalf of one's community from the subjective experience of the work of art."
>
> David Bleich, *Subjective Criticism* (93)

> "Almost every reader will well remember a book from childhood, the circumstance of its reading, and the atmosphere it represented in his mind. Although it is probably not possible to recover original historical circumstances, if the memory of such events has lasted, such residues have important truth value and demonstrable relevance to current, conscious tastes."
>
> David Bleich, *Subjective Criticism* (154)

I well remember my first viewing of the movie *Gone with the Wind* with my eighth-grade class in the mid-1970s. Our history teacher took us to see the movie on the big screen as it made its last rounds in theaters before going to cable. I was so disturbed by the movie's ending, Rhett leaving Scarlett just when she finally realizes she loves him, that I came home and read the last few pages of my mother's copy of the novel in search of a less troubling conclusion. I didn't find such comfort in the novel's closing pages, so I didn't read the novel. I did see the movie again a few times over the ensuing decade and a half and continued to be crushed by Rhett's desertion of Scarlett. Then as we discussed my doctoral exams, my advisor mentioned this novel, which I confessed to never having read. "Well, you certainly need to do so before your exams," she replied. I tried to explain the "trauma" that made this novel anathema to me, but she would have none of it and reminded me that since I was taking the very first doctoral exam on southern literature that the University of Tennessee would give, I simply had to read this southern literary phenomenon—and she added that she would be certain there was a question that could not be answered by familiarity with the movie:

"I'll ask about Will Benteen."

"Who's Will Benteen?"

"Read the novel."

So I read it—and was devastated again by its ending—and then read it again, wrote about it, and continued to return to it over the years, first, compelled to find a happy ending for Scarlett, and then, looking for evidence with which to defend her against her critics.

My focus in this study is on the character Scarlett O'Hara. I do not spend much time defending the rest of the novel. Others have addressed the issue of its historical accuracy, the extent to which it perpetuates plantation mythology, and its depiction of African American characters. Beyond what follows in this introduction, these issues will come up within this study only as they are relevant to the discussion of Scarlett. Here I will repeat and expand on my answer to a question posed to me in an interview on the occasion of the seventy-fifth anniversary of the novel *Gone with the Wind:* "The most common criticisms of the book are that it romanticizes the Old South and that it uses racist stereotypes. How do you respond to those criticisms?" (SSSL).* I noted in my answer that the novel is not romantic from the woman's perspective either. Recall the tableau Scarlett observes during the Wilkes picnic, a scene left out of the movie, as it requires Scarlett's musings on what she sees (and the narrator's musings on what Scarlett misses):

> Under the arbor sat the married women, their dark dresses decorous notes in the surrounding color and gaiety. Matrons, regardless of their

* The following response to this question largely repeats my interview response with some rephrasing and expansion. To avoid the possible confusion regarding who I am quoting when I quote myself from that interview, I have dropped quotation marks from the parts of my response that I reuse here.

> ages, always grouped together apart from the bright-eyed girls, beaux and laughter, for there were no married belles in the South. From Grandma Fontaine, who was belching frankly with the privilege of her age, to seventeen-year-old Alice Munroe, struggling against the nausea of a first pregnancy, they had their heads together in the endless genealogical and obstetrical discussions that made such gatherings very pleasant and instructive affairs.
>
> Casting contemptuous glances at them, Scarlett thought that they looked like a clump of fat crows. Married women never had any fun. It did not occur to her that if she married Ashley she would automatically be relegated to arbors and front parlors with staid matrons in dull silks, as staid and dull as they and not a part of the fun and frolicking. Like most girls, her imagination carried her just as far as the altar and no further. (*GW* 100–101)

Over half a century before Elizabeth Fox-Genovese's book *Within the Plantation Household,* Mitchell had shown with the description of Ellen O'Hara's numerous duties and responsibilities at Tara that the life of a plantation owner's wife "was not easy, nor was it happy, but she did not expect life to be easy, and, if it was not happy, that was woman's lot. It was a man's world, and she accepted it as such" (*GW* 58). While Ellen works herself to an early death, stoically accepting her lot in life, Gerald O'Hara does not seem to do much work at all, his overseer handling the kind of outdoor responsibilities that would parallel what Ellen takes charge of indoors. *A Study of Scarletts* celebrates the daughter of Ellen O'Hara who refused to accept a predetermined role for women that would set such limits on her that she would find her life so dull and burdensome that an early death might not be unwelcome.

Regarding the "racist stereotypes" in the novel, I responded to the interviewer that these are, of course, undeniable. Mitchell employed the tropes of her day, as Mark Twain does in using the term "nigger" in *Adventures of Huckleberry Finn.* When the story emerged in the news that NewSouth Books was publishing an edition in which this and other offensive words would be excised from Twain's classic, I noted to a reporter from a local television station that such a revision seemed an effort to revise history in order to avoid difficult conversations. I believe that it is important for the current generation of readers, who have always known that the term "nigger" is offensive, to see reflected in the diction of such books how people in earlier generations, including generations much more recent than Scarlett's and Huck's, and including people from so-called polite company, regularly and casually employ the term to refer to any African American. One does not defend the ignorance of the prejudiced, racist heritage that influenced Mitchell's descriptions of African Americans.

Writing about Charles Frazier's few references to the institution of slavery in *Cold Mountain,* John Crutchfield notes that "Inman is no abolitionist, much less an enlightened egalitarian. Nor is Ada. Slavery is, *for them,* simply a fact of the world they live in, and primarily, it would seem, an economic and social issue rather than a moral one. In this they are perhaps representative of white people in that historical time and place." Crutchfield notes that "Frazier does no more with the *issue of slavery* than his story requires. It does not, for him, become an ideological point" (*"AppalJ"* 338). So too will race issues factor into my study only as they relate to my focus on Mitchell's novel, which is to defend and explain the behavior of Scarlett O'Hara, whose character is given short shrift in the movie's abridgement of the novel. My study traces Scarlett's development in the course of events in the novel (and the development of other "Scarletts" in their stories). One detail about Scarlett worth calling to readers' attention is that she is as critical of white Melanie as she is of black Prissy, albeit for different reasons. She slaps Prissy, but so too does she slap her own (white) sister at another point in the novel. She tries to manipulate Mammy, yes—just as she manipulates her father. J. E. Smyth observes that Scarlett's egalitarian treatment of people is lost by cutting Dilcey, as well as poor white Will Benteen, from the film adaptation of the novel. Smyth recognizes that the motive for reducing the number of characters may have been "to streamline *Gone with the Wind*'s complex narrative," but the absence of these particular two characters, Smyth argues, removes "Scarlett's close friendships with two racial and class hybrids—the poor white and the Cherokee-African American" (38). Consequently Scarlett is much shallower in the film, as we do not see her respectful interaction with these characters. Mitchell's young heroine, who, as Ann E. Egenriether notes, "survives, triumphs and flourishes in the world of men" (120), does not limit interactions with others based on class or race. Indeed, undeterred by Will's poor white background, she allows Suellen to marry this man, whom her father would surely have considered an inappropriate husband in prewar days.

Unfortunately, raised on a plantation with slave labor, Scarlett does not have an ethical problem with using convict labor as Ashley does, but that is because she is not hypocritical. Her lumberyard management reflects what she has witnessed on plantations her whole life: an overseer put in charge of the field hands. Indeed, when Ashley tells Scarlett he "won't work convicts" because he "can't make money from the enforced labor and misery of others," she replies, "But you owned slaves!" (*GW* 978). One might be reminded here of William Faulkner's Thomas Sutpen modeling his design after what he *saw*, which did not include as clear a reflection of those idealized codes of honor that Quentin Compson would like to think are inherent in the old family dynasties. As Faulkner does in *Absalom, Absalom!*, in the background Mitchell creates for Gerald O'Hara (something else that the movie leaves out), Mitchell does much to dispel myths of the nobility of the southern aristocracy.

In short, *Gone with the Wind* actually does subvert several romantic elements of the plantation novel. Most particularly Mitchell deromanticizes the role of the southern lady, revealing the consequences both to women who dutifully fulfill their role (like Ellen O'Hara and Melanie Wilkes) and to women who strain against the limitations of the role (like Scarlett). Also bringing up *Absalom, Absalom!* in one of her essays on *Gone with the Wind*, Anne Goodwyn Jones points out that "*Absalom, Absalom!* fails to interrogate gender as directly or fully as it does race" ("I" 33). Jones reminds the reader that Quentin and Shreve "hone in on race as the reason for Henry's killing Bon," and "although they report the stories of Sutpen's use and sexual abuse of women, they don't locate the family tragedy there" (33–34). And yet critics have not been as quick to note the implicit sexism of these two young men as they are to note Scarlett's racism. "Why then do Quentin and Shreve—and countless literary critics as well—see the novel as primarily about race?" Jones asks (34). In any case, Jones reminds readers that one should not "assume that Scarlett's racism is Mitchell's" (37). Scarlett may not be able to see a connection between the limitations on women that she resists and the oppression of the slaves on her father's plantation, but as noted repeatedly throughout the novel, Scarlett is not by nature "analytical." Her obtuseness is therefore probably more realistic than her ability to jump right in and take over for her parents upon arriving back at Tara after the burning of Atlanta. Furthermore, as Jones suggests about the limitations of Scarlett's development in the course of the novel, Mitchell's failure "to give Scarlett the kind of growth into autonomy and adulthood that she also denied to her black characters" is ultimately a realistic depiction of the result of oppression (34–35). While I argue that Scarlett's insight after Melanie's death of Melanie's importance to her and her plan to return to Tara after Rhett declares his intent to leave her are evidence of growth, I do not mean to suggest that she undergoes a sudden dramatic change at novel's end. Rather she has developed in the course of the dozen years covered in the novel. She comes a long way from the sixteen-year-old belle with a very limited future in the pre–Civil War South, and there is evidence in the novel's end of the potential for further development.

I agree with Drew Gilpin Faust that "the novel is a bildungsroman, set amidst the turmoil of war, a coming-of-age story in which the transformation of girl into woman involves confronting the transformation of womanhood itself" (8). But as *A Study of Scarletts* reveals, for several generations past Scarlett's, women who struggle against social limitations on their gender will continue to discomfort others and thus attract social censure.

In spite of my own initial resistance to reading this classic southern novel, about fifteen years after finally doing so, I included *Gone with the Wind* in a graduate seminar on southern classics. The last book I put on the reading list for that seminar was Charles Frazier's *Cold Mountain.* Inspired by the sensation this 1997 novel made upon its publication, I posed the question to this class, Is this book the next southern "classic"? It occurs to me now that such phenomenal attention was paid to *Cold Mountain* for much the same reason *Gone with the Wind* was not viewed as just another romantic plantation novel: the untraditional ending that leaves the audience both more and less satisfied. I already knew the ending of *Cold Mountain* before I read the novel—an audience member's question had revealed it during an event featuring the author the year before I read the book for the first time. But *as* I read, unable to keep myself from getting too attached to the character I knew to be doomed, I tried to believe that I had misunderstood the question and had not heard gasps from other audience members who had realized the questioner's faux pas. Of course, I had not misunderstood, and I was deeply saddened to reach the scene of Inman's death, made more tragic in its occurrence at the hands of a scared boy after Inman had finally made it home to his beloved mountain and the woman of his dreams—hence, perhaps, the chapter here on *Cold Mountain*, for I do seem drawn to write about those books that disturb me for one reason or another. Once again I found myself rereading a book to make my peace with an author's choice not to conclude with a traditional happy ending, and in so doing, I found myself focusing on the relationship between Ada and Ruby. Frazier's two women, as different from each other as Scarlett and Melanie, are never rivals. Their partnership is probably the most productive relationship in all of the books covered in this study. And the fulfillment that Ada finds in the life that Ruby helps her to create in Black Cove, under the shadow of Cold Mountain, leaves the reader assured that Inman's death, while a sad loss, will not be devastating to her.

When Anthony Minghella adapted Frazier's novel for the screen, I was not surprised by the movie's emphasis on the tragedy of the novel's ending. After all, Inman's death leaves Ada "alone" again—except that she isn't. She still has Ruby (as well as Ruby's family and her own daughter); she apparently continues to live the productive life that she and Ruby set in motion while Inman was gone. But readers' heterosexist biases likely result in overlooking the fact that Ada now has the survival tools to deal with that loss much better than she was prepared to deal with the loss of her father. In short, she has her own interests now, not just goals tied up with a man's.

For reasons similar to why I find myself returning again and again to *Cold Mountain,* in my classroom as well as in my scholarship, one reason I have incorporated my essay on Ellen Glasgow's 1925 novel *Barren Ground* into this book is that I am also troubled by my students' rejection of Dorinda Oakley's similarly satisfying life, their belief that since she is alone at novel's end (that is, still single and with no romantic interest), her life cannot be considered a successful one—the same reaction of many of the novel's original reviewers almost a century ago, reminding me that attitudes about women are at best slow to change and for many not much changed at all since Glasgow and Mitchell's day. I keep returning to *Barren Ground,* just as I keep returning to *Gone with the Wind,* in order to remind myself as much as my students that the goal should not be the man but the self (a lesson that Ada, it seems, learned before Inman's return, thus allowing her to go on after his death). This book's longer version of my previously published essay on *Barren Ground* and *Gone with the Wind* is based on my first cathartic writing about *Gone with the Wind.* Reading Mitchell's novel with *Barren Ground* culminates in tracing the decline of Rhett Butler and realizing that Scarlett O'Hara is better off without him. She should be viewed by novel's end as being just as triumphant as Glasgow's Dorinda Oakley, who has created a successful dairy on her father's seemingly "barren" farm. Rhett is, by novel's end, a broken alcoholic, like Glasgow's Jason Greylock. We can certainly sympathize with Rhett over the loss of his beloved daughter, Bonnie, but Scarlett has lost *every* person she loves, and she is still thinking hopefully of tomorrow. This is an *admirable* woman, and yet so many readers criticize her harshly, even perceive her to be sociopathic. And Rhett emerges as heroic to such readers, for walking out on Scarlett in the end. In the novel, readers are to be reminded, he merely goes upstairs to pack, not nearly as dramatic an exit scene as what the movie provides for Clark Gable.

After recognizing that Rhett Butler ultimately reveals himself to be no better a catch than Dorinda's first love, Jason Greylock, or Scarlett's once idealized Ashley Wilkes, it is not difficult to defend Dorinda's choice, after being jilted by Jason, to eschew romantic love and focus her attention on her dairy, even if it means her life will be a solitary one. Looking back to the chapter on *Cold Mountain* and forward to the one on *Sula,* one realizes that what is missing in Dorinda's life is not a great romance—she has had that. She has also had a marriage with a man she respected and cared about, Nathan Pedlar. What she has *not* had is a friend—like Melanie or Ruby. The greater tragedy of Scarlett's life, the reader ultimately realizes, is not that she realizes too late that she loves Rhett but that she realizes only upon Melanie's death how much Melanie meant to her, what value Melanie was in her life, and that she loved Melanie, a similar realization experienced by Nel at the end of Toni Morrison's 1973 novel *Sula.**

Sula is another book I am compelled to write about because of students' reactions to it. Students who prioritize romantic love as the ultimate goal of a novel's heroine (and presumably their own lives) find Sula's betrayal of her friend Nel by having sex with Nel's husband to be an unpardonable sin. While the betrayal of a friend is a painful experience, these students' reactions are still prioritizing the heterosexual relationship that is lost as a result of the betrayal, rather than the friendship that is risked (but that does not *have* to be lost). The first time I taught this novel, entering the classroom on the day the students were to have finished reading it, I realized a passionate discussion was already under way and took note, in particular, of the student damning Sula the loudest. To start the class, then, following the example of my own mentor making me read *Gone with the Wind,* I called on this young woman to defend Sula's actions.

"Not me," she said. "I think she's horrible."

"Well, let's say you're a public defender, and I'm the judge, and I've just assigned you as Sula's attorney. Now defend her."

And the student had absolutely no trouble doing so. I have since taught *Sula* numerous times, and in spite of the usual unanimous condemnation of Sula's treachery, I never have difficulty soliciting points in her defense (which will be enumerated in chapter 4) once I get the students to consider this

* While Sula is the Scarlett-like character in this novel, it is interesting that Nel is comparable to Scarlett in being the one left missing her friend and realizing the extent of her loss in the end: in her essay on *Sula*, Anna Shannon notes that "by giving equal time to both characters [Morrison] suggests the powerful, if unacknowledged impact each has on the other" (12). While I don't think readers of Morrison's novel will miss its emphasis on the importance of these women's relationship to both of them, the deep connection that develops between Scarlett and Melanie is something that may be overlooked by readers of *Gone with the Wind* who are more focused on the relationship between Scarlett and Rhett.

particular affair with a best friend's husband, as opposed to just reacting to the general idea of committing adultery with a friend's spouse.

Many years ago, after having an abstract of a paper on *Sula* accepted for a conference, when I prepared to write the paper, which has since evolved into the *Sula* chapter of this book, I began reading the criticism on this novel and discovered that my reading of *Nel's* betrayal of their friendship goes along with much of the scholarship written about this novel. What distinguishes my focus for this study is my identification of the source of Nel's choice to give up her friendship with Sula even after Jude is long gone: traditional communal prioritizing of heterosexual love over platonic friendship even though a friend can often offer as much (and at times more, as in this case) to a person's life as a lover. Terri Apter and Ruthellen Josselyn conclude their book *Best Friends: The Pleasures and Perils of Girls' and Women's Friendships* noting the difficulty of sustaining a friendship in a society that "overlooks the importance of friendship [and] gives little weight to the emotional and psychological significance of 'girlfriends.' Friendship among women continues to exist at the margins of our public social order. . . . The special bond that is women's friendship grows in soil that provides few nutrients. Our society regards women's friendship as somehow trivial—or a footnote to the depiction of women as wives and mothers—despite the fact that women tell us again and again that it is closeness to other women that oils their lives" (287). Toni Morrison explains in one interview: "Black women have always had that [friendships with women;] they always have been emotional life supports for each other" (Denard 16); but, she notes in another interview, when she was writing *Sula* in 1969, "women friendships weren't [yet] considered worthy subjects for fiction" (Denard 204). To illustrate Morrison's assertion, one might note from the focus of readers' attention to *Gone with the Wind* that much more interest is exhibited in the question of whether Scarlett will realize she loves Rhett and he loves her than whether she will learn to value her friendship with Melanie.

Prioritizing friendship is a way of putting oneself first, sometimes our friend first—which is something we, particularly we women, are not taught to do. Rather, we are taught to put our families, particularly our children, but also our husbands first. Friendships are for our own good, as illustrated by the effect Sula has on Nel when she returns to Medallion (and before Nel walks in on Sula with Jude), and thus we are inclined to put friends on the back burner, particularly after marriage but also often during courtship. Friendship is perceived more as a luxury than the necessity that society suggests marriage to be to have a complete life. Nel's failure to see (until novel's end) that Jude is not nearly the loss that Sula is shows that the marriage/friendship hierarchy has not changed much in the time between their friendship and the relationship between Scarlett and Melanie, which is thwarted by Scarlett's inability to see Melanie as anything other than a rival. Also, in spite of the major cultural differences between the two novels, the careful reader sees that suspicion of a woman who rejects limitations set for her sex is cross-cultural.

As Sula ultimately teaches Nel to reassess her priorities, the title character of a little-known novel by Kat Meads, *The Invented Life of Kitty Duncan (Benedict Roberts Duncan),* teaches the novel's narrator how to live a fuller life, free of the constraints of societal pressures to conform. Meads's novel, published in 2006, is set in North Carolina in the 1950s and 1960s; I did not know where the story was going the first time I read it, and when it got there, I had not seen it coming. As I closed the book and reflected on it after a first reading, I recognized Kitty Duncan's similarity to Scarlett O'Hara and was therefore particularly disturbed by my own negative reaction to the title character. Looking back at the experience of reading this novel for the first time, I realize that I had been as discomforted by Kitty Duncan's behavior throughout the novel as Mo (the narrator) and Kitty's mother are, even though what Kitty is doing throughout her story (besides merely whatever she wants to do) is resisting her mother's attempts to make her into a lady. I reopened the book and started rereading and discovered that Kitty, quite simply, lives her life without obsessing over what others think of her. She is no sociopath, but rather a (rare) woman who has not been cursed with self-conscious angst over the need to please other people, even at the expense of her own pleasure. She is an evolved Scarlett O'Hara (for Scarlett does suffer pangs of conscience on occasion and is certainly regretful at novel's end).

Not struggling to survive during and after a war, Kitty is at leisure to enjoy her life, doing whatever she wants regardless of social taboos. Mo, the novel's Nick Carraway, telling the central character's story, does not understand her own obsession with Kitty's life until the end: she has been waiting to see what consequences Kitty will have to pay for such radical behavior, but Mo finds a thirty-something Kitty, not consumed by regrets over past mistakes, not suffering any significant consequences for her untraditional behavior, and certainly not hiding out from the next adventure. Kitty may not be living happily ever after with the love of her life, but one guesses from the lives of such women as Kitty—and Scarlett and Sula and Dorinda and Ada—that the continued *pursuit* of happiness is ultimately more satisfying to them—more exciting, more fulfilling—than settling down would be.

In spite of my efforts to talk myself into believing the ending to Mitchell's novel bodes well for my hero, Scarlett O'Hara, *Gone with the Wind* has continued to haunt me. During the nine months (an appropriate gestation period) preceding the initial drafting of my defense of Scarlett in the first chapter to follow, I listened to an unabridged recording of the novel three times: first, in preparation for teaching the novel; next, in preparation to write a lecture I was invited to give; and a third time, as I wrote the paper. *Gone with the Wind* played and replayed in my head while I walked to and from school, worked out at the gym, did housework, drove anywhere. Three "readings" in such a relatively short period of time allowed me to decide for certain that Scarlett O'Hara has been misunderstood—by the moviemakers and in much of the criticism on the novel, which seems to rely heavily on the movie more so than on double-checking against the full text of the book (some critics seem to just look up the scenes that the movie plays out in order to find page numbers and quotations). Being a romantic, I still *want* Scarlett and Rhett to find a way back to each other, but being a woman who has followed an untraditional path for a girl from the Deep South, I am angered by the negative reaction to this amazing, courageous, defiant, strong, successful woman.

What began, then, as separate essays, lectures, and conference papers has become a study of literature that questions and offers alternatives to our "couple-centric culture": finding fulfillment in one's work, as Dorinda Oakley does; finding unconditional love in friendship, as Melanie offers to Scarlett. Witnessing Nel's grief each time I reach the end of *Sula,* I am reminded of my original devastation over Scarlett O'Hara realizing too late that she loves Rhett Butler after all. I know now that what Scarlett is seeking in the mist *is* the security of love, as we suspect all along about her recurring nightmare, but not Rhett's love, for he never offered secure love to Scarlett. Always there were conditions. Scarlett is longing for the ideal mother love she sought on her way back to Tara during the war. We readers know that it is Melanie who gave that love—not judgmental, unhappy Ellen, who was dead by the time Scarlett arrived at Tara, and certainly not mocking Rhett, who deserted her on the road—and Melanie was right there with her all along. Scarlett's insight about Melanie may be late, but Melanie's is the kind of love that lasts beyond death, for it is an affirming love, which tells Scarlett she is worthy of love, in spite of her flaws, and with that kind of love, Scarlett can live happily ever after.

A Study of Scarletts is a reader-response critical analysis of several books that inspire strong, often opposing reactions in the media, in the classroom, among scholars, and of the general reader. This work reexamines Margaret Mitchell's Scarlett O'Hara, a character long misunderstood, a result, most likely, of her depiction in David O. Selznick's film adaptation of the novel. Going back to the book, one remembers that Scarlett is only sixteen at the start of the novel and twenty-eight at novel's end; that Ashley does not discourage Scarlett's relentless pursuit of him; that Melanie, admired by most as the moral center of the novel, both understands and loves Scarlett; that Scarlett is criticized for behavior that would have been excused if she had been a man; and that Scarlett loses almost every person that she loves in the course of the novel and is still ready to face "tomorrow" as the book comes to a close. For all these reasons and more, Scarlett is an inspiration to female readers, an icon in American popular culture, and yet she is more often than not condemned for being a sociopathic bitch by those who do not take the time to get to know her through the novel.

After providing a more understanding, more sympathetic reading of Scarlett's behavior, which reflects, put most simply, a young woman refusing to accept social limitations based on gender and seeking to be loved for who she is, I examine plots and characters in other novels reminiscent in one way or another of *Gone with the Wind.* These intertextual readings serve both to further develop a less critical, more compassionate reading of Scarlett O'Hara and to expose societal prejudices against strong women. These chapters are ordered chronologically according to the novels' settings, beginning with Charles Frazier's Civil War novel *Cold Mountain,* the characters of which are, of course, contemporaries of Scarlett O'Hara; then Ellen Glasgow's *Barren Ground,* written a few years before *Gone with the Wind* but set a generation later, in the years leading up to and just after World War I; Toni Morrison's *Sula,* which opens after World War I; and, finally, a novel by Kat Meads, *The Invented Life of Kitty Duncan (Benedict Roberts Duncan),* with its evolved Scarlett O'Hara of the 1950s and 1960s.

Chapter 1, "In Defense of Scarlett O'Hara," addresses several points of criticism most often directed against Mitchell's central character: condemnation for her relentless pursuit of another woman's husband and for her attitude about her children, for example. The chapter reminds the reader of Ashley's role in encouraging Scarlett's affections and of the example that Ellen O'Hara, a very detached mother herself, set for her daughter; and the chapter questions Rhett as the perfect match for Scarlett that readers (and other characters) perceive him to be. The chapter also introduces a predominant argument of this study regarding Melanie's love for Scarlett: a love that is less conditional than the love of Scarlett's mother for her daughter.

Melanie's love is based on accepting Scarlett for who she is and on recognizing Scarlett's self-sacrificing nature, but Scarlett does not appreciate the value of Melanie's love until, of course, it is too late.

Chapter 2, "Gone with the Men: Scarlett and Melanie Redux in *Cold Mountain*," examines the working relationship of the two pairs of women in *Gone with the Wind* and Charles Frazier's *Cold Mountain* while the men are away at war. Friendship between women is a relationship only recently valued socially, so it should not be surprising that nineteenth-century Scarlett (created in the early twentieth century) realizes the friend she had in Melanie only at Melanie's bedside just before losing her forever. Melanie may appreciate Scarlett as no other does, but her death as a result of a pregnancy she has been warned against allowing to happen reflects her failure to see past the traditional roles of women in the Old South—wife and mother: Melanie is desperate to have another child with Ashley, even if it means risking her life. With Scarlett, however, she had formed an untraditional family unit that protected and nurtured their children and each other during the worst days of the war—and they survived. Readers of Mitchell's novel have also overlooked the primary importance in the novel of this relationship between the two women, finding the romantic tension between Scarlett and Rhett more compelling and thus missing the fact that Melanie is the greater loss at novel's end—even as many of these same readers condemned Scarlett for not recognizing Melanie's value until it is too late.

It is no surprise that the 2003 film adaptation turns *Cold Mountain* into a more traditional love story, albeit without a traditional happy ending. In the novel, Ada and Inman hardly know each other when they part during the war, and during their years apart they are to a great extent romantic abstractions that keep each other going through tough times. Ruby, on the other hand, provides genuine and tangible support to Ada in the novel. In the film version, Ruby's role as comic relief undercuts her more significant role in Ada's survival in the novel. Many readers, however, have recognized how Ada and Ruby's relationship and Ada's development back home begin to supersede Inman's quest for home in the novel. With Inman's death, then, which leaves Ada and Ruby as the sole focus at the *novel's* end, the reader recognizes that the continued friendship and working relationship between Ada and Ruby provide a satisfactory future for a character who is as uninterested in becoming a southern lady as Scarlett is. Inman may be a greater loss than Rhett Butler was, but his death does not bring a tragic end to Ada's story. With Ruby's help, Ada has developed her own plans for her future, and a life with Inman after the war was only part of that plan and, in fact, the part she was perhaps least sure about the more she came to appreciate her new more active, more responsible, working life.

Chapter 3, "Put your heart in the land": An Intertextual Reading of *Barren Ground* and *Gone with the Wind*," follows a Scarlett O'Hara–type character of the next generation after the Civil War, Ellen Glasgow's Dorinda Oakley. Glasgow's character was created before Scarlett, and Margaret Mitchell read this Glasgow novel just before she began work on her own novel. Dorinda could indeed be the prototype for Mitchell's character with a Glasgow-like "vein of iron" in her soul, but in this study, she is also examined to show how the expectations for and limitations of southern ladies continue from the antebellum days of Mitchell's novel into the next generation (and the following two generations at least, as shown in the subsequent chapters). The role that both protagonists' mothers play in their daughters' dissatisfaction with the status quo is further discussed in this chapter, as is the absence of a male character worth giving their hearts to. Dorinda, like Scarlett and Ada, defies social expectations for women in the South, choosing her dairy over marriage and motherhood, and is criticized by characters within the novel and critics outside of it. Even though the author, a woman who resisted marriage herself, clearly admires her untraditional heroine, many readers have failed to recognize the triumph of Dorinda's life, largely because, as she admires the successful dairy that stands where her father once farmed seemingly "barren ground," Dorinda is alone, without a man. Again the reader is reminded by this intertextual analysis that Scarlett's impending solitude following Rhett's threat to leave her is at least better than being stuck with Rhett or Ashley. Tara, like Dorinda's dairy, is where Scarlett was most productive; therefore, her plan to go back there is not a hearkening back for the days preceding the Civil War, as is Rhett's plan to return to Charleston. And at Tara, the reader should recall, is Mammy. Scarlett may not have recognized in time what Melanie meant to her, but perhaps the loss of Melanie will allow her to reconsider Mammy's value to her life.

Chapter 4, "Sula: 'More sinned against than sinning,'" focuses on Toni Morrison's novel set just after World War I within an African American community that, though not in the South, is still haunted by the oppression of the Old South—certainly more so than the yeoman-class Oakley family was in Glasgow's novel. Such a community survives, in part at least, because of the very untraditional standards it sets, and those who comply with more traditional expectations are the least happy. This community certainly understands (at first) that the Old Order is not worth modeling. In this chapter the focus turns again to a friendship between two very different girls, as different as Scarlett and Melanie and as Ada and Ruby are from each other. When Sula and Nel reach adulthood, however, their differences get in the way of their friendship, and they forget, as did Scarlett and Melanie after Ashley returns from the war, that their relationship is the strongest bond each has ever known. Here again this study looks at the false ideal of unconditional mother love, the failure of which leaves the characters feeling unlovable, seeking another false ideal—romantic love—or asking too much of each other. This chapter explores Melanie's much more accepting love of Scarlett, which is contrasted with Nel's betrayal of Sula after Sula and Jude's affair. Just as chapter 1 defends Scarlett against the usual harsh reader response to her, this chapter defends Sula—even her affair with her best friend's husband—reminding the reader how Sula's defiance of traditional social expectations is a learned behavior once accepted (of Sula's mother and grandmother) by this community. In condemning Sula, the Bottom condemns itself, perhaps to becoming just like the rest of the dominant culture, which is doubly oppressive to black women. Among those who condemn Sula, Nel, like Scarlett, realizes too late that the loss of her friend is a much greater loss than her husband; thus, Nel, too, condemns herself to a lonely life in this oppressive community.

Chapter 5, "'Disregarding the female imperative': Kat Meads's Kitty Duncan, a 1950s-era Scarlett O'Hara," examines a recent novel, *The Invented Life of Kitty Duncan (Benedict Roberts Duncan),* which has not yet received the attention it deserves. The author, Kat Meads, probably the only unfamiliar writer covered in this study, grew up in her native Currituck County in eastern North Carolina. She went to college at the University of North Carolina–Chapel Hill, where she earned a bachelor's degree in psychology, then to graduate school at UNC-Greensboro, earning an M.F.A. in creative writing. She lived in North Carolina until her late twenties, before heading west; she currently lives in California. Meads is the author of several books of fiction and nonfiction published with small presses; consequently her work is not well known. I was fortunate that Chiasmus Press sent her novel *The Invented Life of Kitty Duncan (Benedict Roberts Duncan)* to me in my capacity as editor of the *North Carolina Literary Review.* I hope that the chapter on *Kitty Duncan* in this book will bring much-deserved attention to this provocative novel and its talented creator.

I will not be surprised, given the response to Scarlett and her other literary daughters, if many of the readers who discover this Meads novel regard the title character as a sociopath. Kitty Duncan will inevitably be as misunderstood as Scarlett O'Hara. Reader response to Kitty will probably mirror Kitty's mother's reaction to her and that of her fictional biographer (the novel's narrator), who knew Kitty during Kitty's first brief marriage and who is fascinated by Kitty's rejection of social strictures, her tendency to do whatever she wants to do, even if it is not ladylike. Neither of these more proper southern ladies (or the readers who condemn her) realize that Kitty's behavior hurts no one but herself, that their own discomfort or distress over Kitty's behavior is not Kitty's doing but a result of the continued limited expectations for women, southern ladies in particular. Phyllis Duncan, Kitty's mother, may *be hurt by* (note passive voice) her daughter's behavior, but Kitty does not purposely set out to embarrass her mother. On the other hand, one can imagine that Phyllis's disapproval of Kitty, her efforts to remake Kitty into some other kind of daughter, does hurt Kitty, suggesting, as it might, that Kitty is not lovable for who she is. Kitty, in contrast to her mother, accepts both her mother and her own daughter for who they are, but since the story is told by another character rather than Kitty herself, one might miss these nuances. While the other characters' responses to Kitty reveal that little has changed for southern women in the century between this novel's setting and the mid-nineteenth century of Mitchell's novel, *Kitty Duncan* does end with a note of hope for the next generation of women, as evidenced by Kitty's well-adjusted, self-accepting daughter, a lesbian whose behavior inspires neither shock nor disapproval from *her* mother.

An important, disturbing point illuminated in this study of female rebels against their oppressive society is how southern women have participated in the oppression of their gender. Since before the Civil War, women have defended the patriarchy of the Old South in spite of how the Old Order condoned, if indirectly, adultery and rape (in looking the other way when masters raped their slaves), to name just two of the heinous crimes against women. Many mothers participated in the oppression of their daughters in the Old South and through at least a century of the New South. Unconditional mother love is one of those societal ideals that set these "Scarletts" up for a fall in a society in which the mother's role is to turn her daughters into ladies. When the mother is constantly trying to change the unladylike southern woman, it is inevitable that the daughter is going to feel unlovable. Compare Ellen O'Hara's efforts to turn Scarlett into a lady with Ada Monroe's father educating his daughter in *Cold Mountain,* accepting her rejection of her many suitors, her lack of interest in what marriage seemed to offer to her. I don't mean to remove blame from the patriarchy for the oppressiveness of the culture. My concern is simply with women participating in their own oppression by being the arbiters of manners and mores that set limitations on their daughters. As Rhett Butler puts it, "How closely women clutch the very chains that bind them" (*GW* 183). Where the reader sees progress in these novels is when one contrasts Kitty Duncan's acceptance of her lesbian daughter to Ellen O'Hara's efforts to tame Scarlett.

As it has often been mothers who have resisted change, fearing the unknown, fearing how society will treat their daughters if they don't comply with the rules, it will perhaps be the mothers who bring change to the oppressive Old Order, also for the sake of their children. In the 1970s, in Deep South Louisiana, in the middle of the discussion of "women's lib," my mother was asked whether she was a feminist. "Of course, I'm a feminist," she responded. "I have three daughters." My mother is a brilliant woman, but her father did not allow her to major in engineering as her brother did, since a woman did not need a career but only enough education to attract an appropriate husband. Breaking the tradition of women participating in the oppression of women, my mother did not support societal limitations on her daughters' career goals. If Scarlett had had such a mother, she would have recognized that Melanie's friendship was much more empowering than anything Ashley could have offered, and she would have given up that dream of Ashley much sooner for the sake of that valuable friendship. If she had had my mother, Sula would have known she was *liked* as well as loved. My mother would have applauded Dorinda's dairy farm and would not have been concerned about her lack of interest in marriage.

So I will conclude this introduction and get on with the chapters to follow by recognizing the value of women who support each other. The women in these stories who are most productive and least anxious about their life choices are the ones who have another woman to turn to for support. At times in my life when my speaking or acting out against the norm has resulted in social censure or condemnation, my mother has reminded me of the amazing girlfriends I have always had. Women friends, I realize, give each other the courage to be ourselves and to ignore social self-consciousness that prompts conformity. One can see, as the following chapters examine Scarlett character types and story lines, that one of the major developments between the characters created in the early twentieth century and the ones created as the century came to an end is the move from perceiving a threat in the other woman (Melanie) as a rival to recognizing the value of the other woman (Ruby) as a partner and friend.

Chapter 1

In Defense of Scarlett O'Hara

"She was not a lady, though she wanted to be, but a magnificent woman, a vital, proud, passionate creature, undismayed by life or by death, tenacious of what was hers, acquisitive of what was not, hungry for admiration rather than love, ruthless but capable of tenderness, ambitious but capable of sacrifice, sentimental but without nonsense, deeply rooted in the soil of Tara but uprooted, too, and lost."

Henry Steele Commager, "The Civil War in Georgia's Red Clay Hills," 1936 (13)

"Now her reactions were all masculine. Despite her pink cheeks and dimples and pretty smiles, she talked and acted like a man. Her voice was brisk and decisive and she made up her mind instantly and with no girlish shillyshallying. She knew what she wanted and she went after it by the shortest route, like a man, not by the hidden and circuitous routes peculiar to women."

Gone with the Wind (639)

My first or perhaps summary complaint with the critics of Scarlett O'Hara (including both her own community in the world of the novel and the community of readers outside of it) is this: if she were a man, almost none of her behavior would be found so objectionable—certainly not her enterprising nature or her passion for her businesses, but also not her motives for marriage (marrying for money was probably as common as love matches in the society of this novel) or her lack of focus on her children (beyond providing for their physical needs).

Considering just the double standard in this latter point of criticism often directed against Scarlett, one should recognize that Scarlett's parenting goes along with the role she ends up playing in her family: head of house. She behaves toward her children as many fathers of her culture do—she is the source of security more so than affection and nurturing. But she is considered unnatural, not admirable, while Rhett is praised for his ("motherly") involvement in the care of Bonnie Blue. On the other hand, Rhett's neglect of his ward goes unnoticed, uncensured. Helen Taylor reminds the reader of Rhett's ward, who is "possibly . . . an illegitimate son" (*Scarlett's* 116), evidence for which might be suggested by Rhett's description of the boy as "a perfect hellion," which is what his daughter Bonnie was destined to become, with his spoiling, though in this boy's case his behavior could be due to the absence of a father. Rhett supports this child but admits when telling Scarlet about the boy, "I wish he had never been born" (*GW* 765), and his support (like Scarlett's of her children) is limited to the boy's physical needs. While their community may not know about this child and therefore might be excused for not criticizing Rhett's attitude, neither have readers remarked on Rhett's neglect or dislike of the boy. No one has expressed horror that Rhett would say such a thing about a child as wishing away his existence (which also suggests that Rhett has been around since the child's birth and thus further support for the possibility of Rhett being the boy's father). Consider too that Rhett's behavior is not unlike slave owners' treatment of their black offspring, reminding us that this community has a tradition of turning a blind eye to neglectful fathers. On the other hand, Rhett's parenting *is* remarked on when it goes against the norm by participating in Bonnie's upbringing since such involvement of the father in child rearing is unusual in these times—he behaves in ways more "motherly" than "fatherly," inspiring social admiration of his devotion to his child—and another reason to criticize Scarlett, whose untraditional mothering is emphasized by Rhett's untraditional fathering.

Regarding Scarlett's attitude toward her children, one might ask, How affectionate was *Ellen* O'Hara? Is Scarlett's "tough love" approach to her children so different from how her mother treated her? As Elizabeth Fox-Genovese points out, Ellen O'Hara was "distant and preoccupied . . . having never recovered from an early passion"; consequently she has "little . . .

emotional substance to give to those she so dutifully cares for" ("Scarlett" 404). It is interesting that in spite of Ellen's distance and coldness, she is apparently the source of strength to her family—and so is Scarlett to hers from the moment she enters Tara after escaping the burning of Atlanta. In contrast, however, Ellen rarely receives the kind of criticism that one hears about Scarlett, most likely because in all other ways Ellen's behavior fulfills her community's expectations for southern ladies.

Scarlett may be an untraditional mother, but that does not mean she does not love her children (at least as much as Ellen loved hers). Anne Goodwyn Jones provides an interesting explanation for why, as Jones believes, "Scarlett dislikes children": "because they are so dependent upon her. . . . [S]he does not mind actual responsibility for them, but she resents being reminded of her own childish needs" (*Tomorrow* 344), one of which was the desire for motherly affection. Recall sixteen-year-old Scarlett, on the way to the Wilkes barbecue, watching enviously as the Tarleton daughters tease their mother: "To Scarlett, the very idea of saying such things to her own mother was almost sacrilegious. And yet—and yet—there was something very pleasant about the Tarleton girls' relations with their mother, and they adored her for all that they criticized and scolded and teased her. Not, Scarlett loyally hastened to tell herself, that she would prefer a mother like Mrs. Tarleton to Ellen, but still it would be fun to romp with a mother" (*GW* 86). Scarlett feels guilty about "want[ing] to respect and adore her mother like an idol and to rumple her hair and tease her too" (*GW* 87). This "study of Scarlett" returns again and again to the untraditional woman's desire for her mother's affection, which assures one that she is lovable, reassurance that is particularly needed by those who receive constant social censure.

When terrified by the siege of Atlanta, "Scarlett longed for home and her mother as she had never longed for anything in all her life. If she were just near Ellen she wouldn't be afraid, no matter what happened" (*GW* 329). And although none of the O'Hara daughters, including Scarlett, recognize it, Scarlett is not so different from Ellen in her own awe-inspiring mothering: Wade may be a bit frightened of Scarlett (as Scarlett was of her mother), but he is less frightened of the rest of the world in her presence (just as Scarlett was running home to her mother's protection when she left Atlanta). At some level then, after Ellen's death most members of Scarlett's extended family realize that she is the appropriate replacement for Ellen, for upon Scarlett's arrival at Tara just after Ellen's death, everyone turns to Scarlett (not to the bewildered patriarch of Tara or even to Mammy, the usual source of comfort, or to the unflappable Dilcey).

To save Tara (and those in her care there), Scarlett ultimately sees no alternative other than marriage, even though her first marriage soured her on the institution. When Rhett explains during her visit to his jail cell that he cannot give Scarlett the money she needs, she sets her sights on Frank Kennedy. Marrying for money was not so unheard of at that time—it was probably more common than romantic unions. Scarlett may have married her sister's beau, but so did *he* marry *his* fiancée's sister without first finding out *for himself* if Suellen had, as Scarlett told him, decided to marry another man. And Frank's *choice* to marry the charming and beautiful Scarlett O'Hara Hamilton follows the pattern of defection of Scarlett's other beaux: Stuart Tarleton made clear that he would drop India Wilkes if Scarlett would only say the word, Charles Hamilton did forsake Honey Wilkes to marry Scarlett, and Ashley Wilkes squired sixteen-year-old Scarlett around while betrothed to Melanie. Hayden B. J. Maginnis provides a similar list to illustrate the "strange and *pervasive* moral infirmity" of the Old South, including, along with Charles Hamilton and Frank Kennedy, Aunt Pittypat, who "leave[s] Atlanta during the siege, though Melanie lies upstairs, unwell and a month from childbirth" (645; emphasis added). All of these people's behaviors are shortsighted and self-centered betrayals of others to whom they are obligated, and yet only Scarlett's elicits social censure.

Critics also tend to forget Ashley's role in Scarlett's relentless pursuit of him, but Helen Taylor reports that the more general audience response she heard when researching her book *Scarlett's Women:* Gone with the Wind *and Its Female Fans* is that "Ashley was not straight with Scarlett, and thus contributed to 'ruining her life.'" Taylor notes the interesting contrast between "the extraordinarily one-sided nature of reactions" to Rhett (overwhelmingly positive and uncritical) and readers' negative reactions to Ashley (the most common answer for "least favourite character"; *Scarlett's* 110). In spite of such responses to questions directed toward assessing audience opinion of characters, Taylor observes "how hard everyone is on Scarlett, and how indulgent of Rhett (and hardly anyone attributes blame or responsibility to Ashley)" when responding to questions about the novel's ending (149). Put simply, Ashley led Scarlett on, but many readers seem to forget that, particularly with the movie replacing the novel in their memory of events, for such backstory is difficult to put into a movie. It is so typical for the woman to be blamed in romantic triangles that one is not surprised by the tendency of viewers to recall only Scarlett's relentless pursuit of Ashley until the end of the *movie* when the *novel* makes perfectly clear that Ashley discourages her only after first *encouraging* her—repeatedly. Several times (spread *throughout* the twelve years covered in the novel), Ashley admits to loving Scarlett—and since so many people base their response to Scarlett on the movie, in which she desperately chases a resisting Ashley, I am compelled to enumerate these instances in the novel to remind the reader of how Ashley never comes right out and says to Scarlett that, though he may be drawn to her, he loves Melanie and wants to be married to Melanie and not to Scarlett. He never tells Scarlett he does not love her—quite the opposite!

First, in their first moment alone in the novel (the well-known scene at the barbecue), when Scarlett asks Ashley directly, "Don't you want to—to marry me?," why didn't he just say *no*? Rather, he merely responds, "I'm going to marry Melanie." He continues to equivocate throughout this first of many such conversations: when Scarlett says, "I know I love you," he responds, "Love isn't enough to make a successful marriage when two people are as different as we are" (*GW* 116–17), which suggests to Scarlett that he loves her, too. Again he does not say that he doesn't love her. When Scarlett asks him if he loves Melanie, his first response is not "yes" but "She is like me." In fact, he soon thereafter says, "How could I help caring for you—you who have all the passion for life that I have not?" (*GW* 117).

Second, as Ashley departs from his furlough in Atlanta (when he solicits Scarlett's promise to take care of Melanie), Scarlett runs after him and begs him to kiss her. Again he does not rebuff her; rather "his arms went around her gently, and he bent his head to her face. At the first touch of his lips on hers, her arms were about his neck in a strangling grip. For a fleeting immeasurable instant, he pressed her body close to his" (*GW* 276) before he pulled himself away. Scarlett declares her love again and begs Ashley to declare his love for her ("say you love me!"). Although he doesn't say it, she sees it "written on" his face, "the unhappiest face she was ever to see, a face from which all aloofness had fled" (*GW* 277). One might argue that she is misreading what she sees—which Scarlett is of course quite capable of doing—but again Ashley does not say, *no, he does not love her,* and he *does* kiss her, suggesting that his unhappy visage could reflect his love for someone other than his wife, even if he *also* loves his wife.

Third, after Ashley returns from the war and prison (in the orchard scene that culminates in Ashley handing Scarlett a handful of Tara dirt to remind her of what she loves more than she loves him), Scarlett asks Ashley to run away with her. His response again is not to say he loves Melanie but rather to note that he is too honorable to desert his wife and son. He does, this time, say, "No. I don't love you," but when Scarlett calls that "a lie," he suggests she is right: "*Even if it is a lie* . . . it is not something which can be discussed" (*GW*

532; emphasis added). When he then tries to comfort Scarlett, passion arises again, and "his lips took hers hungrily as if he could never have enough"; and when she asserts, "You do love me! You do love me! Say it—say it!" and moves toward him again, he tells her, "Don't! If you do, I shall take you now, here" (*GW* 533). And then he says it, unequivocally: "You want me to say it? All right, I'll say it. *I love you. . . . I love you,* your courage and your stubbornness and your fire and your utter ruthlessness. *How much do I love you? So much* that a moment ago I would have outraged the hospitality of the house which has sheltered me and my family, forgotten the best wife any man ever had—enough to take you here in the mud" (*GW* 534; emphasis added). And again he does not say that he loves Melanie more than he loves Scarlett; calling Melanie "the best wife" does not deny his declaration of love to Scarlett. It merely reflects a reason he might have for choosing Melanie over Scarlett.

Fourth, it is Ashley who brings up this previous conversation again later in the novel, explaining to Scarlett why he has decided to move his family up north. This is when Scarlett returns to Tara for her father's funeral and asks Ashley to run the mill for her since, in the advanced stage of her pregnancy (with Frank's child), it is long since proper for her to be out of the house. When Ashley then declines Scarlett's offer to sell the mill to him in light of his reluctance to run it for her and thus be her employee, he is adamant in his refusal, and his words do not take back the declaration of love from their previous encounter alone: "You know my reasons better than anyone in the world," he tells her (*GW* 726). And when she reminds him of her promise not to push for a repeat of the orchard incident (she can live on his words if he will just stay around), he says, "Then you are surer of yourself than I am. I could not count on myself to keep such a promise. I should not have said that but I had to make you understand" (*GW* 726–27).

Now in truth, though Ashley clearly does not deny and in fact actually admits love for Scarlett, Rhett may be right that this weak man is merely attracted to rather than in love with this strong woman. But Ashley is not just attracted to Scarlett's body, as Rhett suspects. Ashley, like the Tarleton twins, as well as Charles, Frank, Rhett, and other men, is drawn to Scarlett's strong nature, perhaps as much as he is to her body. Like these other men, too, however—Rhett included—he would not know what to do with her if he got her. Unlike Rhett, who thinks he can tame Scarlett, Ashley does seem aware of the impossibility of taming her; nor does he seem inclined to change her.

Significant as well, like Melanie (and unlike Rhett), Ashley sees the good in Scarlett, sees her strength in positive terms, not as what makes her a "bad girl," which Rhett finds so appealing. Rhett enjoys Scarlett (as long as he isn't hurt by her behavior), but he doesn't seem to respect her, so he doesn't make her feel very good about herself. Even when he is finally admitting to her that he had loved her (past tense), he tells her, "I was the only man . . . who could love you after knowing you as you really are—hard and greedy and unscrupulous, like me" (*GW* 1030). Not only is this characterization insulting, but it is also a confession of narcissism, which would surely detract from Rhett's appeal to Scarlett. Furthermore his assertion is not true—he does not really know Scarlett very well at all. He only understands those qualities in her that he shares. He does not include in his list the fine qualities that Melanie and Ashley recognize in Scarlett: loyalty, courage, and a strong work ethic, for example.

To those who wonder at Scarlett's blindness to Rhett as a more appropriate match for her than Ashley, one might ask why Rhett's love would appeal to Scarlett, expressed, as it is, in narcissistic terms that would contrast negatively with Ashley's ability to see the nobler Scarlett whom others fail to see. Furthermore, if Rhett and Scarlett are so much alike, since Scarlett has not been encouraged to admire herself, why would she like him? A better question might be why *we* do! He is not very nice to this woman he claims to love, constantly insulting her and deserting her each time she really needs him, ultimately angry with her for not usually needing him. All of this leads back to the issue of Scarlett's blindness to Rhett's love for her, so easily discerned by readers (flawed though it may be), and the question then becomes: why *wouldn't* naïve, pragmatic, unanalytical Scarlett fail to see that Rhett loves her?

One might recall here that when Rhett proposed to Scarlett after Frank Kennedy's death (as when he propositioned her earlier in the novel), he told her, "I still *want* you more than any woman I've ever seen" (*GW* 831; emphasis added). He then tries to convince her to marry him with the idea that their marriage might be "fun"—in contrast to her marriages "to a boy and an old man" (*GW* 833). The word "love" is mentioned only in response to her continued hesitation to accept his proposal: he mockingly gets down on his knees and declares—probably the truth but in such a way that she certainly would not take him seriously: "It cannot have escaped your notice that for some time past the friendship I have had in my heart for you has ripened into a deeper feeling more beautiful, more pure, more sacred. Dare I name it? Ah! It is love which makes me so bold!" (*GW* 834). Earlier in the novel, when he also professed love before leaving Scarlett on the way back to Tara during the siege, he similarly prefaced it with poetry that Scarlett would find romantic drivel: "I could not love thee, Dear, so much, loved I not Honour more" (*GW* 390). Rhett's behavior may be an understandable effort to protect himself against humiliation if (and when) Scarlett rejects him, but while Scarlett can perceive sarcasm, she is unable to intuit Rhett's true feelings hiding behind the sarcasm.

On that earlier occasion of first admitting, "I love you, Scarlett," Rhett adds, "because we are so much alike" (*GW* 390). This qualification suggests that Rhett's narcissism is the source of his love for Scarlett, and in any case his assertion of love at this point is also undermined by his subsequent desertion of Scarlett to join the Confederate army. If they are so much alike, why is he joining in a cause they do not believe in, Scarlett might wonder, and if he is so much in love, the reader should wonder as well, why he is leaving her alone to take care of herself, Melanie, and their children, with only a young, scared slave to help her. Rhett, it turns out (and is foreshadowed here), is actually probably more like Ashley than like Scarlett after all, as his departure at the novel's end to seek out the Old South confirms; and everyone, both inside and outside the pages of the novel, seems to agree that Ashley and Scarlett are not a good match. One might deduce, then, that neither are Rhett and Scarlett.

Given Rhett's seemingly sarcastic declarations of love, versus Ashley's angst-ridden, reluctant admissions of same, one should understand Scarlett's preference for Ashley over Rhett through most of the novel. Specifically one might contrast Rhett's final declaration of love even as he insults her ("I was the only man . . . who could love you after knowing you as you really are—hard and greedy and unscrupulous" [*GW* 1030]) and only after he no longer loves her (this comes at the end of the book, when he is telling her he is now *out* of love with her) with Ashley telling Scarlett, "I love you, your courage and your stubbornness and your fire and your utter ruthlessness" (*GW* 534). Yes, like Rhett, Ashley references Scarlett's "bad girl" qualities in this list, but later, like Melanie, Ashley also acknowledges the selfless motives behind Scarlett's "ruthlessness" (in marrying Frank Kennedy): "You wouldn't have let me do anything dishonorable but you would sell yourself to a man you didn't love . . . so that my family and I wouldn't starve." In contrast to Rhett, then, Ashley reassures Scarlett that he isn't "blaming" her, and he tells her she is "the bravest woman I've ever known" (*GW* 724). Ashley does not insult or show disrespect for Scarlett even as he tries to convince her that he is not the right man for her. Rhett may have also recognized Scarlett's courage, and when he deserted her (between Atlanta and Tara) he was correct in assuming that she would make it home without his further help, but unlike Ashley, he is never able to see her motives for anything she does as more than self-interested. Rhett sees Scarlett as a female version of himself, and his actions are usually self-interested, yet he, like so many in their community, condemns her for behavior excusable for a man. Ashley loves Scarlett for herself—including (perhaps most especially) the very aspects of her personality that others criticize. He, like Melanie, accepts Scarlett's difference, her *exceptionalism,* as part of that which makes her lovable. Thus he and Melanie offer Scarlett something more akin to the ideals of unconditional mother love than she received from her mother.

Like Rhett, many readers (and viewers) fail to see beneath the outside veneer that Scarlett projects for the rest of the world, as well as, on occasion, for herself, to keep her own courage up. How vivid is the image of Scarlett O'Hara asserting, "As God is my witness, as God is my witness, the Yankees aren't going to lick me. I'm going to live through this, and when it's over, I'm never going to be hungry again. No, nor any of my folks. If I have to steal or kill—as God is my witness, I'm never going to be hungry again" (*GW* 428). Yes, she first thinks of herself ("*I'm* never going to be hungry again"), but one should not overlook her inclusion of her family ("nor any of my folks") as she expresses her willingness to do whatever it takes. And if she did not take care of herself first, what would happen to the rest of her family? Putting one's own needs aside to take care of everyone around you is what ultimately made Ellen O'Hara "middle-aged" at thirty-two (*GW* 40) and killed her at thirty-five.

With such a strong impression of Scarlett's determination to survive, we sometimes forget the frightened, overwhelmed Scarlett who continues to suffer nightmares from the period of hardship at Tara through her honeymoon with a wealthy man who can assure her of never being hungry again. We forget the fear that haunts Scarlett until the novel's end, when the nightmare comes true. It does not take a psychology degree to interpret Scarlett's recurrent dream, so an explication of this dream is unnecessary, but the description bears quoting in its entirety to remind the reader of how much pressure is on this woman, *not yet twenty years old* when she first has the nightmare, a young woman who was certainly not raised to be in the position of head of a family struggling to obtain the basic necessities for survival:

> She was in a wild strange country so thick with swirling mist she could not see her hand before her face. The earth beneath her feet was uneasy. It was a haunted land, still with a terrible stillness, and she was lost in it, lost and terrified as a child in the night. She was bitterly cold and hungry and so fearful of what lurked in the mists about her that she tried to scream and could not. There were things in the fog reaching out fingers to pluck at her skirt, to drag her down into the

> uneasy quaking earth on which she stood, silent, relentless, spectral hands. Then she knew that somewhere in the opaque gloom about her there was shelter, help, a heaven of refuge and warmth. But where was it? Could she reach it before the hands clutched her and dragged her down into the quicksand?
>
> Suddenly she was running, running through the mist like a mad thing, crying and screaming, throwing out her arms to clutch only empty air and wet mist. Where was the haven? It eluded her but it was there, hidden, somewhere. If she could only reach it! If she could only reach it she would be safe! But terror was weakening her legs, hunger making her faint. She gave one despairing cry and woke *to find Melanie's hand shaking her to wakefulness.* (*GW* 474–75; emphasis added)

The passage also calls to our attention who it is that rescues Scarlett from her bad dreams—Melanie—and reading on we learn that Scarlett is so scared of this recurring dream that "she began sleeping *with Melanie*" (*GW* 475; emphasis added)—like a child, frightened from a nightmare, crawling into bed with her mother.

Once Scarlett is eating regularly, the dream fades, but it is interesting that it recurs during her honeymoon with Rhett—after she has *over*eaten (and has drunk too much wine) and after a fight she has with her new husband about her continued infatuation with Ashley. Rhett is the person who comforts her when she awakens this time, and "he picked her up in his arms like a child and held her," his gentleness perhaps prompting her candid recounting of the dream: "Oh, Rhett, I was so cold and so hungry and so tired and I couldn't find it. . . . I just run and run and hunt and I can't ever find what it is I'm hunting for. It's always hidden in the mist. I know if I could find it, I'd be safe forever and ever and never be cold or hungry again" (*GW* 856). Readers may believe (or want to believe) that once Scarlett recognizes that she and Rhett were meant for each other, she will find that security, but of course Mitchell did not give her novel such a traditional romantic ending. In truth, what Scarlett is seeking in the mist is the security provided by genuine love, love with no strings attached, love in spite of her flaws—the ideal of mother love, which Scarlett did not experience as a daughter (but did experience as a friend, as will be shown later).

Helen Taylor, in fact, compares Rhett to Ellen in the way that he is at times able to comfort Scarlett "with a voice 'so gentle, so quiet', arms 'so tender, so infinitely soothing', not to mention a clean handkerchief" (*"Gone"* 117). And reminding the reader that Rhett is not so different from Ashley after all,

Elizabeth Fox-Genovese connects Scarlett's attraction to Ashley to her desire for her mother's love, noting that "Scarlett perceives Ashley Wilkes to be cut from the same cloth as Ellen. Aristocratic and self-controlled, he possesses self-knowledge and acts according to principles that she cannot fathom" ("Scarlett's" 406). But Taylor reminds the reader that "though we are told [Ellen] has been a major figure to her growing daughters, in book and film she maintains a considerable physical and emotional distance from them" (*Scarlett's* 198). And Taylor notes, too, how "just at the moment [Scarlett] understands her recurrent nightmare of running through the fog, realising finally that Rhett was the only enduring love she had known, he asserts his masculine power and withdraws those enfolding *maternal* arms to deny us all—Scarlett, readers and viewers—the grand finale we have come to expect" (*Scarlett's* 141; emphasis added)—to expect in spite of all the evidence leading up to this final scene suggesting that Rhett's love for Scarlett is no more sustaining, nurturing, and enduring than Ellen's was.

Rhett's way of loving Scarlett was in some ways the other extreme of parenting, in direct contrast to Ellen's emotional neglect: "I wanted to take care of you, to pet you, to give you everything you wanted. I wanted to marry you and protect you and give you a free rein in anything that would make you happy—just as I did Bonnie. I wanted you to stop fighting and let me fight for you. I wanted you to play, like a child—for you were a child, a brave, frightened, bullheaded child" (*GW* 1030). But Scarlett was not a child—and neither is she a southern lady, which, surprisingly, Rhett would have preferred (as evidenced by his appreciation of Melanie). Scarlett may enjoy the security of Rhett's money, which assured her that she would not find herself and her family hungry ever again, but she also enjoyed her expanded role as owner of a lumber mill rather than just manager of her husband's household. She is no Ellen Robillard O'Hara, to be worked to an early grave.

Also similar to Ellen, Rhett deserts Scarlett when she needs him most—or thinks she does. But does she really? Ellen's death comes just as Scarlett exhibits the woman she is capable of being—so different from the belle she was at sixteen—by getting Melanie and their children safely back to Tara. Dawson Gaillard argues that Rhett leaves Scarlett upon realizing that she has grown up, for it is not an independent woman but a dependent child whom he could spoil that he wants (18). Gaillard thus supports the idea that Scarlett is better off without Rhett. Amy Levin agrees, too, interpreting Rhett as "a rather frightening combination of protective father figure, always rescuing Scarlett or bringing her gifts, and rapist," alluding to the night he carries her to bed against her will. Levin concludes, "Rhett is terrifying because he does not ask Scarlett to give up her independent life, but he does ask her to abandon her will" (34–35).

Considering Rhett's decline or regression by novel's end (to be discussed in chapter 3) and his ultimate declaration of his intent to leave her, one understands why he inspired Scarlett's terrifying nightmare to recur on their honeymoon. The security he offered in his marriage proposal was not expressed to her in terms of love (even if the reader realizes he loves her and understands his desire to protect himself from her rejection), and their argument about Ashley before Scarlett went to sleep that night reminded her of that fact, reminded her that she is still looking for someone who will love her for herself—as Melanie and perhaps Ashley do. There may have been a time when Rhett could have provided the security of love, but by the time the dream becomes reality at novel's end, that moment has passed. Rhett's love was not strong enough after all. As Elzbieta Oleksy has suggested, Rhett did not really love Scarlett any more than Scarlett really loved Ashley: "The irony of Scarlett's situation is that when she wakes up from her dream of running in the fog and from her romantic dream of Ashley, and emerges as a mature woman, she confronts another dreamer—for Scarlett was as much a part of Rhett's dream as Ashley was of hers" (180).

Ashley's love is also weak, since he cannot get past his code of honor to follow up on his desire for Scarlett, but Melanie's love is strong and unwavering. In response to hearing that Scarlett has been discovered in Ashley's arms, still Melanie believes in Scarlett, comforts Scarlett, defends her, even to Scarlett herself: "Don't you realize I know you better than anyone in the world knows you?" Melanie reminds Scarlett (*GW* 946), then explains to her that "people are jealous of you, because you are so smart and successful. You've succeeded where lots of men, even, have failed. . . . People just don't understand you and people can't bear for women to be smart" (*GW* 948). What greater test of Melanie's love for Scarlett than the fact that Scarlett would have taken Ashley from Melanie if she could, and still Melanie loves her. Unfortunately (as will be discussed more fully in chapter 4), we are not taught to value the love of a friend the way we are programmed to seek the great romantic love of our life. So Scarlett is comforted by the security of Melanie's love only during their period of isolation from the communal structure that teaches us to value one source of love over another.

Scarlett receives from Melanie the unconditional love that Ellen, in truth, did not really offer. Elizabeth Jane Harrison refers to Melanie "as a kind of mother figure" for Scarlett and comments on Melanie's love for and loyalty to Scarlett: "Melanie stands loyally by her and loves her no matter the cost, welcoming her into her home despite society's censure" (60). Madonne M. Miner points out how "Mitchell links Melanie and Ellen as 'great ladies' in the Southern tradition," which the reader cannot miss, even if Scarlett does not make the connection (26). Miner also compares the deaths of Ellen and Melanie in that "both times she must make a return trip in fear, fear of the absence that might confront her at the end of her trip" (27). However, in contrast to Ellen, Melanie is usually available when Scarlett seeks her. As Hayden Maginnis puts it so succinctly, "Ellen O'Hara is never there for her daughter" (644), and he lists Ellen's consequential absences, from the barbecue to Scarlett's return to Tara after the Atlanta siege. Melanie, on the other hand, gives Scarlett the loyalty and affection that Ellen withheld.

Very early in the novel, we are told of how Ellen, "with soft-voiced admonition" tried to make a lady of Scarlett, instructing her daughter to "be more gentle . . . more sedate" and "to conceal from men your sharp intelligence" (*GW* 59); and, upon learning that Scarlett, while still in mourning for her first husband, danced with Rhett Butler at the Confederate ball, Ellen berates her soundly. Elizabeth Fox-Genovese references Ellen's letter to Scarlett in response to hearing about the ball episode as evidence that "Ellen may have failed decisively as a mother." Fox-Genovese also draws on this incident in the novel to note a significant point of contrast between Ellen and Melanie, who, "on the same occasion, insists on believing the best of Scarlett and defends her" ("Scarlett" 403). Melanie, in fact, defends Scarlett throughout the novel, consistently assuming the best motives behind Scarlett's actions. Some perceive Melanie as a dupe to Scarlett's machinations, too naïve for her own good. Even Scarlett does not give credence to Melanie's unconditional support of Scarlett's actions. When Rhett reminds her that Melanie "has always approved of [her]," Scarlett replies, "It's certainly not to my credit . . . for she hasn't the sense of a guinea hen" (*GW* 680). In an odd response for Scarlett's husband to have to Melanie's constant, unwavering love of Scarlett, Rhett tells his wife that he "can't see why" Melanie loves her (*GW* 936). Hayden Maginnis suggests that what I am referring to as Melanie's unconditional love for Scarlett has its own consequences: "Melanie's strength, her very virtue, is her weakness. . . . She can neither see Scarlett's faults nor be a moral force in her life" (645). I argue, rather, that Melanie simply knows and understands Scarlett and loves her as she is, in contrast most significantly to Rhett, who is *attracted to* the rebel Scarlett, but does not see the unselfishness behind Scarlett's self-centered veneer.

Yes, one may use the word "unselfish" to describe Scarlett O'Hara—at least in the novel's characterization of her (perhaps not the film's, in which the story's compression results in a much shallower Scarlett). As clearly as the novel shows (as enumerated earlier) that Ashley shares the blame for Scarlett's obsession with him, so too does it reveal that Melanie's perception of Scarlett is not skewed. Melanie sees what others, except perhaps Ashley, cannot see, and it is that which explains Scarlett's appeal to readers who at some level seem to recognize what Melanie sees: how Scarlett, grudgingly but repeatedly, sacrifices herself for others, beginning with Melanie. Melanie survives the birth of her first child in Scarlett's care, one of many examples of how Scarlett's seemingly self-centered motives are ultimately unselfish: Scarlett stays with Melanie because she promised Ashley to take care of his frail wife while he is away at the war. Isn't she then putting Ashley's wishes above her own? She will save Melanie if that is what Ashley wants, even though Melanie's death would be, as Rhett notes at the end of the novel, very "convenient" (*GW* 1026) for her. In her more generous reference to Scarlett's actions in this episode as "unselfish," Paula Anca Farca argues that Scarlett is motivated by "an unselfish desire to help others and soothe Melanie's pain" (79). Whatever her reason, Scarlett does stay with Melanie after Aunt Pittypat, who raised Melanie, deserted her niece. And in doing so, Scarlett (albeit unknowingly) misses the chance to say goodbye to her mother and perhaps receive some final words that would assure her of her mother's love and thus make her feel less unlovable.

Scarlett also sacrifices herself when she marries Frank Kennedy. Those readers (and viewers) who focus on Scarlett stealing her sister's fiancé are overlooking the fact that Scarlett is right: Suellen, who misses the luxuries and finery of prewar days so much that she tries to coerce her addled father into signing an oath of allegiance to the Union in order to get restitution money from the federal government for the family's losses, would not have let Frank spend the money he'd saved to pay the taxes on Tara. Suellen's character is another element left undeveloped in the movie, and since Will Benteen is left out of the film entirely, we do not get his long explanation of Gerald's death, in which Will, an unambiguously admirable character, expresses his understanding of why Scarlett did what she did, as well as his explanation of Suellen's selfish treachery of her father. In the novel, therefore, it is much clearer that Scarlett sacrifices herself in marriage to Frank for Tara—and all those living at Tara (her sisters, her son, the Wilkes family, the servants, and Will Benteen). Only Melanie, Mammy, and Will are not appalled; only Melanie, Mammy, Will, and Ashley understand Scarlett's motives. Mammy's race and Will's poor white background would undermine their social credibility were they to defend Scarlett's actions, and in any case they express their understanding of her motives only in conversation with Scarlett herself. Only Melanie defends Scarlett's actions publicly, but others dismiss Melanie's opinion of Scarlett as merely evidence that she is such a good person herself, she is unable to perceive of "badness" in others. Molly Haskell suggests that Melanie's (and others') devotion to Scarlett "work[s] significantly in her favor, or at least modif[ies] the way we see her." Haskell points out "the all-important love and forgiveness of people *we* love or at least trust. Not just Ashley but Rhett, Mammy, and Melanie—three characters with moral authority—love and admire Scarlett not in spite of her but *for* her shrewdness and honesty, even her outrageousness" (176).

However, it is interesting that readers (and other characters) are more inclined to accept Melanie's approval of Rhett, whose scandalous reputation is as bad as if not worse than Scarlett's, while, as noted, many readers perceive her acceptance of Scarlett to be a weakness. Toward novel's end, Melanie does not believe her community's interpretation of what was witnessed when Scarlett was found in Ashley's arms at the mill, and Melanie is right that the embrace was not evidence of an affair. Indeed Scarlett is enjoying being comforted by Ashley, "without passion, without tenseness, . . . *as a loved friend*" (*GW* 926; emphasis added). One might also argue, however, that Melanie's subsequent pregnancy—and the implicit resumed sexual relations with Ashley—are evidence that Melanie is aware of Ashley's attraction to Scarlett and that, as much as she defends Scarlett against gossip, having sex with Ashley is also Melanie's way of protecting her husband from himself.* Note that during this same conversation between Ashley and Scarlett, he admits, "when I was in prison and things got too bad, I'd take out my memories and thumb them over like pictures," including the memory of how Scarlett looked the day she first confessed her love to him. Though he does not bring up their conversation that day, he does tell her, "I'll always remember you as you were that day of our last barbecue, sitting under an oak with a dozen boys around you. I can even tell you just how you were dressed. . . . I know that dress by heart" (*GW* 921). We could therefore add this conversation to the several others that reveal that Ashley was likely as enamored with Scarlett as she with

* This is not to say that Melanie does not also desire her husband. During Ashley's furlough much earlier in the novel, Scarlett notices that Melanie is blushingly eager to turn in for the night with Ashley. But overall, the reader has little evidence in the novel that Melanie is any less inhibited than Scarlett—and there is evidence that she is more modest. But as a dutiful wife, she would not express (probably not even admit to herself) any resentment of the sexual relations expected after marriage, as Scarlett does.

him. Melanie seems not to blame either of these two people, whom she loves so much, for their attraction to each other. More practical than either, perhaps she recognizes that one cannot always help whom one is attracted to; but she is also confident that, in spite of his lust for Scarlett, Ashley does love his wife. Melanie's more mature, less romantic insightfulness in this case results in a state of contentment with her life, which neither her beloved husband nor her dear friend seems to enjoy.

Ellen Glasgow, a writer Margaret Mitchell greatly admired, wrote in one of her prefaces, "It is seldom in modern fiction that a friendship between two women, especially a pure and unselfish friendship, with both women loving the same man, has assumed a prominent place. . . . But more and more in the modern world, women are coming to understand their interdependence as human beings." Just two years before Glasgow's prefaces were published in the 1938 Virginia edition of her novels, probably only accidentally, Mitchell had depicted just such a friendship in her novel. Not surprisingly, the audience (perhaps Glasgow included) has long overlooked the relationship between Scarlett and Melanie just as blindly as Scarlett herself did, focusing instead, again not unexpectedly, on the relationship between Scarlett and Rhett. Consider then the sentence replaced with ellipses in the Glasgow quote above: "Although such an association appears to be not uncommon in life, the novelist, since he is usually a man, has found the relationship to be deficient alike in the excitement of sex and the masculine drama of action" (Glasgow, *Certain Measure* 245). It is interesting that Charles Frazier, a male writer, did not see any such deficiency and gave to his pair of women characters in *Cold Mountain* the same amount of space he gave his returning soldier. Of course, no rivalry over the same man challenges the friendship between these two women in Frazier's novel, but does the suspense regarding whether Inman will make it home to Ada supersede the developing relationship between Ada and Ruby as the question of whether Scarlett and Rhett will get together continues to distract readers from the value of the relationship between Scarlett and Melanie? In any case, reading the two novels together focuses our attention on the positive role that these women play in each other's lives.

Chapter 2

Gone with the Men

Scarlett and Melanie Redux in *Cold Mountain*

"I'll change it any way you want, except to make a happy ending."

Margaret Mitchell (qtd. in Haskell 140)

"But more and more in the modern world, women are coming to understand their interdependence as human beings."

Ellen Glasgow (*A Certain Measure* 245)

Gone with the Wind (the film as well as the novel) is often mischaracterized as a romance. Arguing against such a classification, Harriet Hawkins notes the novel's lengthy focus on the women after the men have gone to war: "Nowadays the film and novel tend to be characterized as deplorably romantic glorifications of a patriarchal slave-state. There is no disputing the racism; the defense of the Ku Klux Klan is the worst feature of the book. But is *Gone with the Wind* all that romantic? No romantic love ever achieves emotional consummation or is ever completely reciprocated within it, while throughout the central section of the novel dealing with hard times at Tara both male love-interests are absent." Hawkins concludes this point asking, "And does [*Gone with the Wind*] extol patriarchy as well as slavery?" ("Shared" 129). I think neither. Rather, this novel's depiction of the plantation South reveals clearly that it was oppressive for women, as well as slaves.

Charles Frazier focuses much of his Civil War–era novel *Cold Mountain* on two women back home while his hero is away, and (like Margaret Mitchell) he gives the novel no romantic happy ending upon the hero's return. He does provide an epilogue with a glimpse of Ada Monroe's "content and expansive" (*CM* 50) future in spite of a heartbreak in her past, a future in which she and her partner and friend, Ruby Thewes, are the apparent heads of household, matriarchs of their small community, situated outside of the kind of social censure that would likely cruelly label Ada's fatherless daughter a bastard and Ada a fallen woman or a spinster, that would also likely assume Ada is unhappily unmarried (for how could an unmarried woman be happy?), and that would probably raise eyebrows at Ruby's indiscreetly passionate relationship with her husband "even after all this time" (*CM* 354). As Linda Wagner-Martin suggests, "What *Cold Mountain* provides is a new definition of community, or perhaps *communitas:* Ruby and her younger drifter husband and their children living with Ada and her and Inman's child, a family built from women's comradeship and women's natural roles in the all-too-gendered world" ("South" 36).

Cold Mountain's epilogue takes place ten years after the action of the novel, and Ada and Ruby are thriving in spite of the loss of Inman, a sadder loss to Ada than Rhett Butler is to Scarlett, Inman being a much more admirable character in the end, and yet Inman is not mentioned in these closing pages. Contrasting *Cold Mountain* and *Gone with the Wind,* Linda Wagner-Martin calls "Frazier's working out of the Inman-Ada love story . . . a surprisingly more positive outcome than that of the romance in *Gone with the Wind*" ("South" 32). By the time of the epilogue, Ada has most definitely moved on; she is not pining for her past love or "thinking of tomorrow." The focus in the end, rather, is on the present; and in that present the relationship Ada and Ruby have maintained may remind the reader of the great loss that Melanie's absence will be in the life of Scarlett at Tara ten years later.

Given the historical time period of the two novels' settings, it is no wonder that *Cold Mountain* draws comparisons to *Gone with the Wind,* though usually simply for the Civil War–era setting and the phenomenal success of Frazier's debut novel, which brought instant fame to the previously unknown author—as well as the National Book Award among its numerous honors. M. Thomas Inge points out that "*Cold Mountain,* published on June 1, 1997, remained at the top of the *New York Times* best-seller list for forty-three weeks, rivaled in southern fiction only by Margaret Mitchell's *Gone with the*

Wind and Harper Lee's *To Kill a Mockingbird*" (19).* Also ultimately associating *Cold Mountain* with *Gone with the Wind,* in this case comparing the movies, John C. Inscoe argues effectively that Anthony Minghella, who wrote the screenplay and directed the film adaptation, "amplif[ied] the roles of women" in the Civil War; Inscoe notes that in the film (and I would add, in the novel), women are "participants and partners" in the war. He believes that in the movie the women are "active agents in their own defense and in the care and protection they provide for males" (again, as they are in the novel). Inscoe compares the role of women in the film to Scarlett's role in *Gone with the Wind:* "Certainly in no other film set in Appalachia and in no other Civil War film since Scarlett O'Hara vowed that she would never go hungry again has this point been dramatized as vividly or as centrally as it is in *Cold Mountain.*" Inscoe therefore determines that "Minghella deserves much credit for how effectively he portrays the gendered nature of this very messy war as it played out on the many home fronts of Southern Appalachia" (319). All of this that Inscoe argues regarding the role of women in the film is actually *more* applicable to the novel *Cold Mountain.* The novel is much more evenly balanced between narrating the story of Ada and Ruby back home and Inman's efforts to return home. The movie does not fully capture Ada's development from southern belle to Appalachian woman as Ruby teaches her how to take care of her land—and herself.

More memorable in the film are episodes in which various women end up taking care of the men, which may be an interesting role reversal that shows these women's strength, as Inscoe notes, but in contrast to Inscoe's praise of Minghella's treatment of the important role of women in the Civil War, Anna Creadick points out "the gratuitous sex and violence against women in the film." Creadick invites us to "contrast Minghella's scripted madonnas and whores with Frazier's focus on Ada and Ruby, two 19th-century women learning independence and interdependence, blossoming in spite of—even because of—their manlessness" (*"AppalJ"* 331). Creadick's point introduces what this chapter celebrates about Frazier's novel: two women finding a source of strength (rather than competition) in each other.

The point of comparison between *Cold Mountain* and *Gone with the Wind* that this chapter focuses on particularly is the partnership between two women that developed in each novel during the Civil War period and

* When asked if he felt "anxious about writing a Civil War epic in the shadow of *Gone with the Wind,*" Frazier admitted that he had never read the novel and only saw the movie "a few years after *Cold Mountain* came out" (Bauer 32).

that ultimately emerges, I contend, as the most profound relationship in both novels: a healthier relationship than Scarlett's with Rhett and a much more developed relationship than Ada's with Inman. To begin, one should note that Scarlett and Melanie were *just fine* while Rhett and Ashley were away during the war, but as I tell my students, "no conflict, no story," so these men have to survive the war and return to interrupt the cooperative—even friendly—atmosphere that develops between these women in their absence. Before the men's return, however, these two women, like the pair of women in *Cold Mountain,* in their own efforts to survive—and save their families—during the war, demonstrate that they are quite capable of taking care of themselves, largely because each pair of women creates a partnership that is more productive and likely more fulfilling than any of their relationships with men. Therefore, while the authors may break with romantic convention as they bring their respective novels to a close that does not send the female and male leads off into the sunset to live happily ever after, the reader does not have to interpret Rhett's rejection of Scarlett as her comeuppance or view Inman's death as a tragic end for Ada.*

In her study of the "female pastoral" in southern literature, Elizabeth Jane Harrison remarks on a distinction of *Gone with the Wind* that applies as well to *Cold Mountain:* "The friendship between Scarlett and Melanie represents perhaps the greatest departure from traditional southern pastoral in the novel. In male versions of the pastoral, bonding between women would digress too much from the romantic plot" (60). Although the friendship between Scarlett and Melanie is overshadowed by the Scarlett/Rhett romance in the novel, I direct readers to Craig A. Warren's reading of *Gone with the Wind,* in which he argues, "In Mitchell's hands, the war and its aftermath existed as transformative experiences shared equally by both genders. And [Mitchell] worked actively to win for her female characters the same respect and honor awarded soldiers" (47). The reader sees Rhett head off to join the Confederate army and hears about Ashley's suffering in prison. But the reader is *with* Scarlett

*That is not to say that Inman's death is not tragic. I agree with John Crutchfield's reading of Inman's tragedy: "Frazier's Inman . . . has to come all the way up out of Hell—no easy task when Hell is himself. When this Inman seeks to spare the young Birch, and dies because of it, his transformation is like that of Aeschylus' Agamemnon: it brings him fully and lucidly to account with his fate. He is struck down by the very arms he is finally trying to bid farewell. He saves his soul, but at the cost of his life and of his future with the woman he loves" ("*AppalJ*" 338). We do well to note, too, that the ending of Mitchell's novel is certainly tragic for Melanie, who dies far too young.

and Melanie as they struggle to produce a crop that will pay the mortgage and feed their families. And for at least a little while in the novel, the story is theirs as much as it is earlier and later the story of the great romance of Scarlett O'Hara and Rhett Butler. Furthermore Melanie is ever present in Scarlett's story, remaining omnipresent even in the pages that follow her death scene; Rhett comes and goes throughout the novel.

Charles Frazier also digresses (repeatedly and throughout his novel) from the traditional male-centered focus of a war story to what is going on back home, with the woman that Inman left behind. Ada's time with Ruby while Inman is gone far exceeds the time she spent with him before he left, and the relationship that develops between the two women is ultimately more grounded than the brief romance between the male and female "leads." Provocatively some critics have argued that *Cold Mountain* "ultimately privileges" Ada's story over Inman's (Merola par. 27). In his *New York Times* review, James Polk calls Ada's story "richer and deeper," and in her *Washington Post* review, Claire Messud finds Ada's development more significant than Inman's. Although he disagrees with such a reading, Brent Gibson points out that several critics have argued that Ada develops while Inman either does not change or changes for the worse (416). While my focus here is not on Inman (and so I will leave that issue for others), I will argue that *Cold Mountain*'s structure, with chapters alternating between Inman and Ada, reflects the equal importance of the novel's two stories.* Inman's quest story is compelling, more so perhaps for its tragic end, but the story back home of Ada and Ruby is inspiring, and it contributes to a fuller coverage of war in literature—telling the story of those left behind when men go to war.

Margaret Mitchell spends much of her novel suggesting that the lesson Scarlett must learn (the hard way) is that like should marry like (*GW* 34). Scarlett ultimately accepts (too late, it seems) what Rhett and Ashley have tried for years to convince her of: that Rhett and Scarlett were made for each other, as were Ashley and Melanie.† Scarlett's parents' history seems to provide evidence that when people so unlike each other as Gerald O'Hara and

* Linda Wagner-Martin observes regarding the novel's evenly divided story lines, "I do not find the designation 'feminist novel' used in the reviews of *Cold Mountain,* but Frazier's willingness to give Ada's life half his book shows his politics" ("South" 35).

† The novel's attitude toward like marrying like is ultimately mixed. Lauren S. Cardon reminds readers of Mrs. Tarleton's views of the results of the kind of the inbreeding between the Hamilton and Wilkes families ("You get good lines, perhaps, but no stamina" [*GW* 89]) and then argues, "It might have been better for Scarlett to 'breed' with

Ellen Robillard marry, they do not live happily ever after—marriage for Ellen, at least, has not been a fairy tale come true. Her role as typical (and typically burdened) southern lady is an example of a deromanticized element of the novel that does not translate into the movie, which shows Gerald O'Hara's devastation at the loss of his wife but does not provide Ellen's background, through which the novel's reader learns that she did not marry for love. Mitchell tells the reader quite directly that "Ellen's life was not easy, nor was it happy, but she did not expect life to be easy, and, if it was not happy, that was woman's lot. It was a man's world, and she accepted it as such" (*GW* 58). And yet, while most of the men are away at war, and life at Tara becomes a "*woman's* world," Scarlett and Melanie develop an effective partnership from which a different message emerges: like should perhaps *marry* like, but when these two quite differently tempered women *work* together, they successfully protect Tara from the Yankees and their extended family from starvation. The reader, if not Scarlett, can see that her relationship with Melanie is a source of empowerment and security.

Melanie's survival of childbirth, with Scarlett's rather than a doctor's help, anticipates the "productive" nature of these two women's relationship as it develops at Tara: *no one dies on their watch.* Ellen dies before Scarlett and Melanie return to Tara, and Gerald dies after Scarlett leaves for Atlanta, but while these two women are in charge at Tara, all who live there survive. While Scarlett focuses on getting food on the table, Melanie provides comfort to Scarlett's frightened son, bewildered sisters, and Scarlett herself. Melanie also sets an example for the rest by going out, without complaining, to try to work in the fields with Scarlett and by being the "only [one who] did not complain" about the scant meals. At first, Scarlett is "irritated" by Melanie's "gentle hardihood" (*GW* 430). But just a few pages later Scarlett's attitude toward Melanie changes.

When Scarlett shoots the first Yankee intruder, she looks up to see Melanie, with Charles's saber in her hand and "a glow of grim pride in her usually gentle face, *approbation* [in contrast to Ellen's typical "admonition"] and a fierce joy in her smile," and Scarlett realizes, "she's like me! She understands how I feel!" (*GW* 441; emphasis added). Then waiting for more Yankee soldiers to arrive some time later, after Scarlett has sent everyone away to hide the

Ashley," both for the sake of the Wilkes line and also because "the marriage between Scarlett and Rhett is a nightmare," support for which Cardon enumerates effectively, reminding us of Rhett's tendency to react violently (or with threats of violence) when frustrated by Scarlett (Cardon 76).

stock in the swamp, she "wished she had Melanie with her, Melly with her quiet voice, Melly who was so brave the day she shot the Yankee. Melly was worth three of the others" (*GW* 461). Scarlett does find the courage to stand up to the men when they threaten to take that same saber, which belongs to Scarlett's son—hence again she is acting on behalf of another—and by the time the thwarted soldier sets fire to the kitchen, Melanie has returned to check on Scarlett (the only one to do so), and the two women fight the fire "side by side." This episode concludes after Melanie saves Scarlett (who catches on fire) with Scarlett "burrowing her head wearily into [the] soft pillow" of Melanie's lap (*GW* 469), the image of the two of them in this position emphasizing Melanie's motherly role in Scarlett's life (which will be discussed further later).

As Melanie comforts Scarlett, who is distraught over the cotton that did not survive the Yankees' torch, by reminding her of what was saved, she begins, "We haven't lost each other," a poignant starting point for a woman whose highest priority is typically her child; "and our babies are all right" comes second in this instance, suggesting that, for this moment in time at least, Melanie understands that what they have together best serves their children (*GW* 469). Regarding Scarlett's assertion of herself before others (as noted earlier), they cannot take care of their children if they do not take care of themselves. Turning her attention to her baby then, Melanie laughs uproariously over finding the dead man's wallet in Beau's diaper and compliments Scarlett's ingenuity: "'Nobody but you would ever have thought of it,' she cried and flinging her arms around Scarlett's neck she kissed her. 'You are the beatenest sister I ever had!'" The chapter ends,

> Scarlett permitted the embrace because she was too tired to struggle, *because the words of praise brought balm to her spirit* and because, in the dark smoke-filled kitchen, there had been born a greater respect for her sister-in-law, a closer feeling of comradeship.
>
> "I'll say this for her," she thought grudgingly, "she's always there when you need her." (*GW* 470; emphasis added)

The respect is mutual; perhaps most telling, when Melanie went to help hide the stock in the swamp, she left her baby in Scarlett's care, reflecting Melanie's absolute faith in her sister-in-law. And Melanie never ceases to understand what drives Scarlett to even her most scandalous acts. Returning to Scarlett's ultimately self-sacrificing actions as an example, to pay the taxes on Tara, Scarlett plans to sell herself to Rhett, and, when that doesn't work, she marries Frank Kennedy, a man she finds repugnant.

To snare Frank Kennedy, Scarlett draws on the one skill her mother and Mammy taught her that is of any use to her in the postwar South—how to attract a man—for she had realized before leaving Tara to find a benefactor that "nothing her mother had taught her was of any value whatsoever. . . . What value is gentleness? Better that I'd learned to plow or chop cotton" (*GW* 434). As Ann E. Egenriether points out, "from neither of her parents . . . does Scarlett inherit the ability to survive in a world where all comfort and security are lost" (121). Lauren S. Cardon lists the qualities in Scarlett's nature—"pragmatism, physical strength, audacity, and willingness to break social and religious mores"—that do allow her "to save her family and plantation." Cardon notes, however, that the postwar "struggle" to survive "strips Scarlett of any loyalty to the values of her mother, for Scarlett resents her upbringing for failing to prepare her for the loss she has just endured" (73).

Like Scarlett, Ada Monroe of Charles Frazier's *Cold Mountain* discovers that she is not prepared for the lean days of the Civil War: "A certain amount of resentment came upon [Ada] when she thought that a measure of applied knowledge in the area of food production and preparation would stand her in better stead at that particular time than any fine understanding of the principles of perspective in painting." Since her father's death, "she had discovered herself to be frighteningly ill-prepared in the craft of subsistence" (*CM* 23). Ada is starving when we meet her, reminding the reader of Scarlett O'Hara's famous line, "as God is my witness, I'm never going to be hungry again" (*GW* 428). One might also compare Ellen O'Hara encouraging Scarlett to "conceal from men your sharp intelligence" (*GW* 59) to Frazier's description of Ada as "educated beyond the point considered wise for females" (*CM* 22).

Upon first meeting Ada, however, the reader may wonder if she has enough Scarlett O'Hara gumption in her to do what it takes to survive the war after her father's death, a point of contrast between the two female protagonists that John Inscoe finds "refreshing": "Given our celebration of southern women's fortitude and resourcefulness . . . it is Ada's very frailties and her obliviousness to even the rudiments of mountain life that make her so compelling a character" (305). Her initial helplessness after her father's death during the war is admittedly more credible than Scarlett O'Hara's overnight transformation as she takes over for her mother immediately upon her return to Tara after the burning of Atlanta. But with Ruby's help, Ada finds the Scarlett within herself, learns how to farm and thus how to survive without a man—or servant—around.

As a very young child Ruby had to learn how to survive without a man—or anyone—to take care of her, and she has years of experience taking care of herself by the time she walks into Ada's life. Frazier's development of Ruby employs the typical characteristics of Appalachian women in literature since the 1930s: "mountain women are portrayed," according to Danny L. Miller in *Wingless Flights: Appalachian Women in Fiction,* "as strong, proud, full of life and indomitable spirit" (2). Miller also notes as "the first and most obvious attribute of women in Appalachian fiction . . . their close, almost mythic, relationship with the natural world" (3). One can certainly recognize Frazier's Ruby Thewes in these characteristics, and such a description might also call to mind Irish-descended Scarlett O'Hara. Like Ruby, Scarlett has a strong, innate survivor instinct, in spite of being raised in a society much like Ada's (and nothing like Ruby's).

The author of *Cold Mountain,* though writing fifty years after the writers Miller is referring to (who were contemporaries of Margaret Mitchell), seems to have created Ruby from the prototype described by Miller: "The emphasis is not on women as victims, although certainly many features of their lives are hard to bear and personal sacrifice is a major characteristic of their existence. Rather the native writers, by focusing on family relationships and the inner lives of women, emphasize the qualities in the lives of Appalachian women that make them admirable rather than pathetic" (2). And one can see too how Ada's relationship with Ruby contributes to the Charleston belle's development into an Appalachian woman, as also described in Miller's study of their depiction in literature: "They have an affinity with nature and the cyclic patterns of life; they love their land, homes and families; they nurture and sustain community and culture; they find solace in the everyday hardships although they are often powerless against the forces that victimize them." Deviating from this type to some extent, Ruby, in contrast to Ada, resists family ties and is not so interested in community, but it is no wonder, for Miller reminds readers of the "subservient role [of women] in the patriarchal system" (3) that typically results in a less satisfying life than the matriarchy that Ada and Ruby create for themselves in Black Cove. Indeed Miller's description of the mountain woman's usual hard life (and brief youth) may remind the reader of the earlier summary of Ellen O'Hara's life: "she was pretty in youth, but married young, bore a houseful of 'youngens,' led a life of endless drudgery often tinged with 'unaccountable' melancholy, became old at thirty-five" (Miller 23)—coincidentally the age Ellen O'Hara was when she died. The consequences of a patriarchy to women were certainly not limited to the hardscrabble life of mountain women.

Ada realizes immediately upon meeting Ruby that this strange woman is proposing "something on the order of equality," not servitude, with her one condition for partnering with Ada: "that everybody empties their own night jar" (*CM* 52). "Ruby insists that she and Ada be equals," Linda Wagner-Martin notes, and Ada recognizes their equality: "Ada, the landowner, understands the wealth of knowledge Ruby has wrung from the land, and tries to learn it for herself" ("South" 35). From this point on in their lives, they share the land and the work: Ruby may allow Ada time to sit over a cup of coffee in the morning, but she also "made Ada work when she did not want to" and "made a point of refusing to tackle all the unpleasant work herself" (*CM* 81). In turn for Ruby teaching Ada how to survive, Ada reads to Ruby, tells her stories, braids her hair. In short each woman nurtures the other—just as in Mitchell's novel Scarlett and Melanie provide different kinds of parenting to those in their care at Tara. These women's relationships reflect a different kind of partnership than what would be found in most marriages of their time and place: a more equitable give-and-take than they would have with husbands in either of their patriarchal societies. In *Gone with the Wind,* Scarlett takes Melanie into Tara and protects her; Melanie mothers Scarlett and loves her. In *Cold Mountain,* Ada gives Ruby a place to live; Ruby shows Ada how to live. One might draw from Margaret Mitchell's mother's philosophy to recognize the value of both women's contribution to their partnership. Mitchell wrote about the lesson her mother taught her with the example of southerners who survived the Civil War: "She talked about the world those people had lived in, such a secure world, and how it had exploded beneath them. And she told me that my own world was going to explode under me, some day, and God help me if I didn't have some weapon to meet the new world. She was talking about the necessity of having an education, both classical [Ada's book knowledge] and practical [Ruby's farming knowledge]. For she said all that would be left after a world ended would be what you could do with your hands and what you had in your head" (Harwell, *Margaret* 38).

Martin Crawford calls Ruby "Ada's alter ego," and certainly she is as different from Ada as Melanie from Scarlett, but one similarity between them is illuminated by comparing the two pairs of women: Ada and Ruby were both raised motherless and thus find with each other the closest thing each has experienced of having a mother in her life. Crawford notes that the two "women forge emotional ties that compensate for their respective familial deficiencies" (188). Melanie and her brother, Charles, were raised by their spoiled, childish aunt, Pittypat, so one might infer regarding Melanie's mothering nature that nurturing all those around her could be a means of filling that void in her own life. While Ellen had been there for almost two decades of Scarlett's life, she was so distant that "Scarlett regarded her as something holy and apart from all the rest of humankind" (*GW* 60), and after Ellen's death, Scarlett must take on her mother's burdensome role at Tara. But Melanie, as we have seen, gives Scarlett the affectionate nurturing that Ellen did not. One might, therefore, apply to these two pairs of women a theory about women's friendships proposed by Luise Eichenbaum and Susie Orbach, who suggest that "woman-to-woman relationships duplicate aspects of the mother-daughter relationship and simultaneously extend the promise to repair some of the hurt and difficulties of the original relationship. Consequently, in adult female friendships we frequently observe an unconscious wish to . . . be mothered and cared for, to receive the nurturance that they continue to crave. Each woman may unconsciously look to the other one to provide whatever she didn't get from her mother; she may depend on her friend for support and encouragement and approval" (75). Certainly Melanie provides encouragement and approval where Ellen provided only criticism. Similarly Ada and Ruby do not criticize each other for their differences; rather they enjoy the new perspectives and experiences each brings to the other during their new life together.

When Ada and Ruby first team up, the description of their daily existence echoes Mitchell's description of life at Tara after Scarlett and Melanie arrive: "Simply living had never struck Ada as such a tiresome business" (*CM* 80). And as Scarlett must drive her extended family to plow fields and plant a crop so that they might eat, Ruby pushes both herself and Ada: "The rudeness of eating, of living, that's where Ruby seemed to aim Ada every day that first month. She held Ada's nose to the dirt to see its purpose . . . made her dress in rough clothes and grub in the dirt until her nails seemed to her crude as the claws of a beast" (*CM* 81). At one point in *Gone with the Wind,* Scarlett recalls that "during the lean months at Tara she had done a man's work and done it well. She had been brought up to believe that a woman alone could accomplish nothing, yet she had managed the plantation without men to help her until Will [Benteen] came." And following this realization comes another shocking (to her) insight: "I believe that women could manage everything in the world without a man's help" (*GW* 620). At first Ada, who believes that only a male hired hand could help her at Black Cove, accepts Ruby into her life merely because Ruby points out that she is the only person available, but Ruby ultimately shows Ada that the two of them can survive without a man around. Then, as *Cold Mountain* draws to an end, when Inman returns, Ruby asserts directly to Ada, "we can do without him. You might think we can't, but we can. We're just starting. I've got a vision in my mind of how that cove needs to be. And I know what needs doing to get there. The crops and animals. Land and buildings. It will take a long time. But I know how to get there. War or peace, there's not a thing we can't do ourselves. You don't need him" (*CM* 325).

Clearly Ruby believes that by how her "vision . . . of how that cove needs to be" is threatened by Inman's arrival. Danny Miller notes that the Appalachian woman's "longing for land is a manifestation of her desire to be free of subservience to her husband." Miller continues, "Mountain women love the land and long for the security it provides" (7). Ruby may not have a husband in mind for herself yet, but as a woman who was raised in this region, she understands the potential threat of a man to the lifestyle she and Ada have enjoyed, their equal partnership with each other, rather than subservience to husbands. Before she answers Ruby, Ada provocatively "took off one of her rings and put it on Ruby's hand." Then "Ruby took it off and twisted it roughly back on Ada's finger." Exchanging this ring with each other might be read as confirmation of their bond to each other, regardless of what Ada decides about Inman. She then agrees with Ruby's assessment of their self-sufficiency: "I know I don't need him. But I think I want him"; and though Inman could be a threat to her own dreams, Ruby accepts her partner's wishes right away: "Well that's a whole different thing" (*CM* 325), she tells Ada, testimony of Ruby's trust in and loyalty to Ada. She puts Ada's desires above her own.

By this time, the reader realizes, Ada and Ruby are in position to be the caretakers of the men in their lives, Inman and Stobrod, Ruby's father. Ruby, having come to know her father in a new way through Ada's appreciation of his music, is able to set aside the memories of past wrongs in order to nurse Stobrod back to life after he is shot by the Home Guard. Ada witnesses this healing in progress (both Stobrod's physical healing and Ruby's emotional healing after a traumatic childhood) and has learned from Ruby that "cures of all sorts exist in the natural world." Ada tells Inman, "I know people can be mended. Not all, and some more immediately than others. But some can be. I don't see why not you" (*CM* 333). Inman is comforted, having perceived while Ada led him back to where she and Ruby were camped with the wounded Stobrod that "she seemed to have a clear destination in mind and that some note in her voice said, Right this minute I know more than you do, and what I know is everything might well be fine" (*CM* 322).

A significant difference between the two novels emerges here. The idea of Ada taking care of the soul-sick Inman and Ruby of her feckless father seems not so burden laden as the idea of Scarlett having to take care of Ashley after Melanie's death, and the reason for the difference in tone is that Ada and Ruby still have each other, while Melanie is *leaving* Ashley in Scarlett's care and thus *leaving Scarlett.* Of course, their partnership had effectively come to an end before Melanie's death. Melanie continued to defend Scarlett to novel's end, but, as Elizabeth Jane Harrison has pointed out, their "teamwork stops when they move back to Atlanta. It seems that Scarlett can only recognize the value of female friendship during moments of great danger like these while the men are away at war" (60)—and, sadly, when she is about to lose that friendship: Scarlett finally fully appreciates the value of Melanie's love at Melanie's deathbed. Her belated insight is at least in part the consequence, as will be argued more extensively in chapter 4, of a male-identified, patriarchal society that privileges the heterosexual marriage over any other kind of "teamwork" between women.

In contrast, before Inman's death, in telling Inman about her life, Ada had been clear about the importance and permanence, she hoped, of Ruby's role in it: "Whatever comes to pass between you and me," she tells her lover, "I want her to stay in Black Cove as long as she cares to. If she never leaves I will be glad, and if she does I'll mourn her absence." When Inman asks if Ruby will "put up with me around," Ada reassures him, with the stipulation: "If you understand that she is not a servant nor a hired hand. She is my friend. She does not take orders, and she does not empty night jars other than her own" (*CM* 337). They are, in short, partners and friends; there is no class (or gender) hierarchy in their new world.

In his discussion of *Cold Mountain,* Kevin Grauke describes Ada's insight by the time of the novel's epilogue, ten years after Inman's death: "Ada has come to realize that society at large is not necessary to be content; in fact, it is a hindrance. All that is needed is the community of the family and the knowledge needed to live off the land." Grauke notes that the idyllic ending of the epilogue occurs "despite [the] calamity" of Inman's death (55), and his death is certainly more permanent than the imminent departure of Rhett Butler (what Scarlett wants, she usually gets, so if she wants Rhett back, one might believe that their separation is only temporary). Still, as will be shown in the chapters to follow, it is Scarlett's decision to return to Tara, to the land that she loves, that provides the note of pending triumph at the end of Mitchell's novel more so than the possibility of Rhett's return to this unforgettable woman:

> She had gone back to Tara once in fear and defeat and she had emerged from its sheltering walls strong and armed for victory. What she had done once, somehow—please God, she could do again! . . . She thought of Tara and it was as if a gentle cool hand were stealing over her heart. She could see the white house gleaming welcome to

> her through the reddening autumn leaves, feel the quiet hush of the country twilight coming down over her like a benediction, feel the dews falling on the acres of green bushes starred with fleecy white, see the raw color of the red earth and the dismal dark beauty of the pines on the rolling hills. . . .
>
> With the spirit of her people who would not know defeat, even when it stared them in the face, she raised her chin. (*GW* 1036–37)

So too does Frazier's novel end "in a positive fashion," as described by Brent Gibson: "The novel gives numerous clues that its ending is to be viewed in a positive fashion. While not negating the pain and loss caused by Inman's death, any grief felt by Ada is kept offstage as the novel ends with Inman's 'bright dream of a home' [353] and the description in the epilogue of Black Cove as a place of fruitfulness, life, love, and reconciliation. The imagery is of order, growth, and life moving forward" (428).

Charles Frazier notes that the whole time he was writing *Cold Mountain* he knew how the real W. P. Inman's life had ended, and thus the story he composed was always moving toward a close in which Inman dies (Bauer 31). Harriet Hawkins points out that so too did Mitchell know from the start how her novel would end, and Hawkins views this ending as positively as Gibson views the end of *Cold Mountain:* "From the beginning—the conclusion was the first part she wrote—Margaret Mitchell directed the course of the action towards an 'open' ending that simultaneously departed from romance conventions and assured a continuing appeal to the reader's imagination. *Gone with the Wind* has been making money without a 'happy' ending for a half a century." And Hawkins sees Scarlett's fate in positive terms: "What Mitchell's heroine opened up to her admirers was the possibility of independence, choice" ("Sins" 492). Frazier reminds his readers that the end of a romance is not necessarily the end of a satisfying life: "In that final chapter of *Cold Mountain,* what I was trying to arrive at . . . is that the damage has been done. They're living with the loss and the damage, but they're living. They've built this little family community" (Bauer 33).

Although the movie adaptation, to some extent at least, reduces *Cold Mountain* to a tragic romance directed toward only a brief reunion for star-crossed lovers, the reader of the novel recognizes that the memories and fantasies that Ada and Inman have of each other to hold on to during the war merely served to keep them going through very hard times. There was almost no time for courtship before they separated, Inman was gone for four years, and he dies soon after returning. The novel is much more about their respective endeavors to survive (for Inman, only to reach his goal: Ada and home) than it is about their great love for each other (they hardly *know* each other). Indeed, before Inman left he told Ada, "If I am shot to death, in five years you'll hardly remember my name," and, though she had protested, "in her heart . . . she wondered, Is anything remembered forever?" (*CM* 196), a question that anticipates the goat woman's later consolation to Inman that "there's no lasting memory" of pain (*CM* 219). Though Inman does not fully agree with the old woman, wondering at her notion that forgetting is one of God's gifts, for he cannot imagine a caring God who would allow pain in the first place, still he passes the theory on to Ada later on. Ada has learned by this time to take such good care of herself that she adds to the woman's theory: "I think you have to give Him some help in forgetting. You have to work at not trying to call such thoughts up, for if you call hard enough they'll come" (*CM* 343). Ada has certainly come a long way by this time from the girl who created some romantic fantasy around her departing soldier, thinking of him as the wayfaring stranger of her romantic stories, to the woman who determined that "to lie down beside him, skin to skin, seemed the only cure" (*CM* 341). And although the daughter evidently produced during their brief reunion would be a constant reminder of Ada's lost love, the novel's epilogue has no direct mention of Inman in it. Ada apparently puts into practice herself what she had advised Inman regarding painful memories.*

Ada's half of the novel (her chapters alternating with Inman's) is about her development (like Scarlett's) from a southern belle into an independent woman rather than into a southern lady. Ada may be pulling her own weight in her partnership with Ruby by the time of Inman's return, but what kind of *wife* would this "New Woman" make?—perhaps a wife something like Mrs. Frank Kennedy / Mrs. Rhett Butler (and how happy were Scarlett's husbands with her?). Ironically Scarlett is perhaps happiest—or at least most "content" with her life—during her marriage to Frank Kennedy, who allows her to have her way. (She's easier to get along with that way.) With the marriage of Scarlett and Frank, as with the partnership of Scarlett and Melanie, one might argue that Mitchell undermines Gerald O'Hara's "like must

* Ada does allude to her reunion with Inman in the epilogue when, finding Ruby and her husband embracing in the fields, she thinks "to make some wry comment. Do I need to cough?" (*CM* 354), an echo of what Ruby had said upon interrupting Inman and Ada ten years before. She does not, however, pursue the memory to a specific evocation of Inman. As noted, he is not mentioned in the epilogue. Ada is living in the present, not the past.

marry like" contention. Although Frank does not have the amount of money her next husband (Rhett) will entice Scarlett with, he has enough to inspire her entrepreneurial nature, and he does not have the courage to thwart her enterprises. Also, since she is not in love with him (or he with her), there is no romance, the source of most of Scarlett's problems—her romanticizing of Ashley's and Rhett's romanticizing of her. During her marriage to Frank, Scarlett's focus remains on business, at which she is more successful than she is at being ladylike and in which she finds more satisfaction than she does in being in love.

Sadly, in her rejection of "ladylike" behavior, Scarlett goes too far in such areas as her use of convict labor. In contrast to Ruby, whose plan for Ada's land breaks with the traditionally oppressive Appalachian patriarchy, it is likely that Scarlett is modeling her business on how Gerald managed Tara. The plantation owner left the handling of slaves to overseers not unlike the man who works the convicts at Scarlett's mill. Once Scarlett witnesses their mistreatment, she steps in and tries to right the wrong but then backs off when the "overseer" threatens to quit. She does not have Ellen behind her, insisting she intervene, as Gerald did when he fired his overseer for impregnating Emmie Slattery. (Gerald, one recalls, was not convinced that the man's crime was so bad and fires the overseer only at Ellen's insistence.) By the time that Scarlett is running a lumberyard, Melanie (Scarlett's replacement for Ellen) is more focused on her roles as wife, mother, and southern lady and resumes her role as Scarlett's partner only when called on to defend her friend to others. Also sad then is that Melanie's restored Old Order priorities are to her own detriment, for Melanie's death can be traced to the high value she places on traditional roles for women. She is determined to have another baby in spite of the doctor's warning that another pregnancy would kill her. Taking up her more "womanly" roles as wife and mother (in contrast to the less "ladylike" roles she played at Tara—as field hand, for instance, and as Scarlett's champion) leads to Melanie's pregnancy and early death.*

Neither *Gone with the Wind* nor *Cold Mountain* has a conventional romantic-plot ending, and yet one might argue that both have happi*er*-ever-after endings for the women protagonists than these women might have lived had they reached the goal they thought they were striving for (and the goal of more traditional romances): a (particular) man. Scarlett realizes upon

* Charles Rowan Beye makes a similar point about Scarlett's mother: reminding us that Ellen dies "from typhoid contracted while caring for the sick," he argues that she "dies for being the stereotypical nurturing woman" (368).

Melanie's death that she is no longer in love with Melanie's husband and that she does love her own husband—but also that these realizations come too late. By this time defeated (as will be shown in chapter 3), Rhett is deserting Scarlett once again to reconnect with the Old South he rejected so long ago. He wants nothing to do with the values of the New South, in which Scarlett O'Hara is still standing, while his precious daughter has died.

The unhappy part of Mitchell's ending is not so much that Scarlett realizes too late that she loves Rhett, but that she has lost Melanie, who, like Scarlett's mother, has died too young. Melanie's refusal to reconcile herself to just one child and thus her own inability, in contrast to Scarlett, to imagine herself beyond the roles of wife and mother has led to an early death. Furthermore Rhett has recently tricked Scarlett into selling her lumber mill to Ashley, leaving Scarlett with neither the friend who loved her nor the enterprise she found fulfilling. But Scarlett will be okay. As Mammy says upon Bonnie's death, "Scarlett kin stan' whut de Lawd sen', kase she done had ter stan' a-plen'y" (*GW* 992), an assertion echoed by Scarlett, who says to herself after Melanie's death and her realization of her loss, "I can stand it. I can stand anything. I've had to stand so much" (*GW* 1015).

Ada will stand her loss, too, in her case with the support of her continued partnership and friendship with Ruby, as evidenced by the novel's epilogue. Who is to say whether Ada could have lived happily ever after with Inman? We do know that Inman felt irredeemably corrupted by his war experience and that the continued violence he witnesses and participates in on his journey home seems to confirm to him that he "could be too far ruined" (*CM* 315) to live out his fantasy of a life with Ada. Recalling to her the night "when I took you in my lap in the kitchen by the stove and you told me you would forever like to sit there and rest your head on my shoulder," he tells her in the letter he writes in the novel's opening chapter, "if you knew what I have seen and done, it would make you fear to do such again" (*CM* 17). John Crutchfield considers "the question of whether or not Inman is now too 'broken' to love and be loved . . . a real question, and Frazier doesn't do much to reassure us." Crutchfield believes that "when Inman expresses the fear that he is no longer worthy of Ada . . . we know that he has good reason to feel this way" ("*AppalJ*" 337). Furthermore Inman's reunion fantasy pictures Ada "dressed in her fine clothes. . . . She would run to him, lifting her skirts. . . . She would rush . . . in a flurry of petticoats" (*CM* 312). Contrasting significantly with this image, with its emphasis on ladies' clothing, when they do finally meet again, Ada is wearing pants, has just shot wild turkeys, and upon seeing Inman, points a gun at him. How will Inman adjust to this new Ada?

For her part, one might recall, too, Ada's willingness to leave Charleston with her father largely because the only goal for her there was to marry, and her prospects had not been especially appealing. Finding a husband is not a primary goal of this young woman. Still, in Inman's absence, Ada does spin a bit of a fantasy around this young man, who seemed so different from her Charleston beaux, and their reunion *is* passionate—and certainly untraditional (since they engage in premarital sex)—but she is also passionate about her new life with Ruby as self-reliant women. Much more of her time and thoughts are taken up by the activities of this new life than indulging in her memories of Inman or fantasizing about his return. Indeed, one day Ada looked around at her "new world" and realized, "On such a day as this, despite the looming war and all the work she knew the cove required of her, she could not see how she could improve her world. It seemed so fine she doubted it could be done" (*CM* 108). Would Inman's presence "improve her world" or intrude on it? Martin Crawford suggests that "there is no place for Inman . . . in this ideal domestic world" (189). Inman would certainly hold no traditional place, for Ada would likely be the one in the role of taking care of him rather than vice versa—which may have been fine with Ada, but would Inman have been okay with such a role reversal?

Considering the question of the couple's compatibility after their respective experiences during their time apart, John Inscoe remarks on how Ada's life has "expand[ed], with more scope and greater range, so that by the time she and her lover are reunited, she has undergone a transformation fully as profound as that inflicted on Inman by the traumas of war" (311). Some critics believe they have grown in different directions (like Scarlett and Rhett)—for example, Paul Ashdown notes how "Ada grows in ability, confidence and self awareness," while Inman "evaporates physically and emotionally as his journey progresses" (215–16). But perhaps (in contrast to Mitchell's lovers) their individual transformations would make them more compatible than they might have been, since they have learned what is (and is not) important in a broader "scope and greater range" than they were probably able to see and consider in their lives before the war. Kevin Grauke remarks on Ada's development as boding well for a relationship with Inman because she "has come to be as self-sufficient as Inman has always been." He perceives Inman as "pleasantly surprised by her metamorphosis" and argues that now "the social barriers that had existed between them before Inman left to fight in the war have disappeared; the couple is able to come together naturally, without artifice" (55). Indeed consider their reunion—Ada wearing pants, later disrobing while Inman watched, and their passionate lovemaking and long conversations—in contrast to their last embrace before his departure for the war, which was impeded by Ada's clothes, described with imagery that calls to mind Mammy tightening Scarlett's corset before the barbecue: "Ada had on about all the clothes women of her station then wore, and so her body was all cased up underneath many lapped and pleated yards of dead fabric. His hand at her waist touched whalebones of corset stays, and when she took a step back and looked at him, the bones creaked against each other as she moved and breathed. She guessed she felt to him like a terrapin shut up inside its hull, giving little evidence that a distinct living thing, warm and in its skin, lay inside" (*CM* 204). By the time of their reunion, Ada has become quite content with the self that had previously hidden underneath layers of social accouterments.

Significantly Ada's contentment seems drawn from the mountains that Inman has been struggling to reach since the novel's opening. Early in the novel Ada realizes that "outsider though she was, this place, the blue mountains, seemed to be holding her where she was. From any direction she came at it, the only conclusion that left her any hope of self-*content* was this: what she could see around her was all that she could count on. The mountains and a desire to find if she could make a *satisfactory* life of common things here—together they seemed to offer the promise of a more *content* and expansive life, though she could in no way picture even its starkest outlines" (*CM* 50–51; emphasis added). Ada wonders, if "the path to contentment was to abide by one's own nature and follow its path," what "if one had not the slightest hint [of] what one's nature was" (*CM* 51). Soon after, significantly, Ruby walks into her life. Ruby helps Ada develop into a mountain woman with the "love of place—land and all it symbolizes" that Danny Miller talks about in his book on Appalachian women in fiction: "Mountain women long for land as the one sure and abiding reality in their lives. . . . [T]he land sustains them both physically and spiritually. For them it represents freedom and independence as well as security" (6). So by the time of her reunion with Inman, Ada has a much clearer picture of her life—she just does not yet know if it will include Inman. Either way, her nature suggests that it will be a *satisfying* life.

Also arguing for the couple's postwar compatibility, John Inscoe points out their similar critical reactions to those who would romanticize war (333–34)—which may remind the reader of Scarlett and Rhett, neither of whom bought into romantic, chivalric notions that led to the Civil War. Ada asserts at one point that "she found the war to exhibit anything but the fine characteristics of tragedy and nobility. She found it, even at a great distance, brutal and benighted on both sides about equally. Degrading to all" (*CM* 141).

Inman admits to the goat woman that he no longer believes in the seemingly noble reasons soldiers are fighting this war. He "now guessed it was boredom with the repetition of the daily rounds that had made them take up weapons" (*CM* 218). But whereas Ada finds it difficult to hold in her laughter as Mrs. McKennet, who "found the fighting glorious and tragic and heroic," recounts "a long and maudlin story she had read about a recent battle, its obvious fictitiousness apparently lost on her" (*CM* 140), Inman is so devastated by what he has witnessed during his experience at war that one could not imagine him able to laugh at the widow's ridiculous story. One wonders along with Inman if he is "ruined beyond repair" (*CM* 333).

The two young heroes of Frazier's novel might have become like-minded ideologically and ultimately share a connection to the region, and their life experiences are by novel's end somewhat less different than they once were, but while Inman has determined that what he has witnessed may make him unfit for human companionship, Ada has developed a more positive and constructive self-confidence as a result of her wartime experience. Though Scarlett and Rhett are both contemptuous of the war and the Lost Cause mentality, consider how Scarlett must hide her hard work beneath the dress made of curtains to fool Rhett into seeing her as unchanged by the war, while Ada greets Inman as a "strange trousered figure, like a mannish boy" (*CM* 319). And while Rhett admonishes Scarlett upon seeing the state of her work-roughened hands, essentially annoyed with her for not being the pretty offering he had hoped, Inman tells Ada upon recognizing her underneath the man's hat she wears, "I've been coming to you on a hard road and I'm not letting you go" (*CM* 320). He is apparently not too disturbed by the difference between his fantasy and the reality of Ada.

Ada writes to her cousin at one point during her transformative new life, "You would not know me, nor, upon seeing the current want of delicacy in my aspect and costume, would you much care to" (*CM* 257), but she attributes the change in herself to "contentment" (*CM* 258), an attitude quite different from Inman's state of mind. Inman tells the goat woman about Ada "and said the verdict he had come to at the hospital was that he loved her and wished to marry her, though he realized marriage implied some faith in a theoretical future, a projection of paired lines running forward through time, drawing nearer and nearer to one another until they became one line. It was a doctrine he could not entirely credit. Nor was he at all sure Ada would find his offer welcome, not from a man galled in body and mind as he had become" (*CM* 220). Later he tells Ada he is worried that "in time we'd both be wretched and bitter" (*CM* 333). But of course Frazier does not allow them the opportunity to find out. Whatever the reader thinks of their future becomes moot—they don't have a future. Inman is killed soon after their reunion, narrowing the novel's focus in the end to the fates of the surviving women.

One might question the validity and usefulness of pondering the fate of a character's life beyond the close of a novel, but it is difficult for me not to seek the comfort of doing so in the absence of a traditional happy ending for characters like Ada and Ruby, Scarlett and Melanie (although I reluctantly accept that there is no future for Melanie). Knowing how the books end (and refusing to read the sequels, Alexandra Ripley's *Scarlett* [1991] and Donald McCaig's *Rhett Butler's People* [2007]), I find myself thinking "what if" each time I reread, but I ultimately agree with Robert Frost that regardless of which road we choose, we end up where we end up, our characters determining our fate, and so, pondering what would have happened had we chosen a different path is needless worry. Projecting the future, what *next* rather than what *if,* on the basis of the actual endings of these novels, however, is comforting, for one can find hope of a happy future for at least Scarlett, Ada, and Ruby, the characters most comfortable with—indeed who thrived because of—the changed, postwar world. Scarlett is certainly better off without Rhett, who, in the end, is going back to Charleston in search of the same Old South he had criticized so insightfully to Scarlett and condemned Ashley for being so devoted to. Inman may have been a more admirable character than Rhett and his death a tragic loss to Ada, but she will be fine—happy even, it seems, according to the novel's epilogue, certainly *satisfied* and *content* (to use the words Frazier employs so often in reference to Ada) with her life within the extended family that includes Ruby's family and her own daughter.

When Ada left Charleston with her father, she did not know what it was she wanted, but she had the courage to leave the familiar in search of it. The Civil War serves the same purpose in Ada's life that it does in Scarlett's, as described by Louis Rubin Jr., who disagrees with those who believe Scarlett "does what she does in order to survive, with the implication that had it not been for the need to sweat and scheme in order to survive, she would have been better off, happier, more contented." Rubin counters that "rather the reverse is more like the truth: she was deeply dissatisfied under the old regime, and the effect of the war and the destruction of the plantation system was to liberate her from the constriction of her traditional role as Southern lady" ("Scarlett" 96). After Ada's father dies, the Swangers ask Ada if she will go back to Charleston. In response to her saying she didn't yet know what she would do, they suggest that she "take a mirror and look backwards into a well" (*CM* 36) to see her future, an image that may recall to the reader of southern literature Allen Tate's reference to the "backward glance" writers of the Southern Renascence took as they "stepped over the border" to enter the modern world, looking back, he suggests, to see what from the past is worth preserving in the present—good and bad since lessons are learned from both (272). Ada's vision in the well seems to predict Inman's return, and she hears lines from "Wayfaring Stranger," which perhaps foreshadow Inman's death ("No toil, no sick nor danger, in that fair land to which I go" [*CM* 38]). She wonders about the vision: "Am I meant to follow, or should I wait its coming?" (*CM* 37). Either way, the focus of her interpretation of this "backward" vision seems to be on what it portends regarding the traditional romance she is waiting for. Significantly, shortly after the vision, Ada looks around at her land, which "showed no neglect from this distance," and she realizes, also significantly, that she would have difficulty finding a hired hand "since anyone fit to work was off warring" (*CM* 39). One might consider this scene part of her vision, a less traditional alternative to looking backward to see what her future holds (the Swangers were, after all, also suggesting she return to Charleston). The vision of her land "show[ing] no neglect" anticipates Ruby's arrival to help her and foreshadows Ruby's effect on the land, which will end up being as important to Ada as it is to Ruby, as Ada develops into a mountain woman more like Ruby than we can imagine at this early point of the novel.

With Ruby, Ada will be able to take care of her land even after Inman, likely the determined figure walking toward her in her well vision, resumes his (spiritual) journey to Cold Mountain rather than staying with her in Black Cove. One may envision Inman continuing on after he is shot to "that fair land" of "no toil, no sick nor danger" that his friend Swimmer had described to him: "Men could not go there to stay and live, but in that high land the dead spirit could be reborn" (*CM* 16), and, presumably, nine months after Inman's departure for that place, his progeny is born to Ada, who stays put, on her land, waiting, as her vision suggested that she do. Perhaps one can find comfort for Scarlett in a comparison: after her nightmare vision comes true, Rhett too will step past Scarlett and go a different way, in his case backward, to Charleston, back to the Old Order he had previously rejected, and Scarlett will find the security of home, which she did not find in her Atlanta mansion, behind the lighted windows of Tara where she too can thrive on her own terms, like Ellen Glasgow's Dorinda Oakley, as will be discussed in the following chapter.

By the time of her brief reunion with Inman, Ada had at least figured out what she did *not* want besides a traditional life, for on the night that she and Ruby agreed that she did not *need* Inman, she says (with more certainty than her beginning, "I *think* I want him"), "What I'm *certain* I don't want . . . is to find myself someday in a new century, an old bitter woman looking back, wishing that right now I'd had more nerve" (*CM* 325; emphasis added). So, with the nonjudgmental approval of her friend, she thwarts tradition again, and the result, we find out in the novel's epilogue, is not only that she has a daughter, but also that she is a woman looking forward, without bitterness, from season to season with this same partner—Ruby—and their not-so-traditional family, living a life not so very different from the one she and Inman fantasized during their brief reunion, in the days when they created their child, when "they agreed they neither gave two hoots now as to how marriages were normally conducted. They would do as they pleased and run their lives by the roll of the seasons" (*CM* 344).*

It is too bad that Melanie could not see past convention to recognize the extended family that she and Scarlett had created, a family in which they took care of each other's children so that, if she could have seen past tradition, Melanie might have realized that she had three children: her own Beau as well as Scarlett's Wade and Ella, who needed the "mothering" affection that Melanie gave them as much as they needed the sense of safety and protection that Scarlett provided.† Certainly there is ample evidence that Wade was comforted by his mother's strength during the war, even as he receives from Melanie and later Rhett the affectionate sympathy and understanding that was not in Scarlett's nature to give.

Melanie ultimately loses sight of the value of her partnership with Scarlett, no longer seeing it any more clearly than Scarlett did (as evidenced by the fact that Melanie is so determined to have another baby in spite of the threat

* In this detail, one can find a way to read Inman's death less tragically by noting the seasonal imagery in Frazier's description of his death, which suggests that in his dying moments Inman's whole (unlived) life flashes before his eyes: "He drifted in and out and dreamed a bright dream of a home. It had a coldwater spring rising out of rock, black dirt fields, old trees. In his dream the year seemed to be happening all at one time, all the seasons blending together. Apple trees hanging heavy with fruit but yet unaccountably blossoming ice rimming the spring, okra plants blooming yellow and maroon, maple leaves red as October, corn tops tasseling, a stuffed chair pulled up to the glowing parlor hearth, pumpkins shining in the fields, laurels blooming on the hillsides, ditch banks full of orange jewelweed, white blossoms on dogwood, purple on redbud. Everything coming around at once" (*CM* 353).

† Paula Anca Farca notes that Scarlett "functions as husband/father figure for Melanie, Wade, and Beau. Scarlett does what any man would have done in her place: she saves her family" (79).

to her life). Once the men return, both of these women accept the communal value of marriage over friendship even when the latter relationship can offer as much (or even more) as the former relationship. The movie *Gone with the Wind* is one of those works (not so much the novel *Gone with the Wind*) that promote the fairy-tale ideology of our culture directing women to a life goal of finding Prince Charming and having his babies. Vivien Leigh's Scarlett is punished at movie's end when the still-dashing Clark Gable walks out the door with the last word. In the novel a not-so-dashing (as will be discussed in chapter 3) Rhett merely goes upstairs to pack, and Scarlett turns her thoughts to leaving herself—to return to Tara, where she had been *just fine* without Rhett. In the novel, too, not only Scarlett but also Melanie ultimately recognizes the value of their friendship, for it is Scarlett whom Melanie first calls to her bedside when she is dying, before she calls in her husband, Ashley (as will be discussed in chapter 4).

Ellen Glasgow once remarked of women of the period both Mitchell and Frazier set these novels in: "When I realize the lives of the women of the South, of the generation before me, I am fairly horror-stricken at the loneliness and depression they must have endured. Even those who married were only occupied for a limited time—say for twenty years of their lives, in bringing up children and preserving their homes. Then what? . . . We should have divined long ago that what we needed most was the spirit of organization. Men have always taunted us on our refusal to do likewise. You realize how often men comment, kindly or caustically, as the case may be, on woman's lack of loyalty to woman" (Raper 24–25). These remarks come at the cusp of the first women's rights movement, in a 1913 interview on the subject of women's suffrage. Here, too, Glasgow describes most women's lives as "absolutely aimless, and, for that matter, actually cruel," continuing with a harshly negative characterization that concludes with her belief in what could help: women "have endured and endured [implying long-suffering endurance, mere survival] simply because they never stood shoulder to shoulder about anything. Each woman has been a host unto herself, as far as she could go, but she was pitifully limited. She needed the help of her sisters, and she could not get it." One can see the lesson Glasgow derives from her observation—"The most important thing for women to learn is co-operation" (Raper 24)—in the successful partnerships created by Margaret Mitchell with Scarlett and Melanie and by Charles Frazier with Ada and Ruby.

At the end of Glasgow's novel *The Miller of Old Church,* a male character observes the strong woman he loves comforting the seemingly weaker woman he is secretly married to: "As they clung together in a passion of despair and of pity—the one appealing by sheer helplessness, the other giving succour out of an abundant self-reliance—Gay became conscious that he was witnessing the secret wonder of Molly's nature. The relationship of woman to man was dwarfed suddenly by an understanding of the relation of woman to woman. Deeper than the dependence of sex, simpler, more natural, closer to the earth, as though it still drew its strength from the soil, he realized that the need of woman for woman was not written in the songs nor in the histories of men, but in the neglected and frustrated lives which the songs and the histories of men had ignored" (*Miller* 410). Relationships between women are less often ignored by contemporary writers. Frazier, as we have seen, gives equal if not ultimately more time to the story of Ada and Ruby's survival back home during the war as to that of Inman's journey home. Ada and Ruby's relationship is not "dwarfed" by Inman and Ada's reunion the way that Scarlett and Melanie's relationship is deemphasized by the passionate story of Scarlett and Rhett. One notes an improvement on the occurrence of women's friendships in contemporary fiction (as well as movies, since *Thelma and Louise* [1991] and television, like *Sex and the City* [1998–2004]). Much less subtly than Mitchell did, perhaps much more consciously, contemporary writers are exploring the value of friendship between women. Even *Cold Mountain,* written by a man, allows both women to survive and continue to thrive, whether or not the men come back.

Chapter 3

"Put your heart in the land"

An Intertextual Reading of *Barren Ground* and *Gone with the Wind*

"Yes, she was not broken. She could never be broken while the vein of iron held in her soul."

Ellen Glasgow, *Barren Ground* (180)

"I wanted to write books, and not ever had I felt the faintest wish to have babies. Other women might have all they wanted, and I shouldn't object. But I was not made that way, and I did not see why I should pretend to be what I wasn't, or to feel what I couldn't. At that age I suspected, and later I discovered, that the maternal instinct, sacred or profane, was left out of me by nature when I was designed."

Ellen Glasgow, *The Woman Within* (108)

When Margaret Mitchell's *Gone with the Wind* was first published in 1936, reviewers compared it most often to Tolstoy's *War and Peace* and Thackeray's *Vanity Fair;* thus, it was likely inevitable that critics would later write extended articles delineating the similarities to these novels, as Harold K. Schefski and Paul Pickrel have done. Only brief mention has been made by Ellen Glasgow scholars noting the similarities between Scarlett O'Hara and

Dorinda Oakley of Glasgow's *Barren Ground,* published in 1925. Criticizing the character of Dorinda, Glasgow's biographer, E. Stanley Godbold Jr., calls her "a sexless Scarlet [*sic*] O'Hara against a setting less dramatic than the Civil War and Reconstruction and without the accompaniment of a Rhett Butler." He continues, "The selfish personality, the feeling of being wounded by circumstances, the bitter determination to rise above tragedy, and the ultimate turn to the land as a source of strength are shared by both characters" (148). Elizabeth Jane Harrison compares Dorinda to Scarlett for "steal[ing] the role of hero from the male characters" and thus having to "'atone' for this sin" (32). She also compares Scarlett to Dorinda, as well as Glasgow's Ada Fincastle, for "return[ing] to the land . . . in order to recover her strength and identity" (43). Harrison later contrasts Scarlett and Dorinda on the basis of Scarlett's "climb to power in Atlanta [which] results not from meaningful work, like Dorinda's, but from her manipulation and exploitation of the labor of others" (58). It is interesting that in a 1979 article on *Barren Ground,* in which Linda W. Wagner[-Martin] compares Dorinda Oakley to numerous characters of American literature, from Hester Prynne to Martha Quest, Scarlett O'Hara is not among them ("*Barren*" 553–54, 563–64). Yet there are enough parallels between the characters and their stories to make a case that Dorinda Oakley is the prototype for Scarlett O'Hara.

In two letters written to Ellen Glasgow, Margaret Mitchell mentions having read Glasgow's books (Harwell, *Margaret* 57, 319). Anne Edwards, one of Mitchell's biographers, notes that Mitchell's husband gave his wife a copy of *Barren Ground* for Christmas in 1925 (125). Mitchell began writing *Gone with the Wind* in 1926, if not consciously thinking of Dorinda Oakley, at least having recently read Dorinda's story. The possibility of a direct influence from Dorinda to Scarlett is there, but for the purposes of this study, since Dorinda's story takes place a generation later than Scarlett's, one might also think of Dorinda as one of Scarlett's literary daughters when reading these books chronologically according to their setting (rather than their publication dates) so as to consider how much (or how little) has changed for women as time passes from the second half of the nineteenth century of the Civil War–era novels discussed in the preceding chapters into the twentieth century of the novels to be discussed in this and the following chapters.

An extended comparison of these two headstrong female characters, their lives, and their fates also serves to replace with a work of literature the David O. Selznick film of *Gone with the Wind,* which is too often used—however unconsciously—as an intertext of the novel, influencing readers' responses to Scarlett O'Hara. As noted by Amy Levin, "for many, [the movie's] images supplanted any experience with the printed text." She points out a consequential disservice to the novel: "Opinions of *Gone with the Wind* [are] thus frequently based on an abbreviated notion of the story, a [movie] version which emphasized the melodrama inherent in the work" (32). In her "study in Scarlett" (the subtitle of her essay in the *New Yorker*), Claudia Roth Pierpont also wrote, "In the public mind, the two versions have merged to the point where it is difficult to say anymore whether 'Gone with the Wind' is in essence a novel or a movie" (88). Remarking on a problem with the film adaptation of the novel, Gerald Wood notes how "Selznick purged *Gone with the Wind* of Mitchell's ambiguity. . . . Rather than dramatize, as Mitchell does, an inconclusive conflict between aristocratic idealism and lumpish realism, the film-maker makes a clear preference for days-gone-by" (131). Harriet A. Deer and Irving Deer point out that "the novel/film seems calculated to affirm the stereotype of a woman who will be destroyed unless she submits to male dominance" (270). But reading *Gone with the Wind* closely with *Barren Ground* illuminates the heroine Scarlett O'Hara's triumph in the somewhat ambiguous ending while revealing how *Gone with the Wind,* the novel, if not so much the film, defies the conventions of popular romance novels and plantation fiction.

In spite of the tendency of many critics to classify *Gone with the Wind* as plantation fiction in the tradition of John Pendleton Kennedy or to dismiss it as a romance, the novel defies the southern literary conventions found in plantation fiction (with the exception of its portrayals of the black characters)—even the glorification of the past. Although it classifies the destruction of the Old Order as a Gotterdammerung, its sympathies lie more with the survivors than with those who are destroyed. And, as Darden Asbury Pyron argues, "The novel rejects the past as a legitimate source of authority" ("*Gone*" 584). It focuses on the present, as Scarlett O'Hara struggles to survive, and looks forward to the future, in which her perseverance will pay off and she will no longer be criticized for her defiance of Old South codes of behavior. In *Barren Ground,* Ellen Glasgow also succeeded in breaking away from southern literary conventions of the era of plantation fiction, as the reviewer for the *New York Times* proposed she had (Brock) and as she believed she had (Glasgow, *Certain* 152). This novel's author does not glorify the "remnants of an older civilization, of a dying culture" about which she writes. Rather she shows that "they had outlived their usefulness" (*Certain* 155). Her focus, then, is on the question of whether "the wasting malady [was] incurable." From the past, however, does come "some deep instinct for survival" (*Certain* 156), which could be put to good use, as Dorinda does, to stop the decline. Like

Scarlett, Dorinda is a survivor, and to survive and thrive, these women have to break with the conventions of their tradition-oriented societies just as their authors break with the conventions of the traditional genres in which critics might want to place them. Glasgow's readers, as Lee Winniford notes, "are led to expect a 'marriage plot'" (142), just as Mitchell's readers expect the ultimate union (even reunion by novel's end) of Scarlett and Rhett. Winniford reminds us, however, that "the heroine of the marriage plot is . . . drawn irrevocably under male domination where identity is subsumed and self-realization curtailed," which "is exactly contrary to" both Glasgow and Mitchell's agendas. The trick is, Winniford adds, to "maneuver [the] protagonist out of the marriage plot that the reader expects and into an alternative plot whose feminist priorities the reader can be enticed to accept" (143). One goal of this *Study of Scarletts* is to help readers to recognize and thus "accept" the "happi*er* ever after" endings of novels like *Gone with the Wind* and *Barren Ground.*

After the role of Scarlett O'Hara was played by Vivien Leigh in the renowned film, it is easy to forget that the novel opens with the words, "Scarlett O'Hara was not beautiful." The narrator then notes Scarlett's green eyes, "without a touch of hazel," and her "bristly black lashes" and "thick black brows." The narrator explains that one could see Scarlett's "true self" in her eyes: "The green eyes in the carefully sweet face were turbulent, willful, lusty with life, distinctly at variance with her decorous demeanor. Her manners had been imposed upon her by her mother's gentle admonitions and the sterner discipline of her mammy; her eyes were her own" (*GW* 3). This opening description of Scarlett connects her to Glasgow's Dorinda Oakley, in spite of the difference in the two characters' backgrounds, for in her description of Scarlett, Mitchell has highlighted the same features that Glasgow points out in her description of Dorinda. Chapter 2 of *Barren Ground* opens with the comment that Dorinda was "not beautiful," and Glasgow's narrator also notes that Dorinda's "eyes were her one memorable feature. Large, deep, radiant, they shone beneath her black lashes with a clear burning colour, as blue as the spring sky after rain" (*BG* 10). Dorinda's thick eyebrows, like Scarlett's, are also remarked on. Although their eye color is different, the connection drawn between the heroines' eyes and their personalities is clearly similar; and both young women will wear dresses to match their eyes on significant occasions throughout their novels.

In addition to the similarities between the central characters of these novels, striking comparisons can be made between the protagonists' mothers. Recognizing the echoes of Eudora Oakley in Ellen Robillard O'Hara serves to deromanticize and deheroicize Scarlett's mother for readers who can easily discern Dorinda's mother as a weak role model but have been as fooled by Ellen O'Hara's reputation and false front as were her daughters, many of the novel's readers, and perhaps the author herself. First of all, these mother characters' backstories are remarkably comparable. Both women suffered early heartbreak from their first loves (as will their daughters). Eudora lost her fiancé, a young missionary, when he died in the Congo before she had a chance to join him. Although she admits to a physical attraction to the man she later married, Dorinda's father, "all the romance in her life, after the death of the young missionary in the Congo, had turned toward her religion" (*BG* 43). Similarly, after the loss of her great love, Ellen Robillard is left "only a gentle shell" of her former self, her cousin Phillipe having taken with him to New Orleans and then to the grave "the glow that was in [her] heart" (*GW* 42). She marries Gerald O'Hara because "he is a kind man" and because he would take her away from the place of her sad memories and from the parents who, in her mind, sent her cousin to his death by forbidding their daughter's union with the family black sheep (*GW* 54). Like Eudora, Ellen then immerses herself in the duties of wife and motherhood, maintaining a similarly strong piety, comprised of her Catholic religion as well as the codes of the Old South.*

These two novels also describe similarly the effects on the mother characters of their duties as mistresses of their respective homes. Both women work "from dawn until after dark," and both are described as thrifty. Both have more sleepless nights than otherwise—Ellen because of the almost nightly calls from the slave quarters as well as the nearby shacks of poor whites, Eudora "because of the jerking of her nerves" after her hard work all day. In contrast, however, Glasgow writes that "the tragedy of [Eudora's] lot [was] that all her toil made so little impression. Though she spent every bit of her strength there was nothing to show for her struggle" (*BG* 39), whereas Mitchell implies that Ellen's hard work improves Tara: "From the day when Ellen first came to Tara, the place had been transformed. . . . She quickly brought order, dignity and grace into Gerald's household, and she gave to Tara a beauty it had never had before" (*GW* 57). Still Ellen remains as unhappy throughout her life as Eudora, and in spite of her achievements, like Eudora, she eventually dies prematurely as a result of being "driven" (the word Eudora uses to describe her response to her duties on the farm) to care for everyone within her reach. Like Eudora, Ellen has apparently been "drained [of] her vitality" (*BG* 39), to

* It is interesting to note, in light of the previous chapter, that Ada Monroe's mother has a similar first love, whom she marries, though not happily. When widowed, she meets Ada's father, and they marry, much more happily, although she then dies in childbirth.

the extent that she is unable to survive, as her daughters do, the typhoid fever she catches caring for a poor white family. On their deathbeds, both women recall their first loves, in spite of the many years that have passed since these young men died. Mammy reports of Ellen's dying hours, "She think she a lil gal back in Savannah" (*GW* 417), and Dilcey adds that at the very end, "she set right up in bed and cry out loud, time and agin: 'Feeleep! Feeleep!'" (*GW* 418). In Eudora's dying moments, "all the years of her marriage and motherhood vanished from her memory, and her mind returned to her early youth when she was engaged to the young missionary" (*BG* 4).*

Even without this comparison between the heroines' mothers in these two novels, it is easy to perceive Glasgow's approval of her novel's protagonist over Dorinda's frenetic mother, but it is likely that even the creator of Ellen and Scarlett O'Hara failed to perceive Scarlett as more admirable than her mother. Noting the comparison between Ellen O'Hara and Eudora Oakley reminds us of how dissatisfied the stoic Ellen really is with her life, but Scarlett, unlike Dorinda, is completely unaware of her mother's unhappiness. Rather than determining to live a different kind of life than her mother's, then, Scarlett feels guilty for not being more like her mother. In her *New Yorker* article on Scarlett, Claudia Pierpont exposes the false idealization of Ellen O'Hara, which should remind us of the effect of such idealizing on her daughters' self-worth: "For Scarlett, the ideal is embodied in her adored mother, the saintly Ellen, whose back is never seen to rest against the back of any chair on which she sits, whose broken spirit is everywhere *mistaken* for righteous calm" (92; emphasis added).

Returning to the similarities between daughters of these women, Ellen's eldest daughter and Eudora's only daughter, one might compare their responses to their mothers. In spite of their long, busy days, these girls' mothers insist on family evening prayers, and during one such evening in each novel it is revealed that neither Scarlett nor Dorinda shares her mother's religious devotion; rather they both find their mothers' piety burdensome. Scarlett, we are told, "wanted very much to be like her mother. The only difficulty was that by being just and truthful and tender and unselfish, one missed most of

* The circumstances leading up to Eudora Oakley's death are also comparable to Gerald O'Hara's death. Eudora fades away after she lies for her son, an action that betrays the piety that has kept her going through all the hardships of her life. Similarly, after Gerald is tricked by his daughter Suellen into swearing an oath of loyalty to the Union, his Confederate heart is awakened, and he briefly returns to his former self and charges away on his horse, from which he falls to his death.

the joys of life" (*GW* 60). After Dorinda becomes annoyed with her mother's selfless dedication to the men in the family, the narrator notes that "the girl had sometimes felt that the greatest cross in her life was her mother's morbid unselfishness" (*BG* 45). The example of her mother leaves Dorinda feeling guilty for giving in to any desires outside of her duties. It is no wonder, then, that upon discovering that she is pregnant and then immediately afterward learning that her fiancé has married another woman, Dorinda "dreaded her mother more than anything that she had to face" (*BG* 178). Thus her flight to New York is in large part motivated by her desire to escape her mother's reproach. Referring to Ellen O'Hara, Darden Pyron notes, "Repressed herself, she becomes a prime agent in her daughter's repression" ("*Gone*" 579). Like Dorinda, Scarlett leaves home to escape her mother's watchful eye on her proper behavior as a widow in mourning. Throughout *Gone with the Wind,* Scarlett feels guilty whenever she thinks about how Ellen would regard her behavior. Dorinda's concern about her mother's response to her pregnancy—"What would her mother say if she knew? When would she know? Who would have the courage to tell her?" (*BG* 180)—mirrors Scarlett's fears of her mother finding out about her behavior at the Confederate ball in Atlanta: "A cold qualm of guilt assailed Scarlett at the thought of Ellen's consternation, should she ever learn of her daughter's scandalous conduct" (*GW* 196). And after the ball, although she largely resumed the life of a belle, Scarlett "clung to her dull black dresses and her veil," not only because she knew "that if she changed them for colors without waiting several more years, the town would buzz even more than it was already buzzing," but, more important, because she does not know "how [she] would . . . ever explain it to her mother" (*GW* 242). Directly echoing Dorinda, Scarlett thinks, "What would Mother say if she knew?" when she reads Melanie's private letters from Ashley (*GW* 210) and later wonders, "What would Mother say?" about her lies about her competitors' lumber (*GW* 662), even though by this time in her life she has realized that "nothing her mother had taught her was of any value whatsoever" since the war (*GW* 434). When Dorinda returns from New York and resumes her life in Pedlar's Mill to help take care of her ill father, the narrator reports that "there were times when it seemed to Dorinda that she could not breathe within the stark limitations of her mother's point of view" (*BG* 298). Similarly Scarlett may be relieved of her mother's censure by the time of her return from Atlanta to Tara, but she never escapes the social censure that was behind all that Ellen taught her.

Although Melanie may be more accepting of Scarlett's unruly nature than Ellen was, she is also a double for Ellen who reminds the reader of how the oppressive life of the southern lady continued even after the Civil War. Melanie is naturally the lady that Ellen was trying to turn Scarlett into, and Melanie, like Ellen, dies too young. Glasgow also uses Dorinda's rival to show the possible consequences of Dorinda getting what she thought she wanted (Jason Greylock). Geneva Ellgood, the woman who does marry Jason, ends up experiencing some kind of mental breakdown and, like Melanie, dies young. Although Geneva and Melanie are ultimately quite different, some similarities are interesting to note, as they not only add to the impressive number of parallels between the two novels but also show how easily the next generation of women could fall into behaviors that lead to lives as short and unfulfilling as those Eudora Oakley and Ellen O'Hara lived. The two authors describe their protagonists' foils in similar physical terms: both Geneva and Melanie have plain, sweet faces and abundant hair. Though Geneva's hair is blond and "arranged elaborately" (*BG* 71), while Melanie's "cloud of curly dark hair . . . was so sternly repressed beneath its net that no vagrant tendril escaped" (*GW* 101), the respective style of each of these women's hair reflects an aspect of her inner nature—Geneva's concern about appearances and Melanie's repression—and the difference in their hair color reflects the difference in their roles in the novel. Geneva is the blond opposite of Dorinda, but Melanie serves more as Scarlett's double than one would expect given the extreme differences in their temperaments. Though not so sexually repressed, as Scarlett is, Melanie is oppressed by social standards that she does not rebel against, as Scarlett does. Melanie is, like Scarlett, a survivor, though only to a point. She is ultimately destroyed, as Geneva is, by her inability to have a child (in Melanie's case, a second child). Both young women insist on having children regardless of the consequences: Geneva convinces herself that she has done so, reflecting her losing her mind over the issue (not unlike Eudora Oakley's frenetic behavior), and Melanie allows herself to get pregnant in spite of the doctor's orders against it (thus dying young like Ellen as a result of her need to nurture). Geneva's madness drives her to her death, and Melanie dies during a miscarriage, both leaving their husbands for the other woman to take care of.

But of course, it will be a while before the novels' protagonists can appreciate the lessons of their mothers—and then their rivals' lives. And in the novels' openings, they are more interested in their romantic fantasies, spun around the men who will ultimately (though unintentionally) lead these rivals to an early grave. One can find similarities too in the scenes describing how the novels' protagonists' romantic dreams are each manifested into a young man. Glasgow's narrator explains that "at twenty, [Dorinda's] imagination was tinctured by the romanticism which makes a woman fall in love with a religion or an idea" (*BG* 12); and indeed Dorinda falls in love with her "idea" of Jason Greylock, who has just returned to Pedlar's Mill. She transforms the young doctor into a man worthy of her adulation, thinking of him as "an irreproachable son who had relinquished his ambition in order to remain with his undeserving old father" (*BG* 13), when in truth, as Jason will later tell her, he "hadn't the heart or the courage to refuse to come" when his father summoned him (*BG* 64). Likewise Scarlett falls in love with the dashing image that Ashley Wilkes made riding up to Tara to pay his respects to her family upon his return from Europe. Ashley, too, shows evidence early on of his cowardly nature when he lacks the courage to tell Scarlett of his engagement to Melanie Hamilton. Ashley does not, like Jason, talk of marriage to Scarlett, but he does escort her around the county for two years without telling her that he and Melanie have an understanding that they will marry.

To please Jason, Dorinda decides to have a blue dress made with the money she had been saving to buy a cow. Though surprised by Dorinda's extravagance, the dressmaker thinks, "After all, you weren't young and good-looking but such a little while" (*BG* 71). This sentiment is found throughout *Gone with the Wind,* beginning at the barbecue with the division of women into belles and matrons, "for there were no married belles in the South" (*GW* 100). Once married, young girls had to put away their brightly colored dresses and were "relegated to arbors and front parlors with staid matrons in dull silks" (*GW* 101). But, like Dorinda, for the time being Scarlett can wear a dress the color of her eyes in hopes of attracting the beau of her choice.

From her dressmaker Dorinda learns that Jason had courted Geneva Ellgood the previous summer. Hearing this, "a wave of dull sickness swept over her. At that moment she realized that the innocence of her girlhood, the ingenuous belief that love brought happiness, had departed for ever. She was in the thick of life, and the thick of life meant not peace but a sword in the heart. Though she scarcely knew Geneva Ellgood, she felt that they were enemies" (*BG* 68–69). So Dorinda begins her campaign to attract Jason's attention away from Geneva by ordering a new hat to go with the blue dress. When Scarlett learns of the possibility that Ashley might be engaged to Melanie, she, too, must confront a harsh reality of adulthood: "There were pain and bewilderment in her face, the bewilderment of a pampered child who has always had her own way for the asking and who now, for the first time, was in contact with the unpleasantness of life" (*GW* 22). And Scarlett also immediately perceives of Melanie as her enemy and begins to plan her strategy for making Ashley jealous at the barbecue so that he will recognize that it is she, not Melanie, he wants.

When Dorinda first learns about her competition for Jason, she feels a "primitive impulse" rise within her, "among the orderly instincts and inherited habits of thought. She was startled; she was frightened; but she was defiant. In a flash the knowledge came to her that habit and duty and respectability are not the whole of life" (*BG* 69). The reader can understand better what is going on within Dorinda by examining her feelings next to Scarlett's actions when she first confronts Ashley about his engagement to another woman. Scarlett's *plans* to win Ashley had ended with, "Of course, she would do it all in a lady-like way. She wouldn't even dream of saying to him boldly that she loved him—that would never do" (*GW* 72); but when she faces Ashley she immediately blurts out a declaration of her love. Like Dorinda, then, her more primitive instincts overpower her notions of respectability.

After seeing Jason with the Ellgoods at church and realizing from his compliment on her new dress that he does not remember asking her to wear blue, the confused Dorinda questions her mother about marriage. Eudora replies, "Grandfather used to say that when a woman got ready to fall in love the man didn't matter, because she could drape her feeling over a scarecrow and pretend he was handsome." Eudora adds her own opinion that a woman's decision to marry is "just the struggle to get away from things as they are" (*BG* 103).* She tries to soften her remarks, which apply so well to Dorinda's attraction to Jason, by telling her daughter, "You'll be all right married . . . if you just make up your mind that whatever happens, you ain't going to let any man spoil your life" (*BG* 103–04). Hearing these words Dorinda feels for the first time "the vein of iron in [her] nature" and "resolved passionately [that] no man was going to spoil her life! She could live without Jason; she could live without any man" (*BG* 104). Although this ultimately proves to be true, Dorinda first suffers from a disappointment that would influence the rest of her life as a result of using her "vein of iron" to attract Jason's attention rather than to resist his charms.

Scarlett's realization about her love for Ashley, which does not come until the second to last chapter of her novel, echoes remarkably Eudora's grand-

* It is an interesting reflection of gender difference that seeking change is also the reason, Charles Frazier's Inman ultimately decides, why men go to war: "Inman now guessed it was boredom with the repetition of the daily rounds that had made them take up weapons. The endless arc of the sun, wheel of seasons. War took a man out of that circle of regular life (218).

father's theory about marriage in *Barren Ground:* "He never really existed at all, except in my imagination. . . . I loved something I made up. . . . I made a pretty suit of clothes and fell in love with it. And when Ashley came riding along, so handsome, so different, I put that suit on him and made him wear it whether it fitted him or not" (*GW* 1016). Like Dorinda's desire to marry Jason, Scarlett's desire to marry Ashley threatens to "spoil her life" after she, too, fails to use her vein of iron to resist him once he first resists her.

The scene of Dorinda's discovery of Jason's marriage is quite comparable to that of Scarlett's discovery of Ashley's engagement. Dorinda's chorus of "*It isn't true*" (*BG* 154) and her waiting for Jason's wagon to pass so that she can see if Geneva is with him are both repeated by Scarlett as she waits for her father's return from the Wilkes plantation on the eve of the barbecue, saying to herself, "Oh, it can't be true!" (*GW* 25). The imagery used to describe the two young women's reactions to their disappointments is also similar. After Dorinda sees the wagon, "she felt cold and wet. . . . Everything within her had stopped. The clock no longer ticked; it had run down" (*BG* 156). Scarlett, after hearing the Tarleton twins' suspicions about Ashley and Melanie, merely goes through the motions of participating in the rest of their banter until they leave, at which time "she went back to her chair like a sleepwalker," feeling her heart "beat with odd little jerks; her hands were cold" (*GW* 22). After Gerald O'Hara confirms the rumor about Ashley's engagement, Scarlett thinks, "So it was true" (*GW* 33), again echoing Dorinda, who finally says to herself, "So it is true" (*BG* 156). And, as Dorinda's body holds onto the earth while she feels her consciousness leave time and space and join temporarily with nothingness, Gerald offers Scarlett the consolation of the land's permanence to ease her pain.

Gerald's words are perhaps the most significant echo in *Gone with the Wind* of Glasgow's novel, published earlier. In one of the most familiar speeches of the novel, Gerald tells his daughter, "Land is the only thing in the world that amounts to anything . . . for 'tis the only thing in this world that lasts. . . . 'Tis the only thing worth working for, worth fighting for—worth dying for" (*GW* 36). Readers will hear these well-known lines in the advice old Matthew Fairlamb gives to Dorinda upon her return from New York: "Put yo' heart in the land. The land is the only thing that will stay by you" (*BG* 323).*

* Dorinda's recollection of her father's view of his farm—"Whatever I give the farm will always be mine. . . . That was the way he felt. The farm isn't human and it won't make you suffer" (*BG* 298–99)—is also quite similar to Gerald's words to Scarlett here. Although Gerald O'Hara, an Irish immigrant who now owns a prosperous plantation,

Both women recall these messages later in their stories as they ponder the losses of their lives and realize that in spite of these losses they have survived. At this earlier, heartbreaking point in their youth, however, neither appreciates yet the resilience of land. Dorinda does recognize the permanence of land, but does not view this constancy positively. Surveying the tired, "overworked" landscape, Dorinda thinks, "The country had been like this . . . long before she was born. It would be like this . . . after she and all those who were living with her were dead. For the one thing that seemed to her immutable and everlasting was the poverty of the soil" (*BG* 11). Although she recognizes the "terrible force" of the land, "whether [this force was] for good or evil she could not tell" (*BG* 38). And for now she is more interested in marrying Jason and leaving her father's farm. Mitchell's narrator explains that Scarlett is not conscious of the beauty of her surroundings: "She loved this land so much, without even knowing she loved it" (*GW* 28). And, to the consternation of her father, Scarlett rejects his proffered comfort of her eventual inheritance of Tara. The only source of interest for her at this moment is in marrying Ashley.

Support for the influence of Glasgow's story on Mitchell's can certainly be found in similarities between the objects of these two young women's infatuation, Jason Greylock and Ashley Wilkes, sons and heirs to homes named Five Oaks and Twelve Oaks, respectively. The reader is reminded, however, by Mitchell's use of *Twelve* Oaks in the Civil War–era novel compared to Glasgow's *Five* Oaks in the post-Reconstruction-era novel that the days of the prosperous (and oppressive) plantation South were limited—and yet Dorinda feels as confined in her community as Scarlett does in hers. The

is clearly not much like the unsuccessful farmer Joshua Oakley, both men are associated with their land. Glasgow employs land imagery to describe Joshua: "The earth clung to him; to his clothes, to the anxious creases in his face, to his finger-nails, and to his heavy boots, which were caked with manure from the stables. . . . [W]henever [Dorinda] thought of him now, his hands, gnarled, twisted, and earth-stained like the vigorous roots of a tree, and that penetrating briny smell, were the first things she remembered. His image was embalmed in that stale odour of the farm as in a preserving fluid" (*BG* 40–41). Similarly "there was something vital and earthy and coarse about [Gerald]" (*GW* 31; emphasis added). And his countenance is "as Irish a face as could be found in the length and breadth of the homeland he had left" (*GW* 30). A second point the two men have in common is their devotion to their horses: "Dorinda had heard [Joshua] talking to Dan and Beersheba in the tone a man uses only to the creatures who speak and understand the ultimate language of his heart" (*BG* 95). As Gerald approaches Tara upon his entrance into the novel, Scarlett hears him talking to his mount.

preliminary goal for these women is a husband, but each sets her sights on the wrong man. The Greylocks' Five Oaks is in a state of utter chaos the first time Dorinda goes inside, seeking the man she believed she would marry, while Twelve Oaks is described in terms of order when Scarlett first sees it upon arriving for the picnic determined to come home engaged to Ashley: "the white house reared its perfect symmetry before her" (*GW* 94). But neither woman accomplishes his first goal of marrying the heir to this house, and by the time Scarlett returns from Atlanta after the Union troops have passed through, Twelve Oaks has been nearly destroyed.

The homes' similar names and ultimately similar decline call readers' attention to the similarities between the two young men doomed to inherit their fathers' legacies. During Jason's first conversation with Dorinda after his return to Pedlar's Mill, he tells her, "I'm trying to enlighten the natives. . . . Nobody seems to ask any more of life than to plod from one bad harvest to another. They don't know the first principles of farming" (*BG* 30–31). Dorinda, however, "was not interested in a discussion of farming. All her life she had heard men talk of farming and of nothing else. Surely there were other things he could tell her!" (*BG* 31). Also different from the people around him, Ashley does not share his peers' views of war. And similar to Dorinda's reaction to the farm talk she has heard all her life, Scarlett is bored with all the talk of war, which, in her opinion, has put a damper on all the parties lately. Reflecting her development, Dorinda, much later in her story, finds herself interested in Nathan Pedlar's talk about farming, and she thinks, "It was surprising . . . what a bond of sympathy farming could make" (*BG* 270). And those critics who argue that Scarlett does not change in her novel should note how years after her youthful reaction to finding war talk boring, when Rhett has taken their daughter with him to London, Scarlett finds herself isolated among her new carpetbagger friends and longs for someone to talk with about the very subject that had bored her in these early years, the war, finally recognizing the bond that this experience created among her older acquaintances.

At this early point in their lives, however, Scarlett and Dorinda are more interested in some vague romantic notion of love than any other subject, and neither young woman understands the man she wants. Dorinda is "sympathetic [to] but uncomprehending" (*BG* 63) of Jason's complaints about the community. And although Scarlett does not want the South to go to war any more than Ashley does, she thinks, in response to his comments against war, "Sometimes there was no understanding Ashley" (*GW* 108). Clearly these two young women are infatuated with romantic heroes of their own creations.

Dorinda finds that Jason's "slight frown . . . made his face . . . more attractive," but the narrator suggests that "the haunting pathos, which she detected but could not explain" is reflective of his "heroic weakness confronting insurmountable obstacles" (*BG* 30). Scarlett sees a "yearning and sadness" when Ashley looks at her, which she believes attests to his love for her (*GW* 26). Ashley explains, however, that he merely admires her "passion for life," which he lacks (*GW* 117).

Ashley's explanation of his attraction to Scarlett is similar to Jason telling Dorinda, "You put something in me that I need. I don't know what it is—fibre, I suppose, the courage of living." This borrowed courage allows Jason to think briefly of running away with Dorinda, and, feeling again "the vein of iron in her soul," Dorinda responds, "I'll go anywhere that you ask me to. I'll do anything that will help you" (*BG* 113). It is further along in *Gone with the Wind,* and it is Scarlett, not Ashley, who suggests they run off together, but she does so after Ashley has told her he envies her strength and wishes he could escape the burdens that have encroached upon his life since his return from the war. Although both men reject these escape plans, both exchanges end in passionate scenes described with similar imagery: Jason kisses Dorinda "with a hungry violence" (*BG* 114); Ashley's "lips took [Scarlett's] hungrily as if he could never have enough" (*GW* 553).

This is the scene that ends with Ashley repeating Gerald's consolation that whatever Scarlett does not have, she still has Tara, "Something you love better than me, though you may not know it" (*GW* 534–35). The reader is reminded then of Gerald's warnings against Ashley as a compatible match for Scarlett. The same Matthew Fairlamb who shares Gerald's view of the value of land is the first to express doubts about Jason's character: "Young Jason is a pleasant-mannered boy, though he looks a bit too soft to stand the hard wear of these here roads. I ain't got nothin' to say against him, but if he'd listen to the warnin' of eighty-odd years, he'd git away before the broomsage ketches him. Thar's one thing sartain sure, you've got to conquer the land in the beginning, or it'll conquer you before you're through with it" (*BG* 16). Miss Tabitha, one of the women of Pedlar's Mill, remarks that Jason "had a sweet nature, but . . . was as light as a feather and a strong wind could blow him away" (*BG* 79). As in these assessments of Jason, Gerald puts a caveat into his criticism of Ashley for preferring his books to such activities as hunting—"I said nothing against the lad, for I like him" (*GW* 34). And finally, Grandma Fontaine's characterization of Ashley is most like Glasgow's characters' views of Jason. She precedes her comments with land imagery similar to that which Matthew ends with, and she uses wind imagery similar to Miss Tabitha's. She calls those who were able to survive the war "buckwheat," since they are the ones with "sap," which allows them to bend "when a hard wind's blowing." She tells Scarlett that "when the wind has passed, [buckwheat] springs up almost as straight and strong as before" (*GW* 717). Grandma Fontaine does not list Ashley among those whom she characterizes as buckwheat, and when Scarlett questions her omission the old lady replies that Ashley has survived because of Melanie, not by his own strength. Just as Glasgow critic Frederick P. W. McDowell notes that "the cruelty of the land to those who do not adjust to its stern power is seen in the fate of the Greylocks" (150), Grandma Fontaine comments on the demise of the whole Wilkes family. As Gerald did much earlier, she remarks on Ashley's being "bred to read books," which "doesn't help a man pull himself out of a tough fix" (*GW* 718). Likewise Glasgow explains that although Jason "had sprung from the soil, he had returned to it a stranger, and there could be no sympathetic communion between him and the solitude. Neither as a lover nor as a conqueror could he hope to possess it in spirit" (*BG* 31). As Grandma Fontaine remarks on Ashley's inability to adjust from plantation owner to farmer, John Abner ultimately observes of Jason's degeneration, "the country goes against you when you ain't cut out for a farmer" (*BG* 399). And finally, even an assessment of Ashley from Scarlett's point of view (much later in her novel) is similar to these Glasgow characters' observations about Jason. As she comes upon Ashley chopping wood in the scene discussed previously, Scarlett thinks to herself, "His hands were not made for work or his body for anything but broadcloth and fine linen" (*GW* 525).

Returning to the early part of the novels, once Ashley's engagement and Jason's marriage become facts that the novels' protagonists can do nothing about, each woman confronts her betrayer, during which time she glimpses the truth about her romantic ideal. After Jason speaks in defense of himself, "with a piercing flash of insight, [Dorinda] saw him as he was, false, vain, contemptible, a coward." She realizes that "nothing that he said made any difference to her. Nothing that he could ever say in the future would make any difference" (*BG* 165). Although Scarlett does not so easily shake the influence Ashley will continue to have on her, she does briefly, recognize his cowardice, too: "Why don't you say it, you coward! You're afraid to marry me!" (*GW* 117), she lashes out at him, realizing, like Dorinda, that his excuses for marrying another woman are indicative of his weak nature.

Both young women then respond to their situations in such a way as to protect themselves from ridicule and shame. Scarlett marries Charles Hamilton in order to save face in front of the girls who suspect her feelings for

Ashley. Dorinda leaves town to escape people's pity and their eyes, for it will not be long before her pregnancy becomes visible. And the two authors then equally conveniently get rid of these burdens on their heroines: Mitchell kills Charles off with pneumonia; Glasgow allows Dorinda to miscarry her baby. The stories of the two survivors, unburdened as yet except for their own heavy hearts over disappointment in love, can thus continue.*

In *A Certain Measure,* Ellen Glasgow defines the vein of iron she refers to in her characterization of her strongest female characters, including Dorinda Oakley, as "the vital principle of *survival,* which has enabled races and individuals to withstand the destructive forces of nature and of civilization" (169; emphasis added). Writing specifically of Dorinda, Glasgow explains, "In the end, she would triumph through that deep instinct for survival." Indeed, Glasgow continues, Dorinda "would be hardened by adversity, but hard things . . . are the last to decay" (160). Darden Pyron compares Glasgow's comments on Dorinda's survival instinct to Mitchell's theme of survival ("*Gone*" 584). Writing of *Gone with the Wind,* Margaret Mitchell explained, "If the novel has a theme, the theme is that of survival. What makes some people able to come through catastrophes and others, apparently just as able, strong, and brave, go under? . . . [T]he survivors used to call that quality 'gumption'. So I wrote about the people who had gumption and the people who didn't" (Harwell, Gone 38). Scarlett O'Hara, of course, is the central survivor of Mitchell's novel. Like Dorinda, she is hardened by her experiences and, consequently, becomes less and less mindful of others' feelings and her own reputation. But Dorinda should be admired for her achievements and sympathized with for her losses, and so too should Mitchell's readers admire and sympathize with Scarlett who, between her sixteenth and twenty-eighth years, loses everyone she loved and life as she knew it, and yet survives to the novel's end and beyond.

As each young woman commences on her journey away from the home that has become loathsome to her since her heartbreak, she feels the stirring of excitement, in spite of her pain. After a while, however, each misses the land of her birth. Living in Atlanta, Scarlett misses Tara and "realize[s] dimly what Gerald had meant when he said that the love of the land was in her blood" (*GW* 155). After two years in New York, Dorinda begins to talk about her family's farm, and as she does so her new suitor notices a change in her

* In Scarlett's tale she does have a child during her first marriage, but, with servants to care for him, she finds him more of an annoyance than burdensome.

and observes to himself, "Strange, the hold the country could get over one" (*BG* 237).

Still neither woman is ready yet to go home. Dorinda does not want to return until "her hate was as dead as her love" (*BG* 228). In contrast Scarlett stays in Atlanta in large part because as long as she lives with Melanie, she will see Ashley when he is on leave. Paradoxically, although she still loves Ashley, she believes herself "done with passion and marriage" (*GW* 215), a sentiment that echoes Dorinda's response to Mrs. Faraday's advice that she should get married: "Oh, I've finished with all that!" (*BG* 243). The narrator explains that Dorinda feels a "revulsion from the physical aspect of love" (*BG* 244). Although she enjoys the company of the young doctor in New York, she recoils from any physical contact: "the thought of love, the faintest reminder of its potency, filled her with aversion. . . . She simply could not bear . . . to be touched" (*BG* 244–45). Like Dorinda, Scarlett rejects sex, seeing it as "inexplicable male madness, . . . a painful and embarrassing process that led inevitably to the still more painful process of childbirth." But unlike Dorinda, she does not reject love: "She was done with marriage but not with love, for her love for Ashley was something different, having nothing to do with passion or marriage, something sacred and breath-takingly beautiful" (*GW* 215). As Kathryn Lee Seidel explains, "To her, Ashley represents a spiritual man, unconcerned with the physical passion that she fears in herself. Scarlett believes she loves Ashley beyond passion, with a 'sacred' love." Seidel points out the incidents in the novel that should show Scarlett Ashley's passionate side but notes that Scarlett "persists in rejecting all the evidence. She is surprised when she learns Melanie is pregnant, a fact that confirms Ashley's 'baser' nature. She is shocked when Ashley kisses her passionately" (54). Unimpressed by the sexual relations of her brief first marriage, Scarlett's obsession with unattainable Ashley is safer, more familiar and comfortable than the libidinous feelings Rhett eventually stirs in her.

As a consequence of their common distaste for sex, both Dorinda and Scarlett aggravate their efforts to get over their first bad experiences with love. Dorinda's rejection of any potential sexual relationship keeps the painful memory of her relationship with Jason alive, so that, when she sees Jason many years later, after not seeing him for ten years, "she felt, with a shiver of terror, that the past had never died." The narrator explains, "In her whole life there had been only that one man. He had held her in his arms. He would remain always an inseparable part of her being" (*BG* 359). Likewise Scarlett will not let herself forget Ashley, who remains her romantic ideal in part because she has shared only passionate kisses with him but not the "inexplicable male madness" of sexual relations. She therefore never gives Rhett a chance to win her heart. And when Rhett does stir her libido, it still does not lead her to thoughts of love for him, for she has separated love from sex.

In spite of their arrested sexual development, both women do mature in other ways during their years away from home. When Scarlett returns to Tara during the war, Mitchell's narrator explains, "She was seeing things with new eyes for . . . she had left her girlhood behind her. She was no longer plastic clay, yielding imprint to each new experience. The clay had hardened. . . . She was a woman now and youth was gone" (*GW* 420). Grandma Fontaine notes that Scarlett has "face[d] the worst that can happen to her" and will thus never "really fear anything again" (*GW* 452). Of Dorinda, Glasgow's narrator explains, "Young as she was she had acquired the ripe wisdom and the serene self-confidence of maturity; she had attained the immunity from apprehension which comes to those only who can never endure the worst again" (*BG* 227).

Neither assessment of the two young women is entirely accurate, however, as is indicated by their nightmares. Scarlett suffers the nightmare that reveals that there is something she still fears—hunger and the insecurity hunger inspires, which Madonne M. Miner associates with the loss of her mother and thus with the loss of love. Scarlett's dream is motivated by her actual return to Tara during the war, rather than the contemplation of returning home, which inspires Dorinda's dream. In looking forward to returning, Scarlett anxiously anticipates seeing her mother again, but, as Miner puts it, "Scarlett's dream of sheltering maternal space becomes a nightmare of absence" (19). Particularly after the ordeals of delivering Melanie's baby and getting herself, her son, Melanie, the baby, and Prissy safely to Tara after Rhett's desertion of them outside of Atlanta, Scarlett longs to hand everyone, including herself, over to her mother's charge. Arriving to find her mother dead, then, is quite a blow, which continues to haunt her in her recurrent nightmare of being hungry and lost in a fog, from which things grabbed at her, trying to pull her down. Ahead, she feels, is security, but she can never reach it in the dream. In her waking life, then, Scarlett determines to find this security for herself and her family, in hopes of stopping the recurring nightmare.

As Dorinda contemplates returning to Old Farm, her nightmare reflects her fear of seeing Jason, her lost love. In her dream his face appears on the millions of thistles that cover the field she is plowing. Just before waking she says, "I am going to plough them under, if it kills me" (*BG* 240). Apparently she is still not over her rage, and it appears, too, that part of her reason for returning to Old Farm is to get even with Jason for the effect he has had on her life. Upon returning to Pedlar's Mill, when she learns of the state of affairs at the Greylocks' Five Oaks, she determines to buy it out from under Jason some day. In order to be able to afford to do so soon, she turns with vigor to her plans to make the Oakleys' Old Farm into a productive dairy.

For their own reasons, then, both young women turn their attention to their land. Dorinda begins to feel "earlier and deeper associations" with Old Farm "reaching out to her . . . groping after her, like the tendrils of vines, through the darkness and violence of her later memories . . . drawing her back across time and space and forgetfulness," and with these feelings she "come[s] to life again" (*BG* 239). She tells her New York suitor, "I can't stay away any longer. I'm part of it. I belong to the abandoned fields" (*BG* 245). She is soon called home to her dying father, and once there, she proceeds immediately with her plans to revitalize the farm. Finding that she, too, has returned to a disabled father, Scarlett also takes charge of her family's farm, and in doing so, she too realizes that "she belonged to the red acres. . . . Her roots went deep into the blood-colored soil and sucked up life" (*GW* 420).

The first obstacle that both young women have to contend with as they take over the two farms is the resistance to change in the people around them. Dorinda had earlier described the people of her community as being "in a rut, but . . . satisfied; they don't want to change" (*BG* 63). Such was a reason for the Civil War, according to Mitchell's novel: the South did not want to change, and, as Jason points out in *Barren Ground,* "people will fight to stay in a rut, but not to get out of it . . . any prejudice, even the prejudice in favour of the one-crop system [or of slavery], is a sacred institution" (*BG* 111). Evidence of the validity of Jason's assessment can be seen in Joshua Oakley's failure to try something new even after years of unsuccessful farming. Earlier Dorinda had realized that "it's being set in a rut . . . that keeps him going" (*BG* 118), but now that she has become interested in farming herself, she sees the problem in the fact that "the experience of generations . . . has taught us nothing except to do things the way we've always done them" (*BG* 238). Hence she believes that her lack of practical experience with farming is to her advantage. She will not be encumbered with the way things have always been done.

Scarlett refuses, too, to allow past ways to hinder the work that needs to be done. At Tara she and her sisters, as well as the house slaves, would all pick cotton. In contrast to Dorinda, however, she looks to the previous generations of her family for strength: "Gerald, penniless, had raised Tara; Ellen had risen above some mysterious sorrow; Grandfather Robillard, surviving the wreck of Napoleon's throne, had founded his fortunes anew on the fertile Georgia coast; Great-Grandfather Prudhomme had carved a small kingdom out of the dark jungles of Haiti, lost it, and lived to see his name honored in Savannah. . . . All had suffered crushing misfortunes and had not been crushed" (*GW* 420–21). This is the kind of backward glance, to use Allen Tate's phrase again, that is healthy: look to the productive examples from history for guidance. It is a different kind of look backward from the kind that debilitates those who would hold on to the destructive Old South, which was so oppressive to women (and, of course, African Americans).

Scarlett's goal is to bring Tara to some semblance of its former self, and Dorinda plans to transform Old Farm into a prosperous dairy farm. In spite of the differences in the two young women's backgrounds, at the time they take over for their fathers, they are starting off with quite similar handicaps. First of all, both women are confronting land devastated by war. Scarlett takes over Tara just after the Union troops have passed through the county during the Civil War, burning the fields and most of the homes and confiscating all valuable items they could find and carry away with them. In the opening of *Barren Ground,* which begins in the late nineteenth century, Glasgow describes the state of the novel's landscape as "impoverished by the war and the tenant system which followed the war" (4). The O'Haras becoming as "land poor" as the Oakleys (*BG* 7) is prepared for in the beginning of Mitchell's novel when the narrator notes that at the edges of the plantations stood forests from which "the soughing pines seem[ed] to wait with an age-old patience, to threaten with soft sighs: 'Be careful! Be careful! We had you once. We can take you back again'" (*GW* 8), just as Dorinda remarks on the threat of broomsedge, pines, and life-everlasting reclaiming her land (*BG* 237). After the war, Scarlett recognizes that these pines will soon take over the cotton fields, and then the "country folks will go back a hundred years like the pioneers who had little cabins and just scratched a few acres—and barely existed" (*GW* 495), an observation that accurately describes the state of affairs on the Oakley farm before Dorinda's management. Like Scarlett, who is determined that the pines will not reclaim Tara, Dorinda will keep away the broomsedge that threatens Old Farm.

In Blanche H. Gelfant's reading of the references to the encroaching wilderness in *Gone with the Wind,* she associates the wilderness with war, seeing both as threats to civilization, as represented by plantations like Tara (15). In *Barren Ground,* too, Dorinda associates the approaching war with the destruction of her hard work reclaiming the land from the wilderness created by the previous war: "That men should destroy one another appeared to her less incredible than that they should deliberately destroy the resources which made life endurable. That they should destroy in a day, in an hour, the materials which she was sacrificing her youth to provide!" (*BG* 446). The war in Dorinda's day (World War I) never actually reaches her land this time, but of course this is not the case for Scarlett. After Scarlett sacrifices her youthful beauty to the hard work of picking the cotton that is left on Tara, Union troops come through and burn it all. Glasgow and Mitchell express similar views of war in these novels, one of which is criticism of the senseless destruction of property; another is summed up by Dorinda when she says, "The worst thing about [war] is the number of people, both men and women, who enjoy it, who embark upon it as upon a colossal adventure" (*BG* 447). Glasgow repeats this notion in an essay, discerning from this attitude "that the only effective way to end war forever would be to make all our ideas of war as unromantic and unheroic as is the average man's daily struggle for his drab-colored existence" (Raper 241). Although Mitchell's novel is full of war heroes, her vivid descriptions of the wounded soldiers and ravished land does as much toward deromanticizing war as Charles Frazier's Civil War novel will over a half century later.

Of course there is a romantic plot to Mitchell's novel, which picks up with Scarlett's efforts to save Tara by seeking financial support from Rhett Butler. Wearing the unforgettable dress made from Tara's green velvet curtains, Scarlett has misgivings about her current desirability after scant meals and long hours working in the sun and is gratified by Rhett's notice of her fine appearance in the new dress. She has no romantic interest in Rhett; her goal is purely economic: to elicit a marriage proposal or a proposition to be his mistress, whichever, as long as she will have available to her in the future any money required to keep Tara. Likewise one of Dorinda's first acts toward improving Old Farm is to buy cows from the Ellgoods. Upon first meeting with Bob Ellgood, "she could see her reflection in his large, placid eyes. . . . It gave her pleasure to feel that she was more distinguished, if less desirable, than she had been two years ago." The narrator explains, however, that "her pleasure was as impersonal as her errand. She had no wish to attract this heavy, masterful farmer . . . beyond the point where his admiration might help her to drive a bargain in cows" (*BG* 283).

Rhett's inability to access his wealth at the parallel point in Mitchell's novel leads to Scarlett's marriage to Frank Kennedy, of whom she had always thought contemptuously and whose appeal to her sister Suellen she could not understand. Such irony can be found too in Dorinda's eventual marriage to Nathan Pedlar, of whom she had once thought, "There could be no drearier lot . . . than marriage with Nathan for a husband" (*BG* 86). Dorinda's marriage brings up another shared detail in the characterization of the two heroines.

Both young women are following in the footsteps of their mothers, as discussed previously, as well as of a female relative of the generation before their mothers. Scarlett's grandmother "married three times and had any number of duels fought over her and she wore rouge and the most shockingly low-cut dresses" (*GW* 680), much of which is echoed in Scarlett's behavior as she pursues her interests during the years covered in Mitchell's novel. Dorinda's great-aunt, for whom she was named, had tried to commit suicide after she was rejected by her first love interest, but when rescued, she, like Dorinda, "sobered down and married somebody else and was as sensible as anybody until the day of her death" (*BG* 102).

Surprisingly, given the characterization of Nathan, Dorinda's marriage to him is also similar to Scarlett's third marriage to Rhett Butler, a character as romantic as Nathan is not. Both women must be talked into the marriage and assured that their new husbands will not interfere with their work. Tonette L. Bond's reading of the purpose for Dorinda's marriage to Nathan—"to gain a strong partner to help her achieve permanence for her ideal" (571)—can be applied to Scarlett's reason for agreeing to marry Rhett. Also Dorinda realizes that Nathan "was at her mercy because he cared while she was indifferent" and thus that "she would be always . . . the stronger of the two" (*BG* 374). Though Rhett makes sure that Scarlett does not realize it, he, too, is at a disadvantage in their relationship because he loves her while she is indifferent about him. And in the fates of Scarlett and Rhett, the reader will learn, too, that she is ultimately "the stronger of the two."

Jan Zlotnik Schmidt's assessment of Nathan and Dorinda's marriage is also remarkably applicable to Scarlett's marriage to Rhett: "Obsessed by her memories of love, Dorinda destroys any possibility of anything more than a platonic union with Nathan Pedlar." Schmidt believes that "Dorinda's desire for revenge [against Jason] has produced her sterile marriage and stunted her emotional growth" (128). All during her own marriage to Rhett, Scarlett remains obsessed with Ashley, the object of immature romanticizing daydreams of her youth. Although their marriage (like her other two marriages) is consummated (unlike Dorinda and Nathan's, it seems), Scarlett apparently participates in sexual relations only as a wifely duty, still finding no enjoyment in the sex act—with one night's apparent exception.

Schmidt terms the effect that buying Five Oaks has on Dorinda "aphrodisiacal." The night of their purchase is the "one real moment of communion" Dorinda has with Nathan. Schmidt concludes from this episode that at this time in the novel "Dorinda's character growth is [still] incomplete" (128). Somewhat similar to Schmidt's reading of this point in Dorinda and

Nathan's marriage is the "one real moment of communion" between Scarlett and Rhett during their night of violent sex after Scarlett is discovered in Ashley's arms (innocently, but still to Rhett's consternation). Thus this episode in Mitchell's novel is also evidence of Scarlett's as yet incomplete character development, since she is attracted to Rhett's ability to overpower her, a reflection of her desire to return to her former childhood state when she was not the one in the position of power with so many responsibilities and dependents. Indeed Blanche Gelfant compares Scarlett's later "determination to get Rhett back" to "a child's regressive longing for home and mother" (13). Recalling the episode of Scarlett's efforts to return to Tara—where she hopes to turn the care of Melanie and their children over to Ellen, only to find Ellen dead and everyone looking to her to take Ellen's place—one sees that the times Rhett appeals to Scarlett come when she is seeking someone to take charge so that she might relinquish power and return to the role of child.

The events leading up to Dorinda's and Scarlett's momentary feelings of connection with their husbands are also comparable. During the auctioning of Five Oaks, Dorinda struggles to keep her mind from recalling the past, realizing that only the present matters. Similarly, earlier in the day that ends with Rhett carrying Scarlett upstairs in hopes of driving Ashley out of her mind once and for all, Scarlett and Ashley had talked about the past, at which time she thinks, "I shouldn't have let him make me look back. . . . I was right when I said I'd never look back. It hurts too much, it drags at your heart till you can't ever do anything else except look back" (*GW* 925). Like Dorinda, she realizes that "no one could go forward with a load of aching memories" (*GW* 924).

During the night of momentary closeness between the Pedlars, Dorinda realizes that her husband "is worth twenty of Jason" but fails in her attempts "to say something affectionate" to Nathan (*BG* 393). Likewise, after their "wild mad night" of passion (*GW* 940), Scarlett and Rhett are unable to communicate their true feelings for each other. At the end of the novel, Scarlett tells Rhett, "that [night] must have been when I first knew I cared about you. . . . I never was happy about Ashley after that" (*GW* 1031). However, whereas Dorinda is "sure that [Nathan] understood her mood and was touched by its gentleness," and the two talked together late into the night about their plans for the future of their farm (*BG* 393–94), Scarlett and Rhett completely misunderstand each other when they confront each other the morning after their passionate night. Still it is not until the night of Nathan's death that Dorinda misses him and realizes how much she has grown to like him over the years, just as Scarlett did not realize until after she had banished Rhett from her bedroom that she would miss their nightly talks, and she does not recognize until she is on the way home from Melanie's deathbed that she loves Rhett. But as Dorinda's discovery is too late, Scarlett too will discover that it is too late for her love for Rhett to matter to him. Jan Schmidt remarks on the consequences of Dorinda's "emotional frigidity," which Schmidt argues "is life-denying for Dorinda" and "demands . . . an unfair self-abnegation" from Nathan. Nathan's death, then, she contends, "provides Dorinda with the final realizations necessary for character building" (129), just as Rhett's abandonment of Scarlett provides her these character-building realizations at the end of Mitchell's novel: as Dawson Gaillard has argued, "when the woman-wife-child . . . awakens to her complete selfhood and matures, the parent-man walks out" (18).

Before reaching the novel's final enlightenment, Dorinda transforms her deceased husband in much the same romantic way she had transformed Jason years before: after Nathan's heroic death, "it was impossible that she should ever think of [him] as unromantically as she thought of him while he was alive. Death had not only ennobled, it had superbly exalted him" (*BG* 442). Even years later she tells herself that though "it was true that she had missed love . . . after all, it was something to have married a hero. Nathan's victorious death had filled the aching void in her heart. Where the human being had failed her, the heroic legend had satisfied" (*BG* 456). As a result, "the years after [his] death were the richest and happiest of her life" (*BG* 446). She had her work and a hero, too—and one who would not interfere with her work. However, Schmidt criticizes Dorinda's "depend[ence] upon this legend to provide 'a sense of purpose in existence'" because "she is not searching within herself for the dimensions of her own legend" (129). Indeed it is not until several years after Nathan's death, when Dorinda painfully contemplates her life as it really was in light of what she had not had in it—love—that Dorinda becomes completely satisfied with herself and what she *has* accomplished with her land.

At the end of *Gone with the Wind,* we see Scarlett begin a similar transformation of Rhett. As Rhett observes, "it's written plainly on your face. Something, someone has made you realize that the unfortunate Mr. Wilkes is too large a mouthful of Dead Sea fruit for even you to chew. And that same something has suddenly set my charms before you in a new and attractive light" (*GW* 1027). A little later in this final conversation, he adds, "I see you are contemplating the transfer of your tempestuous affections from Ashley to me" (*GW* 1033). Rhett is right, and not only does this notion undermine the idea that Scarlett really does love Rhett after all, but also one realizes that it would be better for Scarlett if she were to recognize her own value, rather than turn her attention to another man and begin another obsessive quest for his love. Dieter Meindl sees Scarlett's error here in similar terms: "Scarlett . . . misjudges . . . by offering her love to an ideal image of her husband which, whatever its applicability to the past, does not correspond to the tired, resigned man who will not try to approximate to this idea but cuts off further discussion" (423). Darden Pyron also comments on Scarlett's mistake in turning her sights on Rhett: "Scarlett loses her faith in Ashley too late to transfer it to a more legitimate object, Melanie," as we have seen. Pyron agrees that Rhett, by this point, is "as hollow as his alter ego, Ashley" ("*Gone*" 582).

At the end of both novels the heroines find their original knights in shining armor in their care, dependent on them for survival. When Dorinda sees Jason in the poorhouse, "all connection between him and the man she had once loved was severed" (*BG* 488). And once he is in her care, she realizes, "Whether he had loved her or not made no difference. . . . How futile, how unnecessary, it had all been,—her love, her suffering, her bitterness" (*BG* 492–93). Like Dorinda, Scarlett does not want the responsibility of taking care of Ashley: "But, just the same I've got him round my neck for the rest of my life. As long as I live I'll have to look after him. . . . And if I hadn't promised Melly [just as she had once promised Ashley to take care of Melanie] . . . I wouldn't care if I never saw him again" (*GW* 1017). She is at first disgusted with Ashley for finally admitting, only now that his wife is dead, that he actually loved Melanie all along, but then pity for him replaces her anger, which she soon turns upon herself for not realizing long ago that "her love, her suffering, her bitterness" could all have been avoided had she realized the truth about Ashley sooner. According to Dawson Gaillard, "in discarding the illusion, the image from the past [of Ashley], Scarlett discards completely her girlhood; she becomes an adult, the point toward which the novel has been moving" (17). Her insight, late though it is, indicates that she, unlike Rhett, is developing finally, rather than regressing. At the end of the novel, in contrast to Rhett's backward view, she is looking ahead to "tomorrow . . . another day" (*GW* 1037).

After leaving Ashley, Scarlett hurries home to Rhett, and as she rushes through the streets in the fog, she realizes that her nightmare has come true. She believes, however, that when she reaches Rhett she will finally find the haven that she has been seeking. Though she is soon to learn otherwise, her nightmare coming true, in all its horror, including not being able to reach the security she seeks, can be read more promisingly when it is compared to the positive manifestation of Dorinda's "nightmare dream of ploughing under the thistles . . . into the actual event" when she works to reclaim the land of Five Oaks from the broomsedge and pine (*BG* 401). Dorinda's rejuvenation of Five Oaks reminds the reader that Scarlett, too, reclaimed land from destruction just after a waking nightmare of finding her home ravaged, her mother dead, and the survivors dependent upon her for sustenance. It was in those days of running Tara that she most revealed her strength and endurance. Now, when the nightmare becomes real with Scarlett's arrival home to learn that Rhett, like her mother, will not relieve her of her responsibilities, she determines to return to Tara, where the reader feels sure she can again be strong.

The reader should not consider Rhett's rejection of Scarlett as indicative that he, too, is triumphant at the novel's end. A comparison between Rhett and Jason at this point, in its illumination of the final image of Mitchell's hero, reveals otherwise. Actually Rhett and Jason are comparable from the start. Early on Jason tells Dorinda, "I've known so few girls . . . but somehow you seem different" (*BG* 35). Rhett Butler has known more than "a few girls," but he, too, is attracted to Scarlett's difference: her unladylike behavior and her "rare spirit, very admirable spirit" (*GW* 120), which he points out to her at their first meeting. Since Jason has been compared to Ashley, it should not be surprising that he is also comparable to Rhett, for as Rhett, Ashley, and even Scarlett realize at various points in the novel, Rhett is not so unlike Ashley as they would all, on other occasions, like to think. Even the difference Rhett points to before carrying Scarlett upstairs—that Ashley "doesn't want [her] mind . . . and [Rhett] do[es]n't want [her] body" (*GW* 938)—does not hold, as Blanche Gelfant points out: "for surely Rhett wanted the body he ravished" (27).

Using *Barren Ground*, rather than Selznick's film, as an intertext of *Gone with the Wind* recalls Rhett's condition at the end of the novel (which Selznick ignored in his direction of this final scene between Scarlett and Rhett). Jason's drinking has affected his looks, as Rhett's drinking since Bonnie's death has taken a significant toll on his appearance: "He was untidy now, where once he had been well groomed. . . . Whisky was showing in his face and the hard line of his long jaw was being obscured under an unhealthy bloat and puffs rising under his blood shot eyes. His big body with its hard swelling muscles looked soft and slack and his waist line began to thicken" (*GW* 1000–1001). Quite similar is the condition of Jason toward the end of Glasgow's novel: "He looked [like] an old man, for his skin was drawn and wrinkled, the pouches under his eyes were inflamed with purple, and there were clusters of congested veins in his cheeks" (*BG* 450). When Scarlett first sees Rhett after her return from Melanie's deathbed, "he was sunken in his chair, his suit wrinkling untidily against his thickening waist, every line of him proclaiming the ruin of a fine body and the coarsening of a strong face. Drink and dissipation had done their work on the coin-clear profile and now it was no longer the head of a young pagan prince on new-minted gold but a decadent, tired Caesar on copper debased by long usage" (*GW* 1024–25). His final speech to her—which has long been interpreted as Rhett's triumph over Scarlett (thanks, in large part, to the still impeccably groomed and self-controlled Clark Gable's delivery of it in the movie, followed by his walking out and closing the door on Vivien Leigh's Scarlett)—provides further evidence of Rhett's complete destruction: he is looking and heading backward, toward the Old South values he had rejected early in his life for their hypocrisy and self-destructiveness. Scarlett, in contrast, like Dorinda, is still holding up, in spite of the many tragedies she has endured in the course of her lifetime. Indeed, if one compares the hardships Scarlett and Dorinda overcome during their lifetimes with those suffered by Rhett and Jason, the men's troubles—including the death of Bonnie, since Scarlett has also lost her daughter, as well as many more members of her family—pale in comparison; and yet it is these men who are destroyed by the end of the two novels.

But before emerging triumphant, both women must go through some moments of agonizing contemplation, which contribute to the somewhat ambiguous ending of both novels. As Jason lies dying, Dorinda realizes, "She had never known [him], and now she could never know [him]" (*BG* 497). After Jason's death she regrets her lost youth and "the love that she had never had" (*BG* 504). She wishes she could relive her life differently, and "because it was too late and her youth had gone, she felt that the only thing that made life worth living was the love that she had never known and the happiness that she had missed" (*BG* 507). She recalls Jason "as he was when she had first loved him. Though she tried to think of him as broken, ruined, and repellent, through some perversity of recollection he returned to her in the radiance of that old summer. . . . Success, achievement, victory over fate, all these things were nothing beside that imperishable illusion" (*BG* 508). She revokes her early repeated contention that "there must be something in life besides love" (*BG* 192, 245) with the thought that "love was the only thing that made life desirable" and despairs in this notion since "love was irrevocably lost to her" (*BG* 508).

Scarlett also realizes that "she had never understood either of the men she had loved and so she had lost them both" (*GW* 1036). She too is thinking of a former man, a former Rhett, "who had strong arms to hold her, a broad chest to pillow her tired head, jeering laughter to pull her affairs into proper perspective" (*GW* 1021), as she rushes home to him. Dieter Meindl agrees "that the man she resolves to win back is no longer the man she loves, who represents to her the promise that life can be mastered and peace be found." Meindl then suggests that "what Scarlett, after her pursuit of a knightly Ashley existing only in her imagination, finally purposes to do is to hunt for just another phantom, a Rhett who is no more" (421). Even after seeing and talking with him, she believes that "with the sound of his feet dying away in the upper hall was dying the last thing in the world that mattered." Like Dorinda, she tries an oft-repeated motto—"I'll think of it tomorrow"—but it, too, fails to comfort, leaving her desperate to get Rhett back, even though she, too, recognizes "that there was no appeal to emotion or reason which would turn that cool brain from its verdict . . . that he had meant every word he said" (*GW* 1036).

The morning after Dorinda's painful night of self-evaluation, she emerges strong again: "The storm and the hag-ridden dreams of the night were over, and the land which she had forgotten was waiting to take her back to its heart. Endurance. Fortitude. The spirit of the land was flowing into her, and her own spirit, strengthened and refreshed, was flowing out again toward life. This was the permanent self, she knew" (*BG* 509). She recalls old Matthew Fairlamb's words about the land and takes comfort from her own experience with the truth of them. Thus, as Frederick McDowell explains, although "Dorinda occasionally feels that she may have paid too high a price for her success . . . such misgivings are, for the most part, momentary." McDowell sees Dorinda as "both victor and victim in her struggle with the soil," in that "the grimness of her existence on the land is offset by her sense of a kinship with its strength" (151). Jan Schmidt also remarks on the simultaneous "victory and defeat" that Dorinda experiences at novel's end: "to preserve the [pastoral] legend and the serenity that it promises, she must abandon hopes of romantic fulfillment" (130–31). As Linda Wagner[-Martin] has noted, "Dorinda's reward—for her life of affirmation and deprivation—is not fairy-tale happiness . . . but a kind of constancy, a satisfaction with herself" (*Ellen* 76). Dorinda realizes that "this monotony of contentment had no relation to what she had called happiness in her youth. It was better perhaps; it was certainly as good; but it measured all the difference between youth and maturity" (*BG* 378).

Scarlett also finally recognizes the high price she has paid to insure herself and her family against ever being hungry again. Since Rhett's departure with Bonnie earlier and even more so since Bonnie's death and Rhett's increasing distance, she has felt lonely and questioned the value of her new lifestyle and friends. Now that she has lost both Melanie and Rhett, she is in despair. But she, too, finds a "bulwark against the rising tide of pain" within her by recalling her land: "She had gone back to Tara once in fear and defeat and she had emerged from its sheltering walls strong and armed for victory. What she had done once, somehow—please God, she could do again! . . . She thought of Tara and it was as if a gentle cool hand were stealing over her heart" (*GW* 1036). As Dawson Gaillard points out, Tara is a "boon" superior to Rhett's love (12), which Gaillard perceives to be debilitating, in that Rhett treats Scarlett like a little girl. Therefore, although the reader's sense of Scarlett's development may seem somewhat undermined by her longing for Mammy's arms and her plan to come up with a scheme to get Rhett back, Scarlett is still more triumphant than Rhett. Whereas he is returning to the restrictive codes of the Old South, she, as Gaillard notes, "is free to exert her own vital self" (18). And like Dorinda, who believes in the end that "the best of life . . . was ahead of her" (*BG* 510), Scarlett is contemplating tomorrow. Furthermore the reader should recall that it was at Tara that "the girl with her sachet and dancing slippers had slipped away," leaving "a woman with sharp green eyes, who counted pennies and turned her hands to many menial tasks, a woman to whom nothing was left from the wreckage except the indestructible red earth on which she stood" (*GW* 490). From this earlier passage, one can find support for the idea that Scarlett will conquer again the frivolities of her recent lifestyle and recall, like Dorinda, the value of working with the land. With such an ending Mitchell's book defies the expectations for a traditional romance novel: as pointed out by Helen Taylor, "the happy ending involves not a man but a piece of property/land" ("*Gone*" 131). And Scarlett's longing for Mammy can be read positively, as will be shown in the next chapter: as a manifestation of her belated realization of Melanie's value to her, the value of someone who loves her for who she is.

Like the two novels' endings, their titles are somewhat ambiguous. As Linda Wagner[-Martin] points out, Glasgow "found that readers sometimes misread the title *Barren Ground* (and viewed Dorinda Oakley as defeated instead of productive)" (*Ellen* 94). Louis D. Rubin Jr., for example, believes that "*Barren Ground* is an aptly named novel." He characterizes "Dorinda's life [as] a progressive espousal of barrenness" (*No* 26). Wagner[-Martin] notes that "childless as she is, Dorinda herself might be termed *barren,* but Glasgow shows clearly that Dorinda has never been a barren woman: she has known passion, she has conceived. And what she wrests from the generally unyielding land is fruit, success, promise for the future—the opposite of barrenness" (*Ellen* 74). Glasgow's title, whether it refers to Old Farm or to Dorinda, is ironic by the end of the novel, since neither is ultimately barren. The title *Barren Ground,* rather, sets the stage for the state of affairs at the novel's beginning, describing as it does the condition of the land before Dorinda's hard work. Mitchell's title's reference to the Old South (which is what is *Gone*) also sets the stage for the novel's beginning. And like *Barren Ground, Gone with the Wind* could refer to both the old way of life and the old Scarlett. But this title is not intended to evoke nostalgia for the past, as is the music playing in the background as Mitchell's title appears on the screen in the movie. We might remember here that Mitchell originally entitled her manuscript *Tomorrow Is Another Day* and changed it upon her publisher's suggestion because there were several books with titles beginning with *Tomorrow.* The former title certainly looks toward the future, and the selected title, which is what matters in the long run, attests to the fact that the old days are *Gone.*

In many of the reviews and much of the early criticism of *Barren Ground,* Dorinda Oakley's life is perceived to be a failure. In the *New York Times Book Review,* for example, H. I. Brock says Dorinda is "drearily triumphant" as "a prosperous woman dairy farmer who made barren ground bear rich pasturage and paid the price of it in her own barren life." Jessie Hopkins, reviewer for the *Atlanta Journal Magazine,* notes similarly that although "Dorinda succeeds in conquering the barren soil of her home, . . . she cannot apply the same determination to retrieve her own barren life." And critic John Edward Hardy believes that "the outcome of [Dorinda's] life is meant to be tragic," since "the fertility of the land [is] secured at the expense of human sterility" (245). However, in more recent years, critics have viewed Dorinda more positively. A similar development can be found in the scholarship on Scarlett O'Hara. Still she has been criticized more often than not, and critics continue to explore why she deserves the comeuppance that they perceive in the novel's ending. But eleven years before Margaret Mitchell's publication of *Gone with the Wind,* Ellen Glasgow had shown in *Barren Ground* that being alone is not always a punishment, particularly when one has an occupation about which she feels passionately. Examining Scarlett's life in comparison to Dorinda's, then, should remind those who still express doubts about Scarlett's ultimate development and triumph that ending up without a man is not necessarily evidence of failure.

In *Ellen Glasgow and a Woman's Traditions,* Pamela R. Matthews's reading of *Barren Ground* examines the friendship developing between Dorinda and Fluvanna, a black woman who works in the dairy. I don't find enough of Fluvanna in the novel to be entirely convinced by Matthews's reading, but as we have seen, working together toward a common goal could certainly lead to friendship, even between people as different in both background and temperament as Scarlett and Melanie or Ada and Ruby. In her discussion of *Cold Mountain,* Linda Wagner-Martin asks, "Where in southern literature have we had a narrative of two women working the soil, hunting for medicinal herbs, and building fences?" She answers her question with *Barren Ground:* "when Dorinda Oakley works with her black employee Fluvanna to make her mother's land profitable for the first time." The problem with viewing Dorinda and Fluvanna as potential friends, Wagner-Martin proposes, is that today's readers "have issues with racial difference: we don't believe that the two women are friends, and we resent the plotline that makes Dorinda the source of agricultural wisdom" ("South" 35). Wagner-Martin suggests that "Frazier . . . rewrites that story and makes Ada wise enough to recognize the hard-earned wisdom Ruby has acquired from her own desperately poor, landless majority" ("South" 36). In Mitchell's novel it is when Scarlett and Melanie are working together at Tara that Scarlett is able to see Melanie in terms other than rival. I therefore agree with Pamela Matthews that a friendship between Dorinda and Fluvanna could develop and "overcome 'inherited condescension,'" and I too can "envision a future setting of recurring winter nights' sympathetic talk" (162), just as I believe (and take up at the end of the next chapter) that by the time Scarlett is longing at her novel's end to return home to Mammy, she is capable of recognizing the value of women in her life and thus perhaps ready to make a friend of Mammy.

Chapter 4

Sula

"More sinned against than sinning"

"I have an ongoing interest in outlaw women. They can be wild or they can be ordinary women who learn something fresh. I like very much to see them under duress. I like to see who survives this awful mess, who makes the best decisions, who is left and under what circumstances. If your character knows something at the end of a book she didn't know at the beginning, she is in a better position. Everybody wants a happy ending, but the real happy ending is when somebody really figures something out."

Toni Morrison, in Houston,
"A Conversation with Toni Morrison" (2)

"Womanist . . . Wanting to know more and in greater depth than is considered 'good' for one. . . . Responsible. In charge. . . . A woman who loves other women . . . Appreciates and prefers women's culture . . . and women's strength. . . . Committed to survival and wholeness of entire people . . . Traditionally capable . . . Loves . . . *Regardless.*"

Alice Walker, *In Search of Our Mothers' Gardens* (xi–xii)

Almost fifty years after Glasgow's *Barren Ground* was published, Toni Morrison set her novel *Sula* in about the same period of time that Glasgow left

Dorinda. *Sula* certainly takes place in a different region of the country, Ohio, and depicts a different culture, a community descended from slaves, but still Morrison's novel begins with the community's southern heritage: the "nigger joke" that explains how this community came to be called the Bottom after a man tricked his former slave into working in exchange for good bottom land and then gave him instead land in the hills, claiming it was the "bottom" of heaven.* Barbara Christian calls to mind the previous echo of *Barren Ground* in *Gone with the Wind* when she explains the role of this anecdote in *Sula:* "In presenting the Bottom's origins as a 'nigger joke,' and by juxtaposing its birth to its death, the author signals to the reader that her story will be concerned with the community's philosophy of *survival.* This philosophy, in Morrison's narrative, is very much related to the *land*—for the Bottom is actually topland where survival is precarious" ("Community" 66–67; emphasis added). Christian remarks too on the consequences of such an insular place as the Bottom, particularly on the women, whose lives are limited. Hearkening back to the Civil War–era novels *Gone with the Wind* and *Cold Mountain,* this Morrison novel's two main characters, Sula Peace and Nel Wright, are brought together in friendship by their shared experience of the limited expectations for women—perhaps even more limited by their race than the expectations for Scarlett O'Hara and the other women of her earlier generation who have been considered thus far. Sula and Nel's friendship reminds the reader again of what Dorinda Oakley is missing in her life—not so much a husband, which she is simply not interested in, but a friend—as Scarlett had Melanie and Ada has Ruby.

Pamela R. Matthews examines Glasgow's "lifelong concern with women's cooperative relationships [with each other] and with certain traditions of women's lives, such as marriage, that often threaten them." Matthews asks, "Does the traditional structure of a woman's life isolate her . . . or can it encourage female cooperation and friendship" (18). Luise Eichenbaum and Susie Orbach begin their 1987 book on women's friendships remarking on the changing attitude toward women's relationships in the 1970s (the decade in which *Sula* was published, if not set), "a time when women's roles have been changing and women are demanding of themselves that they get out and fulfill themselves. . . . It wasn't until the seventies that the significance of

* In her interview with the author, Carolyn C. Denard noted that "Medallion—a (northern) Ohio town—. . . was a lot like Black community life in the small southern town I grew up in," to which Morrison's response implies an inevitable intermingling in "what's southern and what's Black" (Denard 184).

women's relationships was recognized. Of course women's friendships have always been important and essential, but until the seventies, friendship between women was rarely graced with the social recognition that befitted it. Friendships were fitted around family commitments and almost every woman understood that her time with a friend was limited" (9). Toni Morrison recognized this failure to appreciate the value of friendship, telling one interviewer: "Women, your own friends, were always secondary relationships when the man was not there. . . . To have heterosexual women who are friends, who are talking only about themselves to each other, seemed to me a very radical thing when *Sula* was published" (Denard 79).

"But it is hardly radical now," Morrison added in this 1993 interview (Denard 79). As noted earlier in this study, contemporary fiction (written and visual) has begun to explore more overtly the value of friendship between women, but even compared to more recent works depicting supportive communities of women, *Sula* is unique. As one ponders Morrison's inversion of the traditional love triangle in her novel, the wronged wife / betrayed friend as the novel's transgressor rather than the other woman / traitorous friend, who in Morrison's novel is more victim than villain, the reader is struck by this means of allowing for a new perspective on that which is so often depicted through the usual triangle story: that is, how so often in literature—and in life—a friendship is thrown away over a person who is simply not worth it—or, as we see in *Gone with the Wind,* the value of a friendship is not recognized by a woman blinded by her focus on getting a particular (and often weak) man, who, if he were worth her attention, would not be torn between two women but fully committed to one of them.

With *The Bluest Eye* Toni Morrison established a reputation for breaking into new territory—exposing in that first novel, for example, how an African American girl embraces Euro-American standards of beauty and dreams of having blue eyes and blonde hair; later exploring in the Pulitzer Prize–winning *Beloved* how the inhumane treatment of slaves often resulted in violence against each other rather than against the oppressor. In *Sula,* certainly, the characters fail to fit any molds we are accustomed to: the matriarchal figure (Eva) is more oppressive than nurturing, the title character difficult to identify with and not very likeable. Indeed Sula commits that cross-cultural taboo of having an affair with her best friend's husband. And yet one leaves this novel with the impression that Sula "is more sinned against than sinning," that Nel, the betrayed wife and friend, is the guiltier of the two: it is she who has rejected her friend and thereby betrayed their friendship more so than Sula did by having sex with Nel's husband.

In an interview with Morrison, Gloria Naylor remarked on the commonness and ultimately inconsequentiality of African American women "shar[ing] men": "We do share our men. We may not like it very much, but there is a silent consensus about that and it hasn't really torn us apart as women" (Taylor-Guthrie 201). First-time readers' negative, judgmental reaction to Morrison's Sula having sex with Jude (especially since, if prompted, it is so easy to defend her) is a reflection of our "couple-centric culture," which automatically prioritizes sexual relationships, particularly marriages, over friendships. As Eichenbaum and Orbach note in their book *Between Women: Love, Envy, and Competition in Women's Friendships,* "In our culture, friendship is often allocated a secondary position while only marriages and sexual relationships are truly significant." These psychotherapists point out the contrast between cultural attitudes toward the importance of friendship and "the experience of many women whose friendships function—for long periods of time—as primary relationships." And yet, they write, "even though we know that close women friends are emotionally dependent upon one another, we rarely acknowledge how important these ties are" (74). Toni Morrison recognizes this truth about the failure to appreciate the value of friendship, which she calls "a discredited relationship." "When I was writing *Sula,*" she told an interviewer for *Paris Review,* "I was under the impression that for a large part of the female population a woman friend was considered a secondary relationship. A man and a woman's relationship was primary" (Denard 79).

As discussed earlier, the general attitude toward Scarlett O'Hara reflects movie viewers' focus on her chasing after Ashley—and their perception of Ashley as a victim of Scarlett's unscrupulous pursuit of another woman's husband. Much less attention is paid to Scarlett's failure to appreciate her friendship with Melanie until Melanie's death, after which Scarlett's loss of Melanie comes so close to the novel's end and Rhett's departure that readers (and viewers) focus their attention on that supposedly more significant loss, the great unrecognized love of Scarlett's life. But with *Sula* it is impossible to miss Nel's eventual recognition of what she lost after Sula's death as the novel ends on Nel's "fine cry . . . of sorrow" (*S* 174) when she recognizes that it is Sula, not Jude, she has been missing. After reading the two novels together, one recognizes that in both, the relationship that emerges as the most nurturing, the strongest, the most valuable to these women is a friendship. However, the *Gone with the Wind* audience often misses what C. Lynn Munro has noted about the triangle in Morrison's novel: "To establish the difference between a love which nurtures and a love which constricts, Morrison juxtaposes the relationships which Nel has with Sula and Jude" (152). One could also see how much more valuable Melanie's love was to Scarlett than Rhett's by recognizing the "nurturing" versus "constricting" relationships Scarlett has with Melanie and Rhett, respectively: Melanie supports Scarlett's efforts to be her strong, independent self, while Rhett wants her to let him take care of her. And yet the focus at novel's end is on the supposedly great loss of Rhett Butler, which overshadows the actually much greater loss of Melanie Wilkes.

Morrison set out, she told Gloria Naylor, to "have one [of a pair of friends] do the unforgivable thing to see what that friendship was really made out of" (Taylor-Guthrie 200). She has Sula break the generally accepted addendum to the commandment thou shall not commit adultery: in particular, thou shall not sleep with thy best friend's significant other. And she develops Sula into a not-so-likable character, making it easier for her reader to condemn this woman for betraying her friend. But Morrison, typically for her, is setting us up. This novel is no traditional story of the femme fatale and her innocent, betrayed friend. In such stories, there is little question of what we are supposed to think about the one woman's self-centered, back-stabbing quest for the other woman's lover—and readers of such have no problem sympathizing with the wronged friend, who cannot imagine that a woman whom she has cared about and whom she considers a friend would betray her. In stark contrast to the traditional version of such a story, Morrison's Sula did not intend to hurt or take anything from her friend; and in further contrast, Morrison's Nel never even gave Sula the benefit of the doubt, did not for years, in fact, ask Sula why she had an affair with Jude. And when Nel finally does ask, Morrison defies expectations with Sula's responding questions: "If we were such good friends, how come you couldn't get over it?" (*S* 145) and "How you know . . . who was good? How you know it was you?" (*S* 146). While it appears to Nel that Sula has chosen an afternoon's pleasure with Jude over their friendship, actually it is Nel who ultimately chose Jude over Sula: apparently out of loyalty to her marriage to this philanderer, she ended her relationship with Sula, and she maintained the estrangement from Sula even after Jude was long gone.

"All's fair in love . . ."—or so we learn from books and movies. Girls often accept an unwritten rule that it is okay to cancel plans with a girlfriend if a boy calls. In her 1973 novel, Toni Morrison seems to question why we aren't taught, instead, to value platonic friendship *at least as much as,* if not more than a sexual relationship. In her discussion of the novel, Renita Weems notes that "along with budding breasts and pubic hair come men, and our love for one another becomes displaced. Like Nel, we allow men to slip in and occupy not only their space but the space once occupied by our girlfriend(s)" (100). In 1983 Morrison remarked in an interview that women's friendship is apparently not considered "a suitable topic for a book": "Hamlet can have a friend, and Achilles can have one, but women don't, because the world knows that women don't choose each other's acquaintanceship. They choose men first, then women as second choice. But I have made women the focal point of books in order to find out what women's friendships are really all about" (Taylor-Guthrie 154). That same year she told another interviewer, "Friendship between women is special, different, and has never been depicted as the major focus of a novel before *Sula*. . . . Relationships between women were always written about as though they were subordinate to some other roles they're playing" (Taylor-Guthrie 157). For example, one might note our tendency to miss the possibility that the friendship between Scarlett and Melanie could be more interesting than Scarlett and Rhett's not so uniquely tumultuous relationship.

Likewise it is easy for the reader as for Nel to overlook Sula's background, which can explain her affair with her best friend's husband. Nel falls readily into the roles of wronged wife and betrayed friend and fails to take into account that Sula was raised by a mother who treated sex casually, teaching her daughter "that sex was pleasant and frequent, but otherwise unremarkable" (*S* 44). Nel has also forgotten the time when she and Sula "shared the affection of other people," including boyfriends apparently, since they used to "compar[e] how a boy kissed, what line he used with one *and then the other*" (*S* 119; emphasis added). Indeed Nel fails to comprehend the significance of the fact that, when she found the two together, Sula "didn't look naked . . . only [Jude] did" (*S* 106), a distinction that reflects Nel's awareness, subconsciously at least, that Sula is not doing anything she is ashamed of, though Jude is. He apparently shares Nel's traditional notions of adultery, as evidenced by his departure after being caught. Sula remains in town, waiting, I would suggest, for Nel.

Since the beginning of their friendship, Sula and Nel have always shared everything. When Sula returns after several years living away from Medallion, she tells Nel about her adventures and in return, it seems, for sharing her experiences with Nel, who had always planned to leave the Bottom but had never done so, borrows Nel's husband for a taste of her life as a married woman. Apparently she never intended to take Jude away from Nel—indeed never intended Nel any harm at all. In fact Sula can be perceived as the "less guilty" of the two women, if not completely exonerated, by the fact that Jude just isn't worth the price Nel pays, the cost of Sula's friendship. Sula apparently knows this all along, for she doesn't leave with Jude, but Nel does not come to this realization until the novel's end, after Sula's death.

In further defense of Sula, Nel overlooks the fact that Sula grew up in a house where more traditional social mores do not apply: her grandmother killed her own son rather than allow his needs to be more important than her own; her mother admitted publicly to loving but not liking her daughter—both women thereby, at best redefining, but also undermining traditional notions of unconditional mother love. In a world where such supposed givens as mother love cannot be counted on, some relationship is needed to replace what is lacking. Consider the earlier discussion of how Melanie provides Scarlett with the affection and approval that Scarlett did not receive from Ellen. Blinded by her perception of Melanie as her rival, Scarlett does not recognize how Melanie provides the kind of love even Ellen, certainly Ashley, and eventually Rhett could not provide. In contrast Sula never considers Nel as a rival and thus inadvertently destroys their friendship by not realizing that Nel's love is no less conditional than anyone else's. Margaret Schramm's "The Quest for the Perfect Mother in Toni Morrison's *Sula*" argues that "the desire for self-sacrificing, unconditional mother love persists and causes the alienation of mothers from daughters and the estrangement of women friends. The quest for the perfect mother fractures the primal relationships of the two protagonists, Sula and Nel, because both unconsciously expect continuous, selfless love, first from their own mothers and then from each other as surrogate mothers" (167). Nel and Sula, we are told when they are first brought together in the novel, both found in each other what they did not receive from their mothers: Nel's mother was always trying to change and improve her; Sula's mother, as Toni Morrison puts it in an interview, is "not particularly interested in her [daughter]" (Taylor-Guthrie 16). Consequently Nel and Sula "were solitary little girls whose loneliness was so profound it intoxicated them and sent them stumbling into Technicolored visions that always included a presence, a someone, who, quite like the dreamer, shared the delight of the dream" (*S* 51). Both girls imagine themselves waiting with someone for their dreams to come true. For Nel, someone with "smiling sympathetic eyes" would wait for her prince with her, while Sula's fantasy puts herself in the prince rather than the waiting role: "on a gray-and-white horse tasting sugar and smelling roses in full view of a someone who shared both the taste and the speed" and who would watch her from the sidelines as she pursued her ambitions (*S* 51–52). In Nel's more traditional fantasy, one notes, the goal is, implicitly, the arrival of the prince; presumably then, Sula would wait with her friend and then step aside as Nel "married and lived happily ever after," which is essentially what transpires at the end of part 1 of the novel. After Nel's wedding, Sula departs down the road, not on a horse, but with a clear intent to taste the sweetness of life and smell the roses. As she tells Nel from her deathbed years later, "I sure did live in this world" (*S* 143).

Incongruous as it may seem to link this post–World War I–era African American female character to a character whom many perceive (wrongly, I think) to be the icon of southern belledom, parallels can easily be seen in critics' descriptions of Sula between Sula and Scarlett O'Hara: "Sula does as she pleases, so completely flouting the rules of the community and so disrespectful of its narrow and orderly boundaries, that Medallion's citizenry look upon her as unnatural" (Matza 51); "her entire life represents a rejection of traditional notions of feminine 'respectability'" (Lounsberry and Hovet 128); "Sula has the distinction of being herself in a community that believes that selfhood can only be selfishness" (Christian, "Contemporary" 40); "Sula refuses to participate in the selflessness that passes for charity and the self-pity that seems compassion in her small-town world" (Middleton 374); "she simply refuses to attribute meaning or to relate to the implications of her behavior" (Guth 577); "she has no sense of, or sensitivity to, cause and effect" (Galehouse 341). Even Toni Morrison's own description of Sula could be applied easily to Scarlett: "the kind of person that would upset everybody, the kind of person that sets your teeth on edge; and yet not . . . so repulsive that you could not find her attractive at the same time—a nature that was seductive and offputting" (Denard 26).

Besides the obvious differences of their race, class, and time, there is another major difference between Scarlett and Sula that effects the two women's lives significantly: Melanie defends Scarlett from their first meeting at Twelve Oaks to the end of her own life, including after India, Mrs. Elsing, and Archie come upon Scarlett in Ashley's arms. In contrast Nel's failure to take the circumstances of Sula's life (and her own) into consideration after walking in on Sula having sex with Jude is a betrayal of Sula at least equal to, if not greater than Sula's affair with Nel's husband. Whereas Sula knows that Nel was raised by a socially hyperconscious mother, she also knows that Nel had once preferred the less conventional Peace family's household. Thus Sula has reason to expect Nel to give her the benefit of the doubt, to at least ask her *why* before ending their friendship. Since Nel doesn't ask, Morrison defends Sula through the novel's narrator with the information that Nel should have known:

> She had no thought at all of causing Nel pain when she bedded down with Jude. They had always shared the affection of other people. . . . Marriage, apparently, had changed all that, but having had no intimate knowledge of marriage, having lived in a house with women who thought all men available, and selected from among them with a care only for their tastes, she was ill prepared for the possessiveness of the one person she felt close to. She knew well enough what other women said and felt, or said they felt. But she and Nel had always seen through them. They both knew that those women were not jealous of other women; that they were only afraid of losing their jobs. Afraid their husbands would discover that no uniqueness lay between their legs. (*S* 119)

This passage suggests the occurrence of discussions between the two friends from which Sula might infer that Nel and she were still simpatico regarding relationships between men and women. Morrison's narrator then proceeds from this defense of Sula into an implicit condemnation of Nel's betrayal of Sula: "Nel was the one person who had wanted nothing from her, who had accepted all aspects of her. Now she wanted everything, and all because of *that*. . . . Now Nel was one of *them*. One of the spiders whose only thought was the next rung of the web. . . . Now Nel belonged to the town and all of its ways. . . . It had surprised [Sula] a little and saddened her a good deal when Nel behaved the way the others would have. Nel was one of the reasons she had drifted back to Medallion" (*S* 119–20; Morrison's italics). And since her return to Medallion, Sula has given to Nel as much as she received from her: Sula "made her laugh . . . made her see old things with new eyes"; made her feel "clever, gentle, and a little raunchy"; allowed her to "be foolish"; and finally, perhaps most applicable to the crisis at hand, "never competed [but] simply helped others define themselves" (*S* 95). But Nel forgets these gifts as she takes on the role of victim after discovering Sula and Jude together. Again Sula's intent was not to take someone who belonged to Nel; and Nel might have used the experience to recognize how her values had changed since she and Sula were children, how she was becoming more like the mother whose conventional ideals she had resisted when she and Sula were girls. Nel does eventually achieve this self-recognition, but not until after Sula's death.

Twenty-five years after Sula's death, Nel realizes, "'all that time, I thought I was missing Jude.' And the loss pressed down on her chest and came up into her throat" (*S* 174). Diana Gillespie and Missy Dehn Kubitschek explain that when she married, Nel was "expected to refocus her commitments from her female friend to her husband, an expectation so strong that Nel thinks for years that she has done so" (84), but in this recognition scene, these critics point out, "Nel abandons the conventional fiction of her supreme attachment to her husband to mourn her greater losses, Sula's friendship and Sula herself" (75). The extent of the devastation Nel experiences upon realizing her mistake is another example of Morrison's fiction going against the grain. She suggests in this novel that much more important than Nel's marriage or Sula's affair with Jude is that Nel and Sula were "girls together"—that is, that their friendship is more valuable than any other relationship in their lives. The novel concludes with Nel's "fine cry" of grief—the adjective "fine" suggesting the grief's redemptive power—"loud and long—but it had no bottom and it had no top, just circles and circles of sorrow" (*S* 174). Nel recognizes that she lost the most important person in her life, the woman she was "girls together" with but only briefly women together, because of Nel's abandonment of their friendship rather than Sula's betrayal of it. The reader is reminded of Scarlett's devastating realization at Melanie's deathbed: "Why, oh, why, had she not realized before this how much she loved and needed Melanie? But who would have thought of small plain Melanie as a tower of strength? . . . But now, as Scarlett looked sadly back, she realized that Melanie had always been there beside her with a sword in her hand, unobtrusive as her own shadow, loving her, fighting for her with blind passionate loyalty, fighting Yankees, fire, poverty, public opinion and even her beloved blood kin" (*GW* 1012).

Yet we are taught, from the fairy tales told to us as children, through the movies and books that reflect the general ideology of our culture, that the single most important relationship in our lives, excepting our bonds to our children perhaps, is supposed to be with our life partner. And, even given the value of parent/child relationships, our children will leave us to join with another and go on with their lives without us, so this notion of who the single most important person is supposed to be holds. The ideology of this culture being predominantly heterosexist and given that same-sex marriages are still not recognized by law in most places, this person is *supposed* to be our spouse and a member of the opposite sex. This is the person whose name is *supposed* to be on our lips on our deathbeds, indeed the person we imagine will be with us in our dying hour or waiting for us on the other side. Perhaps this person might be replaced in some scenarios with the dying one's child, but certainly one's spouse or lover over a mere platonic friend. "So what's the problem?" psychologist Brenda Hunter asks and then answers, "By emphasizing heterosexual relationships above all else, our culture trivializes the importance of female friendships." Hunter notes too that "until the seventies the subject of women's friendships was largely ignored by writers and researchers alike" (24). And yet, as Louise Bernikow points out in her book *Among Women,* in contrast to social expectations, women "have died in each other's arms far more than the romantic novel or cinema would lead us to believe" (101). Recall that it is Scarlett whom Melanie calls to her deathbed.

In a 1980 interview, Morrison remarked on social expectations about whom one can love: "there was a time when you could love god, or your race, or your brother, or your sister, or your mother, but all those things have been taken from us in a way, because if you love god they think you are backward, if you love your mother they think you got some Freudian thing . . . if you have a friend that you love somebody will think that you are lesbian or homosexual. So what's left? There's nothing left to love, except the children and the member of the opposite sex." The consequence of such limits, Morrison adds, is that "the person on the other end of that gets everything. It's too much; the lover expects so much from the beloved. If you loved five things intensely, no one of them would receive that hysterical responsibility for yourself, emotions would be diversified" (Taylor-Guthrie 73). The reader is reminded of Rhett's aversion to Scarlett redirecting the intensity of her passion for Ashley to him: "Don't look so determined, Scarlett! You frighten me. I see you are contemplating the transfer of your tempestuous affections from Ashley to me and I fear for my liberty and my peace of mind" (*GW* 1033).

As noted previously, neither Scarlett nor Melanie can stretch their imaginations beyond the traditional expectations for women—winning the handsome prince and living happily ever after—in spite of their own broad experiences outside of their married lives. For Scarlett, albeit unconsciously, finding true love (she assumes with Ashley) will make up for the love she did not get from her mother; Melanie longs for many children to love. Neither realizes they are much more suited to each other and that Melanie already directs the mother love she longs to give toward Scarlett and Scarlett's children. It is likely that the novel's author did not even realize how these women could have given each other what they each longed for and thus could have lived happier lives with their respective husbands (a longer life, too, in Melanie's case). In contrast to Mitchell, Morrison is directly, consciously reexamining the value of friendship in *Sula:* why shouldn't the last person one thinks about be a friend rather than a child or lover? While Sula dies alone, still it is Nel's name on her lips at the moment of her death. In contrast to Nel's overwhelming sense of loss at the end of the novel is Sula's surprisingly peaceful death, which she immediately anticipates sharing with Nel: "Then she realized . . . that there was not going to be any pain. . . . Sula felt her face smiling. 'Well, I'll be damned . . . it didn't even hurt. Wait'll I tell Nel'" (*S* 149). Sula's wish to share this experience with her friend, even though they have been estranged for years, reflects her view of the vitality of their friendship in spite of the years of separation—indeed its vitality beyond the grave. At this moment of her death, her thoughts reveal that she anticipates being reunited with Nel some day—not her mother, who died before her; not Ajax, the one man she loved beyond the moments of sexual pleasure; but Nel, the friend who completed her.

The reader may recall how Sula anticipated a reunion with Nel before her death, during her last conversation with Nel, when she tried to explain how eventually everyone (presumably including Nel) would love her ("It will take time, but they'll love me" [*S* 145] she tells Nel); lists all the deviant (nonconforming and untraditional, that is) behaviors that will eventually lead to a recognition of Sula's value; and concludes, "then there'll be a little love left over for me," adding, "And I know just what it will feel like" (*S* 146). Though she says nothing more to Nel, she recalls to herself at that point, presumably to illustrate "what it will feel like," the day she ran to Nel after hearing her own mother say she didn't like her daughter. Nel's love once made up for her mother's rejection, and Sula apparently believes that she will know that kind of love again, when Nel remembers how she once loved Sula and once recognized the value in deviating from the norm. Sula longs to experience again that unconditional love, often associated with a mother but which she once received from her friend (as Scarlett did from Melanie).

So finding herself dying alone after Nel's departure, Sula envisions returning to a paradisiacal womb: "It would be here, only here, held by this blind window high above the elm tree, that she might draw her legs up to her chest, close her eyes, put her thumb in her mouth and float over and down the tunnels, just missing the dark walls, down, down until she met a rain scent and would know the water was near [symbolic of death to her after what happened to Chicken Little], and she would curl into its heavy softness and it would envelop her, carry her, and wash her tired flesh always" (*S* 148–49). It is significant that Sula alludes to the deaths of her mother and Chicken Little in this passage: the "blind window" is the boarded-up window through which Eva jumped to try to save her burning daughter, Sula's mother, Hannah, thus demonstrating the kind of self-sacrificing mother love that Sula never received, perhaps because she is not worthy, the child might have reasoned, finding evidence of her unworthiness in the fact that she "killed" Chicken Little. The reader knows that his death was an accident, but as the narrator tells us, its occurrence so soon after finding out her mother does not like her taught Sula that she could not count on anything in this world—not even mother love, not even herself, and later, not even Nel: "The first experience taught her there was no other that you could count on; the second that there was no self to count on either. She had no center, no speck around which to grow. . . . She had clung to Nel as the closest thing to both an other and a self, only to discover that she and Nel were not one and the same thing" (*S* 118–19). It is no wonder Sula might long to return to the womb—ironically she is longing to do exactly what Eva feared Plum was trying to do and killed him for (which perhaps explains why Sula put Eva in a nursing home). But the unconditional mother love that Sula may be seeking in her vision of returning to a fetus state is as much an ideal as the fairy-tale happily-ever-after promised to good girls who follow the basic tenets of society. It is not surprising, therefore, that Sula spent her life thwarting tradition, which she recognized as limiting to women, in particular. Even living a life of rule breaking, Morrison reminds us, Sula "never does anything as bad as her grandmother or her mother did," but, as Morrison suspected would happen, few realize this (Taylor-Guthrie 16).

In the novel Morrison explains that the community's "evidence against Sula was contrived, but their conclusions about her were not. Sula was distinctly different"—a nonconformist, in essence. With "Eva's arrogance and Hannah's self-indulgence . . . she lived out her days exploring her own thoughts and emotions, giving them full reign, feeling no obligation to please anybody unless their pleasure pleased her" (*S* 118), behavior reminiscent of Scarlett O'Hara. Yet neither woman's behavior would be so out of the ordinary if they were men. Morrison observes of Sula, "She will do the kind of things that normally only men do, which is why she's so strange. She really behaves like a man. She picks up a man, drops a man, the same way a man picks up a woman, drops a woman. And that's her thing. She's masculine in that sense. She's adventuresome, she trusts herself, she's not scared, she really ain't scared. And she is curious and will leave and try anything. So that quality of masculinity—and I mean this in the pure sense—in a woman at that time is outrage, total outrage. She can't get away with that" (Taylor-Guthrie 26–27). Susan Neal Mayberry suggests that Chicken Little's death is "the means by which Sula is set dangerously free from any context, any community; having killed, even accidentally, she is no longer afraid of death" (526). Morrison's and Mayberry's analyses of Sula are reminiscent of Grandma Fontaine's concern for Scarlett because, as she tells Scarlett, "it's a very bad thing for a woman to face the worst that can happen to her, because after she's faced the worst she can't ever really fear anything again. And it's very bad for a woman not to be afraid of something" (*GW* 452). Through the observations of Scarlett's husband Frank, Mitchell describes Scarlett's "masculine" traits as well: "her reactions were all masculine. Despite her pink cheeks and dimples and pretty smiles, she talked and acted like a man. Her voice was brisk and decisive and she made up her mind instantly and with no girlish shilly-shallying. She knew what she wanted and she went after it by the shortest route, like a man, not by the hidden and circuitous routes peculiar to women. . . . Scarlett was guided by no one but herself and was conducting her affairs in a masculine way which had the whole town talking about her" (*GW* 639–40). So too is "the whole town talking about [Sula]."

When they finally confront each other at Sula's sickbed, Nel tells Sula, "You can't have it all," and Sula asks, "Why? I can do it all, why can't I have it all?" Nel's response is simply because Sula is "a woman and a colored woman at that. You can't act like a man. You can't be walking around all independent-like, doing whatever you like, taking what you want, leaving what you don't" (*S* 142). Michael Wilson points out that "part of the difficulty in the community's inability to understand Sula's radicalness is that she is a woman. . . . [H]er actions are neither different nor worse than those of Jude or Ajax, both of whom are easily accepted into the community" (34). But for readers, Diane Matza suggests, it is this very independence that allows us to sympathize with Sula, in spite of her behavior: "Although Sula's selfishness is sometimes ugly to us, we find her sympathetic because her non-conformity is motivated by her profound desire to be her own person" (51). Sula admits to Nel that she may be lonely, but at least "my lonely is *mine.* Now your lonely is somebody else's. Made by somebody else and handed to you." Sula chooses to be alone if that is what living her life her way requires; Nel is alone because Jude left her and because social decorum dictates that she not continue a friendship with a woman who had an affair with her husband. Sula reminds Nel that they are all ultimately doing the same thing—"Dying"—but, in contrast to those who are "dying like a stump," she is "going down like one of those redwoods" (*S* 143). In other words, people will notice when she is gone.

Sula would have liked to share her life, but not with a man or children: "She had been looking all along for a friend, and it took her a while to discover that a lover was not a comrade and could never be—for a woman." So she returned to Medallion, to Nel, only to find "that no one [not even Nel] would ever be that version of herself which she sought to reach out to and touch with an ungloved hand." This left "only her own mood and whim, and if that was all there was, she decided to turn the naked hand toward it, discover it and let others become as intimate with their own selves as she was."

She would do whatever she wanted and thus not protect others from truths revealed about themselves via their interactions with her. But Medallion was stifling: "in a way, her strangeness, her naïveté, her craving for the other half of her equation was the consequence of an idle imagination. Had she paints, or clay, or knew the discipline of the dance, or strings; had she anything to engage her tremendous curiosity and her gift for metaphor, she might have exchanged the restlessness and preoccupation with whim for an activity that provided her with all she yearned for. And like any artist with no art form, she became dangerous" (*S* 121). When she is dying, Sula tries to explain to Nel how exploring her own mind was more fulfilling than any passion she had ever felt for a man. Nel merely perceives further self-centeredness in this remark: "You own the world and the rest of us is renting. You ride the pony and we shovel the shit" (*S* 144). The horse metaphor, however, should remind the reader of Sula's childhood fantasy, in which she was in the role of Nel's knight—Sula's adventurous nature as not completely selfish. She would have gladly included her friend Nel in her explorations.

Scarlett O'Hara cannot imagine having a female friend: "She had never had a girl friend, and she never felt any lack on that account. To her, all women, including her two sisters, were natural enemies in pursuit of the same prey—man" (*GW* 60). And yet, as Drew Gilpin Faust has pointed out, "the shortcomings of men are at the center of Mitchell's novel" (11). Although Scarlett does recognize many of the "shortcomings of men," it takes her until the end of the novel to see that Melanie is her greatest source of support. In *Sula,* in direct contrast to Scarlett's negative attitude toward female friendship, Toni Morrison questions, among issues of community and individuality, prioritizing marriage over friendship. The men of the Bottom have their "shortcomings," too: in particular they cannot be counted on to stay around: Eva's husband leaves her with three children; Hannah's husband dies; Jude deserts his family; Ajax flees Sula's love. If Hannah "could break up a marriage before it had even become one" (*S* 44), what does that say for the men's devotion to their wives even during the honeymoon period of their marriages? Compare Sula's reaction to noticing Ajax's name on his driver's license (A. Jacks)—she is dismayed by the thought of having never really known him—to Nel's dismayed reaction to Jude's betrayal—horror that someone who (supposedly) *knew* her could do such a thing. Anna Shannon also compares the two women's failed relationships, seeing both as reflecting "the limits of women's relationships with men in the novel" (11). In such a world, Morrison asks, why would one value marriage over friendship? Shannon points out that "the dormant love of Nel for Sula survives long after Jude and Ajax are vague memories" (19). As Gloria Naylor observed while talking with Morrison about *Sula,* "black women have always had each other when we had very little else." Naylor notes, however, that "what we didn't dare do was to put it in black and white like you did in *Sula*" (Taylor-Guthrie 201), reminding the reader of Morrison's observations, quoted earlier, about how little literature focuses on women's friendships.

Indeed one can see how living in a culture of double standards regarding adultery—where men's transgressions are often overlooked or more easily forgiven, as we see in reader/viewer sympathy for the pursued Ashley Wilkes in comparison to their condemnation of femme fatale Scarlett O'Hara—would result in the notion of women betraying women as the unpardonable sin: women must have someone to count on; if their lovers cannot be counted on to be loyal, then their friends must be. And notice again that it doesn't occur to Sula to leave Medallion with Jude. Her affair with Jude was not about getting Jude for herself, that most serious of crimes against friendship between women. As for Jude's departure, since Nel is focusing her blame on Sula's betrayal of their friendship, there is no reason he has to leave his family—yet he does. Sula, in contrast, waits patiently, does not intrude on Nel's choice to stay away from her. Then, when Nel shows up at her house upon hearing that Sula is sick, Sula's behavior reflects her willingness to pick up right where they left off—as though Nel's visit is what she stayed in Medallion for: she was waiting for Nel to realize that their friendship has a stronger foundation than Nel's marriage did and thus that the two of them can work through their betrayal *of each other.*

With *Sula,* Morrison moves readers to question traditional hierarchies: in truth, aren't our platonic friendships so often of stronger foundations and longer lasting than our relationships with lovers? Why, then, do we invest more in our relationships with our lovers than in our friendships?—or do we? Morrison asks in this novel. Regarding the first question—why do we value marriage more than friendship?—Morrison emphasizes with the novel's ending that the loss of the relationship between these two women, the years that Nel's loneliness might have been replaced with Sula's vibrant company, is much more significant than Nel's broken marriage. But Morrison also questions whether we really do have more invested in our sexual relationships than we do in our friendships. Again there is the implied question, Don't our friendships often help us through our failed relationships with lovers? Consider that while Nel is figuring out how she will handle losing Jude, she naturally thinks of turning to Sula: "Here she was in the midst of it, hating it, scared of it, and again she thought of Sula as though they were still friends and talked things over. That was too much. To lose Jude and not have Sula to talk to about it because it was Sula that he had left her for" (*S* 110). Apparently Nel not only recognized from the first that "[Jude] had left her" (which Sula never did), but she also at some level perceived from the first that Jude was not the loss that Sula was—"because," as Morrison explains to an interviewer, "when you don't have a woman to talk to, really talk to, whether it be an aunt or a sister or a friend, that is the real loneliness. That is devastating" (Denard 16).

Here one might consider, as Susan Mayberry does, the question of "why Jude has sex with Sula" (526). Mayberry's angle on this subject, which calls to mind Ashley's attraction to Scarlett, reveals why Jude is not worth crying over, much less giving up a friendship for: "Along with Plum and Tar Baby, Jude is one of the most passive male figures in *Sula,* and, true to form, he allows Sula to use him merely to fill up some space. A second answer is that, since he cannot usurp white male power, he will conquer the masculine black female. A third is that his incomplete masculinity is attracted to the masculine in Sula" (526–27). Here again we are reminded of the problem of like marrying like, as discussed in chapter 2 and as explained by Anne Goodwyn Jones in her chapter on *Gone with the Wind:* "the marriage of like to like leaves both yearning for what is missing," which explains, Jones says, Ashley's yearning for Scarlett even though he loves Melanie: "Ashley the dreamer sustains a certain attraction to earthy Scarlett that is formed partly out of physical lust and partly of admiration and envy of her physical and psychic strength" (*Tomorrow* 340). Jones's reading of Ashley is certainly echoed in Mayberry's reading of Jude. With men like Ashley and Jude, one can see why women like Melanie and Scarlett, Nel and Sula need each other. According to Morrison, "if Anna Karenina had just one female friend who would say, 'Don't throw yourself under that train, over that man—that's crazy,' her life may have been very different" (Denard 16).

Of course Nel suppresses the realization that *Jude* (not Sula) left her, along with her knowledge of Sula's background. Nel blames Sula for betraying their friendship and ruining her marriage, thus ignoring what—or rather *whom*—she still had after Jude left. And Nel is not the only one in this novel who fails to understand Sula's potential value. It is interesting that in a community so accepting of eccentrics, Sula's untraditional behavior meets with disapproval. Given how this community allows Eva to get away with murdering her own son; tolerates the same sexual freedom from Hannah that Ajax, a man, enjoys; accepts Hannah's admission that she does not like her daughter with no expressions of horror from her listeners; even incorporates Shadrack's insanity into its communal calendar, one can be pretty certain that Sula is not ostracized for her betrayal of Nel. Rather, like Nel, the community finally forgot itself, forgot its usual tendency to accept eccentricity, and judged Sula by more traditional standards of socially acceptable behavior. Also noting the discrepancy between the communal response to Shadrack and then to Sula, Carlyle V. Thompson points out that, "while Shadrack has been accepted into the body politic of the black community and tolerated by whites, Sula will remain an outsider, a pariah who will be demonized." Thompson attributes "the critical difference in their subjectivity and community acceptance" to their respective genders (156), but that does not take into consideration what is noted here—that Eva and Hannah, like Shadrack, are accepted by the community, in spite of their untraditional behavior. Going back to the earlier list of the numerous instances of men deserting women in this novel, consider Desiree Lewis's observation that Eva and Hannah "devote much of their time to bolstering male egos" (42). One of the reasons that Sula is condemned by her community is her refusal to waste time that way. In contrast to Hannah, Sula "would lay [other women's] husbands once and then no more. . . . Sula was trying them out and discarding them without any excuse the men could swallow," but paradoxically this behavior serves the marriages in that "the women, to justify their own judgment, cherished their men more, soothed the pride and vanity Sula had bruised" (*S* 115).

The community that condemns Sula does not realize until it is too late that they will miss her. Nel's sorrow over losing Sula has "no bottom and no top"—suggesting that it is a sorrow she will take to her own grave, that the rest of her life will be filled with grief over the loss and pain at the realization of the wasted years she could have had with Sula. So too is the community likely to suffer for their treatment of Sula. Sula's return to Medallion had led those around her to treat their loved ones better: mothers are more nurturing to their children, wives more forgiving of their husbands' transgressions. They become better people to distinguish themselves from one they consider evil. This is Sula's role in Medallion, a role she accepts without resistance or concern. In turn, however, the community does not take care of her as they do Shadrack, Tar Baby, and the deweys, and when Sula dies, taking away their negative example of how *not* to act, the people revert to previous behaviors—Teapot's mama returns to drinking and abusing her child, for example.

It is not insignificant that the community's failure to attend Sula's funeral is shortly followed by the earth opening up and swallowing many of its citizens, a fate more reminiscent of the wrath of the traditional (patriarchal) Old Testament God than the merciful nature of the more tolerant and accepting (and more feminist) New Testament values. In southern literary terms (applicable given the novel's opening history of the setting, telling how the Bottom land was given under false pretenses to the freed slaves), one might consider how the citizenry of Medallion have begun living by the value system of the Old Order, as reflected in the fact that others in the community have come to share Helene's (and now Nel's) more conventional values. Anna Shannon notes how in this novel, "hostile . . . public opinion often mirrors white opinion" (12). Diane Matza has pointed out how in *Sula* Morrison "emphasize[s] the individual's conflict with the larger group in order to explore the real tragedy in the minority group's need for a united community speaking often with a single voice. This is a need Blacks did not create themselves. To get services, jobs and some necessary acceptance, and to fight injustice, a united front is usually imperative. The united front, however, is often sustained only by a preoccupation with questions such as, how do we best present ourselves? and what is best for the group? And so, the individual voice must often be suppressed" (54). One should recall here that the novel opens during the same period as the Harlem Renaissance, when African American philosophers, writers, and other artists were debating whether to emphasize shared human traits or celebrate cultural differences in their art and lives. Once the folks of Medallion become less accepting of each other's differences, reflecting the more traditional values that Helene had emulated and passed down to Nel, they become as oppressive of each other as the dominant culture was to their race. Noting that "*Ms.* Magazine was founded on the premise that we [women] really have to stop complaining about one another, hating, fighting one another, and joining men in their condemnation of ourselves," Morrison warns that such infighting and condemnation are "what dominated people do" (Denard 79).

Sula's final question to Nel, "How you know . . . who was good?," may start Nel on the path to reconsidering which of their behavior was "good" (and thus, which "evil"): as has been suggested, she begins to think about her own desertion of Sula after the transgression with Jude. Readers have tended to focus on Sula's follow-up question, "How you know it was you?" (*S* 146), the implicit answer being that Nel dumping Sula's friendship over Jude was also bad if not worse, as Anna Shannon also suggests (11), than Sula's affair with Jude. But the initial question could be asking, how do you know good? And the answer to that question is by contrast to evil, as illustrated in that earliest of stories, about the Garden of Eden. So Medallion, like Nel, will miss Sula, and Medallion, like Nel, is doomed to become more like the rest of the (fallen) world after all, condemned to live by the more traditional rules of a less accepting society. Once tolerant of the behavior of Hannah, they judge Sula's promiscuity, and as Michael Wilson points out, they do not recognize their "inconsistent moral standards" (34): they reject Sula for reputedly having sex with white men, though one of the town prostitutes, who was properly buried by the community, has a white son. No one condemned Eva for killing her junkie son, but they find Sula's decision to put Eva in a home despicable. I suggest that it is the matriarch of this community, Eva Peace, whose intolerance of her own son may have begun the change in the community's values. Even after killing Plum, she is offended by Hannah's questions about whether she loved her children, but the reader understands, explains Lucille P. Fultz, that Hannah is wondering about the lack of "affection" she received from her mother (235), which Fultz equates with Sula hearing Hannah say she did not like her—did not approve of her (just as Eva did not approve of Plum's life) (233).

Defending Eva (for we do not want to show the kind of intolerance that the novel critiques), Fultz also reminds the reader of the difficulty in hard times for a mother to show affection to a child, which the reader might apply to Scarlett's treatment of her children, Wade, born during wartime, and Ella, during Reconstruction to a mother still haunted by her fear of starvation. In further defense against the criticism about Scarlett's mothering (from both readers and the people of her community), like Sula and Hannah, Scarlett did not have an affectionate mother herself; as we have seen, Scarlett's experience of her mother's "love" was Ellen's disapproval of Scarlett's behavior as Ellen tried to make a lady of her young belle. Yet Ellen is not condemned by her community as Scarlett is for her failure to show affection to her children. Certainly Scarlett did not learn how to be affectionate from Ellen, in spite of the O'Haras' prosperity during Scarlett's childhood. It is interesting that the one child Scarlett does feel affection for, Bonnie, was born into prosperity: perhaps there was time then to enjoy the child. Yet it is Rhett who is praised for his involvement in Bonnie's upbringing, while Scarlett's softening in her mothering of this child goes unnoticed (that is, until a 2007 essay in which Paula Anca Farca points out evidence toward the end of the novel of "Scarlett's growing interest in motherhood and her attempts to become a good mother" [84]). Scarlett's seemingly uncaring attitude toward her other children (though they were not uncared for under her watch, as we have seen) is certainly noted by those who find her unmotherly and thus unwomanly. Rhett's nurturing behavior, in contrast, is not perceived as unmanly, another instance of a double standard for the men and women in the novel.

In "Identity Formation and the Relationship between Eva and Sula Peace," Lizabeth A. Rand's discussion of Eva may also recall Scarlett O'Hara to the reader: "When [Eva's] husband, 'BoyBoy,' suddenly leaves, and with only three beets to feed her children, she must set off on a journey for survival." The situation is comparable to the scene in *Gone with the Wind* when a starving Scarlett tries to eat an old radish and vows to never be hungry again. The subsequent chapters narrate Scarlett's various means of keeping this vow to herself, culminating in her marriage to the wealthy Rhett Butler. And further establishing the parallel, Rhett immediately builds Scarlett a ridiculously huge house. When Eva returns with money (and missing her leg), Rand reminds us, "she orders the building of a house with many rooms" (343), in which she takes in various orphans, including her own children, previously abandoned. Both Eva and Scarlett are matriarchs caring for an extended family, but, as Rand points out of Eva (quoting Morrison), they are simultaneously "generous [and] selfish" in doing so (344). One may also think of Scarlett when reading Victoria Middleton's characterization of Eva's mothering: "Eva, though fiercely protective, gives her children not motherly love but life, keeping them alive by mysteriously sacrificing her own flesh" (374). Sula apparently learns from her grandmother's example that people would not thwart a woman who, if the rumors were true, would give up a limb for the money to bring home to her family. She too mutilates herself to protect Nel from the boys who threaten them. "If I can do that to myself," she asks the boys after cutting off the tip of her finger, "what you suppose I'll do to you?" (*S* 54–55).

Pascal P. Buma suggests that this scene evokes the knight-in-shining-armor fantasy that Sula and Nel share, with Sula in the role of "the knight who saves the daintier Nel from the prowling rogues" (82)—just as Scarlett is Melanie's rescuer in *Gone with the Wind,* not only by delivering Melanie's baby and then keeping both mother and baby alive through the arduous journey to Tara, but then at Tara, where Scarlett and Melanie set up the untraditional household that is ultimately more productive and less destructive than their more traditional marriages. Though one might at first perceive the communities of *Gone with the Wind* and *Sula* to be worlds apart, they could both be characterized as Victoria Middleton describes Medallion: "a self-destructive, closed world that functions at the expense of the self-esteem of its individual members." Middleton notes that Morrison's pair of young black female characters "become friends because they recognize that, as black girls, they are nothing in their community's eyes" (369). When even their mothers do not seem to love them and certainly do not contribute to a positive self-image, Nel and Sula turn to each other. Scarlett and Melanie do not find each other so quickly, but perhaps never really expecting an intimate friendship with each other, they never really disappoint each other and thus manage to sustain their relationship until Melanie's death. Jane S. Bakerman considers "the real tragedy in *Sula*" to be that they never experienced the lesson of their friendship in their adult lives: "Just as their friendship is essential to their well-being as children, so would their learning from one another's faults have made them adult women capable of well-being" if only they had accepted each other for who they were as adults the way they did as children. When they instead judge each other's behavior, "their friendship ruptures and they live isolated, frustrated lives" (549).

Bakerman argues that "one of Morrison's most important points in *Sula* [is that] the personalities of Sula and Nel, could they have been merged, would have amounted to one whole person" (549). Alisha R. Coleman calls Sula and Nel "two halves of a personality that combines to form a whole psyche . . . two parts of a psychological self: individually or apart, Nel is the superego or the conscience, and Sula is the id or the pleasure and unconscious desire of the psyche; together they form the ego, the balance between the superego and the id, and what is usually considered to be a single identity" (151). Anne Jones calls the two women "two parts of a complicated vision of southern women" (*Tomorrow* 332); Louis Rubin argues that "Melanie Wilkes, the traditionalist, the lady, and Scarlett O'Hara, the opportunist, the woman, were not really two persons, but . . . one and the same flawed human being" ("Scarlett" 102). When Nel visits Eva years after Sula's death, Eva remarks, "You. Sula. What's the difference? . . . Just alike. Both of you. Never was no difference between you" (*S* 168–69). Martin Crawford believes that *Cold Mountain*'s "Ada and Ruby have become virtually one person" (189). Coleman points out "the conflict and dissatisfaction" that results from two such friends as Sula and Nel losing each other (which does not bode well for Scarlett after Melanie's death, except that Scarlett recognizes the significance of her loss immediately upon the death of her friend rather than years later, as Nel does). On a more positive note, the potentially productive bond between each of these pairs of women illustrates what Sula means when she thinks of the time when she and Nel "were two throats and one eye" (*S* 147). Women who come together in their views are empowered by the doubling of their voices against those who might oppress them.

In *Frankly, My Dear:* Gone with the Wind *Revisited,* Molly Haskell remarks on "how unusual it was to create a heroine of such wicked proportions and treat her in such a nonjudgmental fashion" (139). Diane Matza makes a similar observation about Sula: that "despite [the] acts that the community and we as readers judge cruel and selfish, Sula is a sympathetic character" (51). Outside of the pages of her novel, even Mitchell criticized Scarlett, insisting that Melanie was the novel's real heroine. In contrast Morrison recognized that the "rule-breaker" Sula would be more interesting than Nel, who "knows and believes in all the laws of that community." Morrison tells interviewer Robert Stepto that Nel "*is* the community. She believes in its values. Sula does not. She does not believe in any of those laws and breaks them all. Or ignores them. So that she becomes more interesting . . . because of that quality of abandon" (Taylor-Guthrie 14). Mitchell may have been surprised by her readers' reaction to Scarlett, whom Haskell calls "an unlikely heroine, even an unwanted one." Haskell argues that "here may be the source of her staying power—we move in to fill the gap of sympathy withheld by her creator" (89). In contrast to Mitchell, Morrison did not withhold sympathy for her untraditional heroine. She defends Sula, criticizes Nel (and she presents Eva and Hannah, who are at least true to themselves, without judgment). The reader comes to recognize that while unconditional love is asking too much of mothers, still it must be disconcerting to be raised by a grandmother who kills her own son and a mother who openly and unashamedly expresses her dislike for her daughter. And so we are able to pity Sula, as we should be able to feel sorry for Scarlett.

Once estranged from Nel, Sula turns to sex and, upon meeting Ajax, eventually tries the kind of relationship that Nel would give up their friendship for. But Ajax, like Nel, is attracted to Sula's untraditional nature—as Morrison describes her to Gloria Naylor, "If it wasn't unconventional, she didn't want it" (Taylor-Guthrie 200)—so when Sula behaves conventionally, cleaning the house and putting a ribbon in her hair in anticipation of her lover's arrival, he makes love with her one last time and then leaves her to experience the loss of another love, the rejection of another beloved. The reader may be reminded of Rhett finally giving up on Scarlett after their last sexual relations, which, though many readers consider rape, Scarlett seems to have ultimately enjoyed: "The man who had carried her up the dark stairs was a stranger of whose existence she had not dreamed. And now, though she tried to make herself hate him, tried to be indignant, she could not. He had humbled her, hurt her, used her brutally through a wild mad night and she had gloried in it" (*GW* 940). Has he finally conquered her and thus lost interest? Recognized that she has finally enjoyed sexual relations only to then punish her for the years of rejecting him? The reader might be suspicious of Rhett's sudden inability to read Scarlett's thoughts when he has so easily understood her prior to the morning after that passionate encounter. At least one of the readers Helen Taylor surveyed noted the inconsistency between Rhett's usual ability to read Scarlett's mind and his failure to perceive her enjoyment of their passionate relations that night, though the reader wonders, then, "if he does not recognise his achievement in at last showing Scarlett sexual ecstasy, how can he be said to recognise anything else about her?" (*Scarlett's* 133). I have argued that Rhett really doesn't know Scarlett as well as he claims, but also I suggest here that his departure after that night might be connected to his belief that he (in contrast to any other man) can tame Scarlett. Once he has conquered her in bed, he has accomplished this goal. And her morning-after sweetness makes her more like other women and thus less desirable, just as Ajax finds Sula less interesting with a ribbon in her hair, waiting for him in her tidied house. Ironically Ajax presumably goes home to his mother after leaving Sula, another untraditional woman who inspired his attraction to Sula in the first place, and Rhett turns his attention to his precocious daughter, who reminds him of the Scarlett who first attracted him.

Rhett's rejection of Scarlett at this point anticipates his eventual desertion of her when she realizes she does love him after all. Many readers (and movie viewers) believe Scarlett deserves the comeuppance of Rhett's ultimate rejection. Molly Haskell reminds us that Mitchell "refuse[d] the consolations of a romantic ending" (139), agreeing to "change it any way you want, except to make a happy ending" (qtd. in Haskell 140). Haskell explains that the novel's ending "is precisely what's singular and uncompromising about Mitchell's vision: there is no eleventh-hour epiphany, none of that conventional change of heart so beloved of second-rate dramaturgy. Scarlett, unchanged and unchanging, lives in an eternal present. Remorse and regret, anything connected to the past, is emotional baggage that must be shrugged off, as she invokes the denial that allows her to forge ahead" (140–41). I do not agree with the "unchanged and unchanging" part of this summation of Scarlett at novel's end. Scarlett's ability to live in the present is due in part to her ability to change, and in the preceding chapter I noted how her development is evident in the final pages of the novel. Furthermore, unlike Melanie, she does not hold onto their past, the Old South with manners and mores that instilled in Melanie the urgent desire to have more children, a desire that ultimately killed Melanie. And Scarlett's refusal to wallow in "remorse and regret" may not result in a happy ending, but it does, as Haskell says, allow her to continue on, as Kat Meads's character does as well in the novel to be discussed next.

In the absence of traditional happy endings, readers may miss the ultimately positive endings of these novels. The deaths of Melanie and Sula are great unrecoverable losses to their friends, but the surviving friends are left with new insight—hard-earned but valuable—which, as in all good tragedy, the reader gains with them. Victoria Middleton compares Nel to "a revisionary critic" (perhaps like myself) in the way that she "learns to read Sula's character and her story correctly; her example teaches us how to interpret Sula's heroism" (369). Perhaps then our understanding of Sula may serve to help us to better understand Scarlett as well. Neither character is by any means an ideal heroine (but neither is a "bad bitch" either). Carolyn M. Jones argues that Sula's "absolutely unbounded and free" self is both "beaut[iful] and "danger[ous]. . . . This immense, unchecked power is destructive both for the self, as we see when Sula dies alone, and for the community, as we see when the people of Medallion refuse to recognize Sula's importance and are destroyed by the angry spirit of the dead Sula." Jones continues, reminding us of the need for the kind of balance that these pairs of women experience and exhibit during the most constructive periods of their lives: "Alone, Sula . . . is a warning. Balanced after death, however, with the loving and stable power of Nel, who takes on the task of mourning and memory, [Sula's birthmark] becomes tadpole and not snake. That is, it signals the development of the self and creates the compassion—the ability to be a self but also to see with the 'other'—that is the basis of true community" (625). And, as Diane Gillespie and Missy Dehn Kubitschek point out, "no longer oversimplifying her experience and denying her feelings and her own needs, Nel has the potential to attain moral maturity and enjoy authentic relations with others" (75).

At the end of Mitchell's novel, Scarlett may be confounded by losing Rhett just as she realizes that she loves him after all and by gaining the responsibility of Ashley even as she realizes not only that she does not want him but also what a burden he will be. I have earlier suggested that by novel's end, Scarlett may be better off without Rhett, who is so devastated by the loss of Bonnie that he has turned to alcohol and the past, heading home to Charleston and the traditional manners and mores of the Old South he had rejected—which rejection was a source of his appreciation of Scarlett, another rebel against the old ways. Scarlett too thinks of going home: to Tara and to Mammy, "the last link with the old days" (*GW* 1037). While associating Mammy with "the old days" may suggest that Scarlett is also turning toward the way of life she had previously rebelled against, we might remember instead that toward the novel's end, just after Bonnie's death, when Scarlett misses the people from home, she thinks of them, not as they were in the pre–Civil War days but rather as people "with common memories of war and hunger and fighting" and "common roots going down into the same red earth. . . . For they knew. They had known war and terror and fire, had seen dear ones dead before their time; they had hungered and been ragged, had lived with the wolf at the door. *And they had rebuilt fortune from ruins*" (*GW* 1003; emphasis added). Going home to Tara is not about trying to recapture her carefree youth ("the girl with her sachet and dancing slippers") but about knowing what she has accomplished there as "a woman who turned her hands to many menial tasks" and recognized that the one constant in her life was "the indestructible red earth" of Tara (*GW* 490). As Anne Jones has suggested, "freed from the self defined in loving Ashley and then Rhett, back at private, agricultural, feminine, antebellum Tara with her skills and self learned in the public, business, masculine, postbellum world, she may manage to solve simultaneously the riddles of Southern womanhood and of Southern history by incorporating the new into the old" ("*Gone*" 373).

It is significant that Scarlett names women as the people she misses from her old life: "Maybelle . . . Fanny . . . Mrs. Elsing . . . Mrs. Meriwether" (*GW* 1003). Even before Melanie's death, Scarlett has begun to recognize the value of these women; finally, Scarlett, who never had girlfriends, might be ready for women friends. Of course these women may be difficult to win over, but Mammy, like Melanie (and ultimately unlike Rhett), loved Scarlett in spite of seeing her for who she is. Longing for Mammy in the end further reflects what drives Scarlett from the start: to be loved for (and in spite of) herself. Calling attention to "Mammy's knowledge of Scarlett and her acceptance of her," Elizabeth Fox-Genovese calls Mammy "the compelling double for Ellen," arguing, however, that to Mammy "Scarlett's recalcitrance elicits disciplinary action but not condemnation" ("Scarlett" 410). Helen Taylor also contrasts Mammy with Ellen, reminding the reader of Ellen's "physical and emotional distance" from her daughters, in contrast to Mammy's "day-to-day detailed vigilance, discipline and concern" (*Scarlett's* 198–99). Scarlett did not get such unconditional mother love from Ellen, but Mammy has loved her as Melanie did—for herself. The reader is told early on that "Mammy was under no illusions about [Scarlett]" (*GW* 59). Like Nel's insight on realizing "all that time" she had been missing Sula, the insight that Scarlett gained at Melanie's deathbed could allow her to accept Mammy's love, to understand the value of a woman's love, with which she can face "tomorrow" with or without Rhett Butler.

Chapter 5

"Disregarding the female imperative"

Kat Meads's Kitty Duncan, a 1960s-Era Scarlett O'Hara

"I set out to depict a far-from-admirable woman."
Margaret Mitchell, qtd. in Pyron, *Southern* 258

"Mrs. Hopewell would say, 'If you can't come pleasantly, I don't want you at all,' to which the girl, standing square and rigid-shouldered with her neck thrust slightly forward, would reply, 'If you want me, here I am—LIKE I AM.'"
Flannery O'Connor, "Good Country People,"
in *A Good Man Is Hard to Find*

Kat Meads's fictional biographer for her novel *The Invented Life of Kitty Duncan (Benedict Roberts Duncan),* Mo, is, like *Sula*'s Nel, drawn to a woman seemingly her complete opposite: for Meads's biographer-character, it is the title character of Meads's novel. Readers may find Kitty Duncan reminiscent of Moll Flanders and Becky Sharp, and by novel's end, we realize she is a twentieth-century Scarlett O'Hara, a woman who simply does not conform to the expectations of southern ladies. Since the novel is told from the perspective of those who interact with Kitty from her childhood in the 1950s through two marriages and into her thirties, we do not know if she repeats any mantra to herself—like Scarlett's "I'll think about it tomorrow"—when she knows her behavior is considered "unladylike." From others' perspectives she seems to be a self-absorbed sociopath. But a closer reading reveals that Kitty is simply refusing to live by social standards that would thwart the pursuit of her own desires and thus stand in the way of her living a fulfilling life. During Mo's ultimate confrontation scene with Kitty at the end of the novel, we find, along with Mo, that Kitty (by then pushing forty) is satisfied with her life, that she is not consumed by regrets over past mistakes, and that Kitty's daughter loves and accepts her for who she is (as she loves and accepts her daughter for who she is). In short Kitty does not suffer dire consequences (as Mo expects) for her nonconforming, rebellious behavior simply because she does not care what society—or anyone—thinks of her.

Indeed Kitty might be perceived as an evolved Scarlett O'Hara, following her own desires (like Scarlett), unmindful of her mother's censure (in contrast to Scarlett). One recalls that Scarlett's conscience is most often pricked when she is doing something she knows her mother would not condone. We leave Kitty about ten years older than Scarlett is by her novel's end. Like Scarlett, Kitty has not been defeated by the trials of her life, but neither has she conquered: as Scarlett is heading back to Tara at novel's close, Kitty is back home with her parents at the end of her story. If one is troubled that so little has changed for women in the century between these two (anti-)heroines' stories, Meads provides hope for further evolution in much less time with Kitty's daughter, incongruously but not inappropriately named Caesar, who, with no experience of a mother's constant criticism of her behavior, may conquer rather than just survive.

Though Kitty grows up in the South a century after Scarlett O'Hara, reader response to her is likely to be similar to first impressions of Scarlett—that is, she is likely to be labeled as spoiled and self-centered, but as one reviewer responds to Kitty's adventures, "we're happy to go along for the ride. Kitty, with her total lack of propriety, frequently causes us moral pause, but never so much that we stop *liking* her, admiring her energy, wondering where she'll head next" (Heberlein 190). Certainly this description is similar to reader reaction to Scarlett O'Hara. Like Scarlett, too, Kitty has a mother with a hyperactive social conscience, so one should actually question the perception of these two young women as "spoiled": who spoiled them? No one. Their insistence on having their own way is not a result of being pampered but merely their resistance to the limitations of life as a southern lady, which they both witness in the drab existences of mothers who are obsessed with a clean and orderly house and well-behaved daughter (plural in Ellen O'Hara's case) at the expense of their own lives. It should be no wonder that these headstrong offspring would learn by the unhappy examples of their mothers *not* to put everyone's needs ahead of their own.

Scarlett does on occasion wish she could be more like her mother (or rather, she *wants* to want to be more like Ellen), but her failure to be as "good" as Ellen saves her from her mother's (and Melanie's) shared fate, an early death. One might consider Sula's question regarding "who was good" in this context. The "good" women in *Gone with the Wind* are certainly not rewarded with long or even happy lives. Perhaps it is "better" not to be so "good"—certainly, it is healthier. Kitty Duncan has apparently figured out very early in her life that she does not want to be like her mother at all. She may not live happily all her life, but as Sula said to Nel, she "sure did live in this world" (*S* 143), and, like Scarlett, Kitty still has many years before her when the novel comes to a close. The reader feels certain that both Kitty and Scarlett will live exciting lives even if they never find fulfilling love with a man. These are not, in short, traditional romance novels.

But neither are these novels' protagonists traditional in any way. Amy Levin distinguishes Scarlett "from the feminist picture of a strong superwoman" on the basis of her "unanalytical" nature: "Scarlett's obtuseness becomes frustrating for the reader who is accustomed to protagonists who confront difficulties. Scarlett instead seems not to change; her story is no *bildungsroman*," Levin concludes (33). Scarlett may remain largely "unanalytical" to novel's end, but, as argued in the previous chapter, she does *develop* in the course of the novel—like Frazier's Ada, from a southern belle into a southern woman rather than lady. She may not *analyze* the codes of her society, but she does rebel against them. She is "adaptable," as Ann E. Egenriether points out (121), if not analytical. And her failure to analyze the world around her is not unique: southern belles and ladies were not encouraged to examine the manners and mores passed on to them by their mothers. Levin notes that Melanie is no more analytical than Scarlett (35); indeed none of the women (or men, for that matter) who hold onto their illusion of the Old South is being very analytical about this culture. The narrator tells us directly that Melanie "refused to change, refused even to admit there was any reason to change in a changing world" (*GW* 733). Ultimately it is the South, of which Melanie is a manifestation, that needs to *change*, beginning with raising girls into thinking, *analytical* women who might join Scarlett in resisting the limitations imposed on their gender and *adapting* to a changing world.

As Meads's novel shows, the South continues for another century (and longer) to hold onto its narrow sense of propriety, and readers will balk at Kitty Duncan's audacious behavior—just as they continue to do so at Scarlett's. Significantly the theme of Kitty's high school prom is "antebellum . . . Mansions. Magnolias," and "attendees were encouraged to dress 'plantation-style' in keeping with the decorations." As Scarlett wears to the picnic at Twelve Oaks a dress with a low bodice more suitable, according to Mammy, for an evening occasion, Kitty demands a black dress for her prom, which her mother considers inappropriate for a teenager.

The reader familiar with the novel *Gone with the Wind* will hear in Phyllis's objections to black an echo of Scarlett's observations of the married women at the picnic, who had to wear drab colors now that they were respectably married rather than belles seeking husbands: "whereas drab dark colors remained at a woman's disposal for life, one could *only* wear pretty pastels to their truest advantage as a young girl," Phyllis tells Kitty. It seems, however, that if Kitty is going to be considered some femme fatale for her unabashed exploration of her sexuality, she will dress the part. With no hoop skirt hiding what is beneath her waistline, she tells Dale, "I'm going to look sooooooo good, you'll be all over me" (*KD* 35).

In 2007 I asked Kitty Duncan's creator, Kat Meads, whether she had intended her character as a 1950s–60s Scarlett O'Hara. She had not, she replied. The next year, in an interview for the *North Carolina Literary Review*, I brought up the subject again, asking Meads what she thought of the comparison after having had a year to think about it. She responded, "Who knows what's going on in the back of your head as you sit down to write? *Gone with the Wind* was a very, very important book for me—as for so many." She noted that although "the resemblance" wasn't intentional, once it had been called to her attention, she "saw parallels," particularly the fact that "when push comes to shove, like Scarlett, Kitty has to rely on herself" (Bauer and Wieland 197).

Meads's tone in her affirmation of the similarity between these two characters is positive. She does not apologize for her heroine the way that Mitchell seemed compelled to criticize Scarlett. The tone and style of *Kitty Duncan* is also strikingly different from *Gone with the Wind.* For example, even as Mitchell opens her novel with the line "Scarlett O'Hara was not beautiful," her subsequent description of Scarlett's compelling "charm" and voluptuous body are in keeping with the romantic conventions of a beautiful heroine at the novel's center (*GW* 3). Meads's opening physical description of Kitty is more consistently unromantic: "belly-huge [she is pregnant] . . . [b]ored, restless, and very blonde, thanks to bleach. Vaguely pretty. . . . A young woman at once unremarkable and unmistakable" (*KD* 3). While Mitchell has been praised for her meticulous research while writing her historical novel, Meads's narrator admits from the start, "my research methods were shoddy, half-assed and half-hearted." She also explains that the person at the center of the story she tells is "a woman I met and briefly mingled with but cannot, in good conscience, genuinely claim to 'know'" (*KD* 1). This admission of ignorance is another parallel between the two novels, as I do not believe that Margaret Mitchell "knew"—as in *understood*—the woman at the center of her novel either.

Margaret Mitchell wrote in a letter that she "set out to depict a far-from-admirable woman" and then "found it wryly amusing when Miss O'Hara became somewhat of a national heroine," which she thought "looked bad for the moral and mental attitude of a nation" (qtd. in Pyron, *Southern* 258). In response to questions about her creation of Kitty Duncan, Meads explained that she was inspired by "reviews in which the writers were being taken to task for writing about 'unsympathetic characters'" (listing Brontë's Heathcliff and Nabokov's Humbert Humbert as examples, but not Scarlett O'Hara). Like Mitchell she set out "to create an unsympathetic character," but she says that "by the time I had finished the novel, I didn't find Kitty all that unsympathetic."

Meads admits that she shares her narrator "Mo's interest in Kitty," which "was in watching her push the limits and then seeing what would happen. What would be the fallout?" (Bauer and Wieland 196). Many have read the ending of Mitchell's novel as suggesting that Scarlett O'Hara was ultimately punished for her (mis)behavior. Meads has a less dramatic but much happier closing for her character's story, even as it is not at all a romantic end to the novel.

Meads's novel's narrator meets Kitty Duncan (now Benedict) at college—Mo is in college; Kitty is the wife of a college student and soon thereafter the mother of a baby girl oddly (but ultimately not surprisingly, Mo realizes) named Caesar: "a girl named after a pet grows up to name her own girl child after an emperor" (*KD* 14). Kitty hires (but does not pay) the narrator to babysit, nicknaming her "Mo, a derivative of MOM, in honor of [her] various momish ways" (*KD* 111), and the two develop, not quite a friendship, but some kind of bond. Mo is at first horrified by this new mother's seemingly irresponsible behavior toward her baby, from smoking while pregnant (though such was not so unusual or known to be unhealthy at the time—Mo simply finds it unladylike) to hosting wild parties with a newborn in the house, but Mo is soon also fascinated by Kitty, "a female I would, repeatedly and rotatingly, despise, curse and violently envy. . . . From the get-go, [Kitty] went her own way, unconcerned with convention, undeterred by criticism, unfazed by societal expectations and all the rest of the machinations by which females are brought to heel. Her audacity amazed and confounded. I couldn't begin to fathom how she'd managed to *escape* those machinations, to *avoid* being brought to heel. But I was curious—very, very curious—and blithely assumed I could satisfy that curiosity by observing, from a safe, chaste distance, the iconoclast at work and play (okay, totally at play); that I could spy without threat of ricochet" (*KD* 13). Mo's conclusion to this passage reflects her expectation that Kitty will suffer consequences for so thwarting social expectations of the behavior of southern ladies. And the interesting thing about this novel is that, while Kitty's actions are consequential—she didn't use birth control and so eventually got pregnant, for example—she is not tortured—or even pricked—by a guilty conscience or social censure. Amy Levin says of Scarlett O'Hara, "she refuses to think about the consequences, moral or otherwise, of her actions" (33); according to Mo, neither does Kitty.

But Scarlett does suffer pangs from her conscience, which Kitty does not, as far as the reader can tell. Kitty does, however, experience bouts of depression, first after the birth of her baby and later after her second marriage begins to bore her, in both cases evidence that she is dissatisfied with her life. It is easy to overlook this sign that Kitty is more than just a self-centered, spoiled brat since so much of the novel focuses on her seemingly but ultimately not-so-destructive behavior: from her early sexual activity, to the wild parties and violent fights with her first husband, to her campaign to marry the wealthy Brandon Roberts, to running off with a schizophrenic teenager (and leaving behind her daughter). One is ultimately surprised to realize that Kitty's behavior hurts no one except, occasionally, herself. Upon realizing the effect that having a baby will have on her life—only after the child is born, for the stigma of being pregnant before marriage never troubles her—Kitty falls into a depression, but her mother arrives to take care of the baby as well as Kitty's husband, cooking better meals than he and Kitty had been eating, cleaning up their apartment, and seeming to understand exactly what Kitty is going through (a rare moment of understanding her daughter's behavior). Even when Kitty shakes her depression by hosting wild college parties, Caesar does not suffer either neglect or harm, for Kitty recognizes her mother's responsible nature in Mo, whom she assigns to babysit Caesar. Furthermore Mo is not enjoying the party and is ultimately not really unhappy with the responsibility thrust upon her and the excuse it gives her to hide away with the baby in the bedroom. And Caesar lies quietly oblivious to the chaos around her, certainly much less discomforted by it than her guardians are (both Mo and Phyllis, Kitty's mother). From the time she is a baby, we see evidence that this child is learning early how to live in rather than struggle against the world around her.

The reader might contrast Caesar's early years with what Mo relates about Kitty's childhood: the failed play dates Phyllis sets up for her, inviting little girls over to play with Kitty but then entertaining them herself when Kitty gets bored and excuses herself to go to the bathroom, from which she then does not emerge until the other child has gone. Further evidence of Kitty as an evolved Scarlett can be found in Kitty's lack of concern for or interest in popularity, her refusal to allow her mother to negotiate friendships for her. Ann Egenriether notes how "Scarlett learns the outward trappings of gentility from her mother because it enables her to become popular with the young swains of the County" (121). Like Scarlett, Kitty is popular with the boys—though in her case because of her interest in exploring her sexuality, certainly a major point of contrast to Scarlett. But also like Scarlett, Kitty doesn't have girlfriends as a child or in her teens, and her relationship with Mo after high school is not, as already noted, a developing friendship, at least not by any traditional definition of "girlfriends." Mo is torn between her own rebellious nature (hence Kitty's appeal to Mo) and the rules of proper behavior for a young lady, which she, too, learned from her mother. Perhaps recognition of the possibility of their common rebellious natures is why Kitty tolerates Mo's fascination with her, answers Mo's questions, listens to Mo's ranting—until she gets bored, that is. In turn Mo provides Kitty with a diversion from Kitty's unsatisfying life as wife to a college freshman (who spends most of his time in the library) and mother to a new baby. Kitty enjoys sparring with Mo, cutting through various masks to unveil for Mo the truths of Mo's life.

Bored, Kitty also spars with her husband, Dale, who continues to escape his wife and baby in the library, afraid of himself since their fights had become increasingly more virulent and then even violent during Kitty's pregnancy. Kitty has at least one affair (with a student she meets through Mo, thus breaking the girlfriend rule of finding out whether one's friend has any interest before getting involved with someone the friend introduces). Kitty and Dale ultimately recognize that their marriage is doomed. Kitty and Caesar go home to Kitty's parents; Dale enlists in the military. Mo contemplates the shame of the failed marriage, recognizing that Kitty and Dale did have something together, which might have worked out if Dale weren't trying so hard to be more like Kitty's father (in order to make sure he is nothing like his own physically abusive father) that he never contemplated his own ambitions and, more important quit having fun—if he had been more like his wife, in other words.* Kitty was repulsed by the Dale "who poured over books, tossed and turned in his sleep and cringed when some old fart in tweeds called out his name in class" (*KD* 86); she missed the Dale she had loved. As Mo reports, Kitty's assertion that she did not care was "uncharacteristically dishonest. . . . She desperately wanted, needed, Dale to reclaim his former confidence and bluster so that she could follow his example" (*KD* 95). Overwhelmed by the concept of being a mother, being responsible for a child, Kitty wants Dale to step up and reassure her, but he can't do so—he too is overwhelmed. Mo muses sadly as she brings this chapter of Kitty's life to a close, beginning, ironically, with fairy-tale language: "Once upon a time they shared a connection worth preserving, made themselves vulnerable to each other in a manner neither would risk again. A regrettable waste, such an excellent match. Moreover, as the future would reveal, what existed between them before it peaked and sputtered represented their best chance at making a success of the man/woman thing. Only with each other did togetherness seem worth the effort, no need to fake affection, that survival skill yet to be acquired. Their bond, during the best of times, was automatic, intense, true. But it didn't last. It just didn't last" (*KD* 119). Mo's sadness for Kitty and Dale is akin to reader reaction to the ultimate failure of the marriage of Scarlett and Rhett, another "regrettable waste [of] an excellent match."

As indicated previously, these novels are not traditional romances: they may begin "once upon a time," but they do not end "happily ever after." And yet Kitty understands that such is life. Much later in the novel, she will get caught up in watching soap operas, which surprises Mo: "Blunt, impatient, anti-secretive people don't, as a rule, warm to convoluted, preposterous story lines that unwind at something very near real life pace. And yet Kitty thought the writers should draw out the 'action' even further to accommodate the daily incidentals of teeth brushing, mail opening, yawning and snoring" (*KD* 226). Kitty realizes that "some days there just aren't any big scenes to play" (*KD* 227), and her acceptance of this reality is how she enjoys a life that does not follow a traditional romantic story line. Like Scarlett, Kitty is drawn to romantic love, as evidenced by her enjoyment of soap operas, but, in contrast to Scarlett, she does not allow her disappointment in her first love to dictate the rest of her life.

* Kitty's visit to Dale's parents' house on the newlyweds' way out of town is comparable to Dorinda's experience at Five Oaks, where she confronts Jason's violent, alcoholic father. Like Dale, Jason fears turning into his father—though in Jason's case, he actually does.

Living back in her parents' home after the breakup of her first marriage, with the perfect babysitter at her disposal (her mother), Kitty focuses only on getting a tan until her next adventure, which comes up, ironically, when a high school acquaintance, hearing of Kitty's return, decides it is her duty to call on her former schoolmate, even though she and Kitty were not friends. During this visit Pauline Roberts tells Kitty about her successful, wealthy, and divorced brother, from which moment Kitty, having arrived at the conclusion during her pregnancy that "marriage isn't supposed to be about love. . . . It's about bucks, not backseat thrills. Always marry the bankbook, never the man" (*KD* 87),* set out to win over Pauline: "she strove to appear as fainty, neurasthenic, helpless and dependent a Southern Belle as the Confederacy ever produced" (*KD* 134). Meads's description of Kitty's "ridiculous charade" in front of Pauline, just to be invited to meet brother Brandon, would be hilarious if not for its testimony to the continuation of women hiding their true natures even from each other well into the twentieth century. Reflecting the continuation of such behavior, the reader might first recall Scarlett's outburst as Mammy fusses over her before the picnic at Twelve Oaks: "I wish to Heaven I was married. . . . I'm tired of everlastingly being *unnatural* . . . of acting like I don't eat more than a bird, and walking when I want to run and saying I feel faint after a waltz, when I could dance for two days and never get tired. I'm tired of saying, "How wonderful you are!" to fool men who haven't got one-half the sense I've got, and I'm tired of pretending I don't know anything, so men can tell me things and feel important while they're doing it" (*GW* 79). Compare Scarlett's frustration over not being allowed to be herself with Kitty's behavior in front of Pauline:

> During interminable Jackson City luncheons, she waited for Pauline to order, ordered the same, then forced herself to leave three-quarters of the meal untouched on the plate while her stomach rumbled and howled. She complained endlessly of headaches, heart palpitations, the countless sleepless nights endured since her "break" with Dale—every syllable a lie. Kitty had never had a headache in her life, her heart beat with the strength and regularity of a grazing bull,

* Note the provocative similarity between Kitty's theory of marriage and Anne Goodwyn Jones's characterization of how Margaret Mitchell viewed marriage. According to Jones, Mitchell "looked at marriage with a highly pragmatic and calculating eye. [She] saw clearly that marriage was a job like any other and that bagging a husband was the equivalent of getting a promotion" (*Tomorrow* 331).

> and she slept as easily and as soundly as a divorcée as she had slept as an adolescent. In addition to lying outrageously about nonexistent frailties, she covered her tan with the whitest of scented powders and learned to imitate, precisely, Pauline's round-shouldered "Kill Me If I Offend You" posture. She made sure to inject vocal curlicues of doubt into every sentiment expressed, to sound weepily undecided about eating sherbet. (*KD* 134–35)

"Pretense can be quite exhausting," the narrator concludes, reporting that upon returning from these excursions with Pauline, "Kitty stumbled in the door and took to her bed, utterly and genuinely spent. All that reigning in, all that biting back, all that acceding to the wishes of anyone and everything. Eee-gods! She couldn't believe how hard she had to work to impersonate a drip" (*KD* 135).

It is no surprise that seducing Brandon is easier than seducing Pauline: in spite of Brandon's lack of sexual appeal to Kitty, sexual seduction comes more naturally to her than behaving like a lady. Not surprisingly Kitty wins her campaign to be the next Mrs. Brandon Roberts. What *is* surprising is to realize that everyone benefits from this arrangement. Brandon, whose wife has deserted him and their sons, has none other than Kitty Duncan, who never would have paid him any attention in high school, as his trophy wife. In one of the rare glimpses into Kitty's thoughts (at least Mo's theory regarding her line of thinking on the matter), the reader learns that, upon realizing there is certainly enough money for everyone, Kitty determines that she will share her windfall with Brandon's sons. Thus she is no threat to them even if she is also not all that interested in replacing their mother—but then again their mother was not all that "motherly" either, as evidenced by the fact that she deserted them as well as their father. In short the boys are certainly no worse off than they were before Kitty's arrival. During her marriage to Brandon, Kitty also helps Pauline, who is even more uptight than Mo, broaden her horizons so that she is not so focused on Brandon's life (and thereby Kitty's). While the benefit to Kitty is that Pauline quits trying to undercut Kitty to Brandon, the greater benefit is to Pauline (since Brandon wasn't listening to his sister anyway); Pauline, put simply, learns how to have a good time. Kitty's marriage to a successful lawyer certainly pleases Kitty's mother. And finally, Kitty's second marriage means financial security for Caesar.

Eventually, in fact, Brandon determines to adopt Caesar, and in another surprising moment of the novel (surprising if one is still viewing Kitty as some femme fatale), Kitty resists, even though it would strengthen her and her daughter's financial security should her marriage fail, as is so likely. Before making a decision on this matter, perhaps because Kitty loved Caesar's father (in contrast to her feelings for Brandon), she takes Caesar to meet Dale's mother, Alma, another oppressed wife (in Alma's case to the extent of having been physically abused by her husband). Whatever the reason (if there is a conscious reason—like Scarlett, Kitty may just be acting on instinct), just as when Kitty chose a name for her daughter, her actions about Caesar's adoption show much more respect for her daughter than was ever shown to her by her own mother: Kitty leaves the decision up to Caesar. Sure Caesar is young and does not really understand what adoption means or who the man is in the photographs her "new" grandmother shows her, but Kitty at least refuses to make such a life-altering decision for her daughter without asking for Caesar's input. After explaining the situation as best she can, she leaves the decision to the person most affected by it: Caesar. And when Caesar goes along with the adoption, Kitty still makes certain her daughter learns about her biological father. Kitty also continues to help Dale's mother, not only emotionally, by allowing Alma a role in her granddaughter's life, but also financially, showing that she (Kitty) is not so self-absorbed as not to recognize—and, when she has the means, to help—another woman in need. One should note here that Kitty had actually helped Mo in college, not financially, since she never paid Mo for babysitting, having decided Mo didn't need the money, but emotionally, allowing Mo to talk with her, showing Mo a philosophy of life that did not focus on pleasing others and that was not motivated by guilt.

It is interesting to note here the surprising information that "by the age of five, Caesar had been granted full confidante status" (*KD* 166). Although Kitty was not one to have girlfriends, her talks with Mo in college anticipate somewhat her later relationship with Caesar. Perhaps Kitty was merely waiting on a girlfriend who has not yet been socialized toward certain expectations of a friend. Referring to their relationship as "adventuring buddies," Kitty takes Caesar on "long, meandering drives," during which "Kitty shared her uncensored thoughts and ruminations, some of which Caesar grasped, some of which she couldn't even slightly comprehend. No matter. She liked listening to her mom talk and when it was just the two of them riding, talking, she felt very grownup. . . . By intention or merely from habit, Kitty didn't water down, pretty up or sugarcoat during those gabfests, but she did leave room for dissension, often finishing off her sentence with the qualifier: 'Just my opinion, you understand. You probably have another'" (*KD* 166–67). Kitty is fine with "dissension"; one recalls that she had no qualms about arguing with Dale or

Mo. It was Dale's conformity, not their fighting, that brought their marriage to an end. And it should be no surprise that Kitty encourages her daughter to think for herself, even if it means Caesar develops views different from how her mother sees things.

As Mrs. Brandon Roberts, Kitty can develop her tan without interruption—there is household help to watch the children. But eventually she gets bored again and once again slips into a depression that reminds the reader that there is more beneath the surface than the other characters can see (and of course the story is not told from Kitty's perspective, so we are only rarely privy to Kitty's thoughts and even on those occasions, we are getting Mo's interpretation of Kitty's thinking). Kitty eventually lets her appearance go, reminding the reader that her attention to her dress and her body has always been more for her own enjoyment than to improve her appeal to others. Her obsessive tanning, the conscientious darkening of her skin, one might interpret to be a physical expression of her rejection of her mother's attempt to make a southern lady of her: white skin, of course, being a signifier of gentility.* And from the time she began to develop breasts, Kitty also began exploring and enjoying her sexuality, in contrast to the traditional stereotype of the practically asexual southern lady. Once Brandon, to whom Kitty is not physically attracted, resumes Phyllis's efforts to make Kitty into a lady, the mistress of his house, Kitty rebels, first acting out, fighting back, as she did with Dale, and then sinking into a depression as she did after giving birth to Caesar.

When Brandon pressures Kitty to have her hair done and go shopping "because you've become something of a laughingstock in this community" (*KD* 171) for not, as Pauline has reported to him, "keeping herself up" (*KD* 172), Kitty, never one to tolerate hypocrisy, is outraged:

> For all his talk of despising first wife Leanne, he meant to make Kitty her clone: a church-going Junior Leaguer, a coifed and boot-licking Barbie doll. . . . They'd made a pact! They'd struck a deal, wherein she got her goodies and he got his. And now the warty little turd, the insufferable bozo who called himself her husband, was trying to renege on the agreement??? Trying to turn Mrs. Brandon #2 into

* When asked about the significance of tanning in the novel, Meads responded, "I miss the indolence of sunbathing, so I *awarded* it to Kitty. . . . But I also liked the notion that she's layering. . . . The tan is taking on a different look. The interior was the same; the exterior was played with" (Bauer and Wieland 200; emphasis added).

> some autopilot ding-a-ling? Some twit who professed to like doing GOOD WORKS for OTHERS??? . . . The idea, the fucking idea, that the laughingstock of the universe [Kitty realizes who is really being laughed at], Brandon Roberts, imagined he could bend *her* to *his* will! . . . [I]t galled Kitty like nothing Brandon had previously insinuated or attempted. (*KD* 173)

Kitty is likely reminded of the beginning of the end of her marriage to Dale, when he started trying to tell her how to act, for appearance's sake. Perhaps it is this reminder—of lost love—that prompts the depression that follows her anger. But first Kitty gets her revenge on her self-righteous, hypocritical husband.

Taking Brandon up on his insistence that she go shopping, Kitty brings Pauline with her, and Pauline, to her own surprise, enjoys the initial shopping spree, which concludes with the two women getting drunk at Brandon's club. Kitty then becomes (outwardly at least) the hostess Brandon wants, and it is during Kitty's "party-throwing spree" that Pauline learns to have fun, in spite of Brandon. Also during this period, Kitty buys extravagantly for her frugal mother, her long-suffering former mother-in-law Alma, and her bewildered daughter, but none of her activity is self-satisfying, the reader realizes. Brandon misses the signs of danger ahead: "It didn't occur to him that frenzied entertaining might indicate profound despair and/or a prelude to explosion" (*KD* 180). He does not balk at Kitty moving into her own room until, "in the middle of a swim party, half the household's crystal at the bottom of the river, she and her white bathing suit disappeared into her white bedroom and didn't bother for the sake of Pauline, Brandon or appearances to return. From that night on, her bed became her empire" (*KD* 181). The reader is reminded of the wild parties that preceded the end of her first marriage. Apparently the parties can stave off depression for only so long. The reader might also recall how Kitty would seek solitude in the bathroom and refuse to come out when her mother would force play dates with other little girls on her. Not one to have developed friendships, as noted before, and knowing that she does not share her mother's values and her mother certainly doesn't understand her choices, Kitty has no one to turn to for comfort when disappointed by her life. And therefore she isolates herself and sinks into another depression.

Still trying to "fix" Kitty, Brandon sends his wife to a psychiatrist, where she meets a schizophrenic teenager in the waiting room, a young man who will be the catalyst to her next adventure, on the way to which Kitty once more behaves unexpectedly. Before she runs off with the young man, she invites her mother out to lunch, refusing Phyllis's suggestion that she just make something for them: "Let someone else serve for a change" (*KD* 195), she responds to her mother's offer. Then at lunch she offers the suggestion that "Dad should retire. . . . You guys should take some time, travel, enjoy yourselves." To Phyllis's incredulity over her daughter's concern about her welfare, Kitty responds, "Well, sure, I'm concerned. . . .What do you take me for?" Indeed, what *have* we taken Kitty for? Just because she has refused to be what her mother wanted does not mean she did not care about her mother, as evidenced by her parting advice to / request of her mother: "Do something for yourself every now and again, okay?" (*KD* 196). Though Phyllis seems to find it incongruous that Kitty, who has been the source of so much stress to Phyllis over the years, is concerned about her, the reader should recognize that Kitty's behavior has thus far *only hurt Kitty.* Kitty is the only character in this novel who falls into the debilitating depths of depression, for example.* Her interest in Phyllis's well-being, on the other hand, is reminiscent of her treatment of Alma and even of her behavior toward Mo, whom she has also tried to shake out of her limiting conformity. It may surprise readers to realize, finally, how magnanimous Kitty can be (just as readers might be surprised to recognize unselfish motives behind some of Scarlett's actions).

Also before leaving her second husband, Kitty stops in Caesar's bedroom to kiss her (supposedly) sleeping daughter good-bye and to leave a note that says, "*Good luck, Pumpkin*" (*KD* 198). Though Caesar has spent the rest of the night secretly hoping that her mother will change her mind and still be there in the morning, she does nothing to stop Kitty and is not cooperative with Brandon's attempts the next morning to figure out when Kitty left. While Kitty's mother and husband are once again scandalized by Kitty's behavior, Kitty's daughter seems more concerned about her mother than about herself, even though the reader knows that Caesar has issues of her own by this point in her young life. That may be, but Caesar does not blame those issues on her mother, and the reader should recognize them as typical of a child striving to fit in (though of course not holding her mother responsible for her unhappiness is pretty *a*typical). At this point in the novel, Caesar is not following in her mother's footsteps onto her own rebellious path. She, in fact, has tried to "buy" friends by sharing her bounty, and when that strategy went out of

* In the present, that is. Her mother's grasp of the situation after Caesar was born, with only what Dale tells her over the phone to go by, suggests that Phyllis has been there herself, as will be discussed later.

control, she started changing into an old dress on the way to school so that her schoolmates would believe her story that she and her mother have fallen on hard times. Kitty, one recalls, never courted friendships, never cared about popularity or what people thought of her. In contrast to Kitty, whose unhappiness she witnesses, Caesar is going through a stage of at least trying her grandmother's more socially conscious philosophy of life.

Before moving on to Brandon's search for Kitty and Kitty's adventure with her schizophrenic, teenage lover, Mo digresses to tell the reader a bit about how her own life is going. Mo has pursued a career as a journalist (the same career that Margaret Mitchell pursued before writing the story of Scarlett O'Hara). A newspaper reporter now, Mo, being a woman, is assigned human interest rather than hard news stories and, when assigned to actual news, she is encouraged to take a human interest angle (interview the wives and girlfriends, for example). Mo gets her big break, however, when the sheriff she sits next to during a murder trial, not taking her seriously as a woman reporter, makes a racial slur against the defendant in her hearing, and the resulting news story and its aftermath of threats and vandalism directed at Mo, her property, and her employer "made [Mo's] journalistic reputation" (*KD* 128). But that occurred around the time of Kitty's relationship with Brandon, and by the end of Kitty's second marriage, Mo is dissatisfied with her own life and thus perhaps curious to find out what will happen to Kitty for running out on hers.

The reader here begins to understand Mo's interest in Kitty: finding out what happens to those who are not good girls. "It's a women-centered book," Meads says, explaining, "In the 1950s, in the particular South that I lived in, there weren't a whole lot of ways women could wield power. . . . It took a while before women—Southern women in particular, I think—felt they could live their own lives and make their own choices, go out into the wider world, not behave exactly like their mothers, and still qualify as good Southern daughters" (Bauer and Wieland 196). Thirty-something Mo is still unmarried and on a career track—certainly not following in her mother's footsteps—and yet she is startled to see in the bathroom mirror that she is still turning into her mother: "I was, in every sense, bombarded by my own marginality. In the bathroom mirror, I looked less and less like myself and more and more my mother's twin." Her lifestyle may be different from her mother's, but she realizes she is still "Miss Goody Two Shoes" on the inside (*KD* 202).

In recalling her first encounter with Kitty back in college, Mo had asked herself, "Why (attempt to) commune with one's polar opposite?" (*KD* 12), asserting that "Kitty and I weren't remotely alike" (*KD* 13). In truth Kitty is not Mo's opposite except in her lack of angst over her nonconformity. When teenaged Kitty noticed her breasts growing, she was horrified by the idea that they would grow as large as her mother's, apparently seeing this as evidence that she could turn into her mother, and from that moment on (much earlier than Mo), she had resisted being anything like Phyllis. The source of thirty-something Mo's unhappiness is not having sacrificed having a family to pursue a career but rather, it seems, still behaving like a lady, while the rebel Kitty Duncan is twice a wife, also a mother, yet never a lady. Mo may worry that she has given up marriage and motherhood for nothing, since she is not finding her career fulfilling, but the reader knows that both times that Kitty suffers depression it is not because she is a housewife but because she is being asked to be someone she is not. And Kitty's depression lifts both times when she resumes her more natural behavior of pursuing her own interests even though doing so goes against the norm. The lesson here seems to be that the issue is not whether a woman follows a career path or has a family, but whether she does what she wants to do and is who she is, without pretense.

Resuming Kitty's story after the digression on her own unhappiness, Mo reports that Kitty is easily found after her departure from Brandon's house. Brandon can, after all, afford a private detective, but also Kitty makes no effort to elude the agents spying on her and in fact, makes their surveillance easier by keeping them apprised of her comings and goings so that they don't have to wait around in the hot sun (she's in Florida). She treats the schizophrenic boy she has run off with as she treats everyone: she is completely herself with him and accepting of his behavior and tolerant of his demons. But the truly interesting part of this section of the novel is that she goes to work and enjoys it—not unlike Scarlett O'Hara, who finds more satisfaction working in her lumberyard than in spending Rhett's money. Kitty is perhaps happiest in this section, and her enjoyment of her life has little if anything to do with her current lover (the schizophrenic teenager). Rather, her platonic friend/eventual employer Hank, the owner of a local bar, accepts Kitty's offer to help him out and thereby gives her the most purpose she has had since perfecting her tan—and more of a challenge than tanning ever was. It is off-season, the beach is largely deserted, except for the locals, and no one is interested in pedigree or ladylike behavior at the Junket. They *are* interested in the drinks Kitty finds she has a talent for concocting, and Kitty thrives—like Scarlett with her lumberyard. Mo calls this "Kitty's most personally satisfying epoch" and, alluding to Kitty's past bouts of depression, notes that during Kitty's time at the Junket "she left bed every morning willingly and for a purpose she enjoyed, her abilities and projects converged nicely, effort and achievement overlapped, the square pegs found the square holes and results were good all around." This last metaphor alludes to Kitty's popularity among the locals—finally people accepting her for who she is as she has always accepted others. Kitty makes friends, including Hank, the Junket proprietor, who benefits from giving Kitty a job: he can now take a day off occasionally to go fishing. Their friendship is a willing, open, and honest give-and-take, perhaps for the first time in Kitty's life. Mo describes Kitty in the Junket as "quintessentially Kitty, doing what she pleased with whom" (*KD* 249).

Mo admits to being tempted to end Kitty's story in Florida, with "Kitty finishing out her days as a tart-tongued, gray-haired barkeep, a Junket icon and confirmed tourist draw" (*KD* 248). But not unlike Kitty's first husband Dale, Hank eventually tries to be what he is not by changing the bar's look to attract the transient tourists, and the permanent locals no longer like it. Without the support of the off-season crowd, Hank loses the bar, and so Kitty loses her job. She heads home—to her parents—returning shamelessly, knowing they will take her in—because that's what parents do—and seemingly unembarrassed about being nearly forty, alone, and unemployed. She is perhaps waiting on the next adventure—and she is not to be disappointed: in walks Mo, coming to call like Pauline did, but in Mo's case more for her own curiosity than a sense of duty. Mo is *not* in the neighborhood as she pretends to be but on a story several miles away and on a deadline, which she ignores in order to find out how Kitty's story is going. She is apparently at least subconsciously considering walking out on her life and has sought out Kitty to find out what happens to a single, thirty-something, unemployed (and unladylike) woman before doing so. In hindsight Mo realizes that she went "in search of hard evidence, of incontrovertible, unimagined proof, that my heroine had not only survived but succeeded on her own quirky terms; that willful, contrary Kitty Duncan had eluded the consequences of being willful and contrary" (*KD* 266).

Mo's timing is excellent, as not only is Kitty at home when Mo calls but Caesar is on her way home, too (presumably from college). Kitty is obviously pleased to hear from Mo and surprised by Mo's memory of her "stealing" the boy Mo was interested in. "Why would you remember all that?" (*KD* 266), she asks, a question that may remind the reader of Sula asking Nel, "How you know . . . who was good?" (*S* 146). Like Sula, Kitty questions who the victim is, in actuality rather than in memory: has Kitty been the victimizer or the victim—or perhaps *a* victim who has fought back? All of the women in this novel are oppressed, but Phyllis, Alma, Pauline, and Mo have accepted their oppression, even participated in it by maintaining the manners and mores of the society that oppresses them: from Phyllis's humiliation by her daughter's behavior to Alma staying with her abusive husband, even though a very nice man is willing to help her leave Ted. Kitty has refused to participate in such victimization, rejecting the rules of behavior for southern belles and ladies, although she has been oppressed by the limitations of her life: she goes to college as the *wife* of a student, not as a student herself; her way out of one marriage is to go home to her parents, and with a child to take care of she regains her independence from them again only by marrying a wealthy man whom she does not even like. She doesn't *need* a lot; the ability to buy all the clothes and toys that she and Caesar could want was just fun in the early days of her marriage (and in the absence of love and passion), but eventually these *things* bored her—just as Thomas H. Pauly observes of Scarlett: "Rhett's gifts—the house and even Bonnie—all simply deprive [Scarlett] of the thing she needs most—a challenge" (226). So like Scarlett managing the lumberyard, Kitty found work that she enjoyed, but it was still not her own business, and thus she had no control over the business decisions; her advice was not taken, and she lost her bartending job, then found herself again under her parents' roof. But the important point here, as suggested before, is Kitty's unapologetic attitude about returning. Though her mother has never accepted her for who she is, Kitty accepts *her* mother for who *she* is and knows that Phyllis will take in and take care of her wayward daughter, in spite of the embarrassment she feels about Kitty—Kitty calls it the "insurance" of "the prodigal daughter" (*KD* 250).

Upon first seeing Kitty again, who "did appear the worse for wear: bulkier, sloppier, if possible," but "didn't look as bad as a woman should have looked with her track record," Mo realizes what it was that so intrigued her about Kitty, simultaneously repulsing and attracting her: "Not caring: that's the lure that reeled me in. Every time. Without exception. Her native genius for disregarding the female imperative" as evidenced, for example, in the fact that, when Kitty greets Mo at the door, she does not display any usual reaction but rather, "she didn't look like she gave a fig how she presented—to herself, to me, to anyone dead or alive" (*KD* 264). So not only is Kitty unselfconscious about being caught back home with her parents at her age, single after two failed marriages, and unemployed, but also she is not self-conscious about her physical decline. She is simply not embarrassed.

Nor is she suffering from guilt or remorse or any other such emotion, which would suggest that she were at some level ashamed of herself. Mo asks her, "Thinking back, if you could do anything differently, would you?" (*KD* 266), and she receives another enlightening response: "What's to change? It was what it was. And if it wasn't that, it'd just be something else," Kitty says, and adds, "Face it, Mo, I'm not like you. . . . I'm not an agonizer. Never was." And Mo's response: She recognizes, "Goddamn it, how I envied her! There she lazed, on the far side of thirty-five, sloppy, almost chunky, ruled by neither burning ambition nor grievance, living with her goddamn parents, and none of it seem[s] to bother her a goddamn bit!" (*KD* 267). One might apply what Amy Levin observes of Scarlett's inability to "analyze herself" to Kitty's lack of interest in doing so: "she [Scarlett] is given the intelligence to question the code, but not to analyze herself or to make a clean break from its strictures. This lack of consciousness or consistency ultimately appears dishonest." But, Levin continues, "one must wonder about self-analysis as a virtue. Is it a value encouraged by the society in which Scarlett lives? Of what value would it be to her? Or, is analysis a luxury? Can a woman in a rigidly structured society afford to analyze herself too deeply? To what will analysis lead?" (34). Kitty may have realized (we can't know since this is really Mo's interpretation of Kitty's story) that thinking too much about her situation at any given point would only add to her frustration with the limitations people keep trying to enforce upon her.

Mo has one more test, however, to see if this living according to one's own morality and desires rather than inherited values and drives is worth the risk. She eagerly takes advantage of the opportunity presented by Caesar's curiosity about her biological father and his relationship with her mother, about which Caesar recognizes that she is likely to get a more objective perception from Mo than she has from either of her grandmothers (and Kitty, of course, does not dwell on the past, so is unlikely to be much help). Mo answers Caesar's questions about what she remembers about Kitty and Dale back during their college days and then asks one of her own, her "gut . . . in turmoil" (or does she ask? The question is put within quotation marks but the introduction and follow-up to it don't make clear whether she asked out loud): "And you don't resent your mother? What she's done? Who she is? You're not sorry you weren't dealt a mother who performed in strict motherly fashion? Provide and protect? Stay the course? Pledge her devotion, mean it? Put your welfare/well-being before her own? Sacrifice her happiness to yours?" Mo gets her answer, whether she actually asked the question or not. Caesar comments on what she has heard from Mo, "I guess Mom was a bit of a free spirit. For back then." To Mo's judicious "a bit" Caesar then says, "But, you know, to me she was just mom," the biggest whammy of Mo's day:

> *Just mom.* My God. Kitty Duncan in the guise of just mom.
>
> The just mom who—it now hit with the force of concrete sludge—at least partially contributed to the formation of this calm, curious, centered being who seemed to incorporate neither her grandmother's roiling hysteria nor her mother's gruff obstinacy. Insight laced with humor. Could any parent hope for better? (*KD* 274)

Kitty may be "just mom," but also Caesar is *just fine*! She did not suffer irreversible psychological harm from the behavior of her mother; indeed she seems to be even healthier than Kitty is—there are no reports of her going through the serious depressions Kitty has suffered—and she is certainly better than Kitty at not discomforting others with her own "misbehavior"—her grandmother, for example, is oblivious to not only the smell of marijuana on Caesar and her visiting girlfriend or their slightly stoned condition but also the fact that the two young women are lovers. But Mo and Kitty stumble (literally) upon this proof of Kitty's daughter's own avant-garde lifestyle, and Kitty "stepp[ed] across a naked tangle of feet . . . let loose a belly laugh and left her daughter to it" (*KD* 277).

Like Scarlett, Kitty lives in the "eternal present," but she is not in any kind of denial—at least as far as we know from Mo's story (it is, after all, Mo's story). As I suggested earlier, Kitty is an evolved Scarlett: Scarlett never gets around to thinking about it tomorrow; Kitty never plans to do so. She won't put off for tomorrow what isn't worth thinking about today. And Caesar will ultimately benefit. Kitty does not spoil Caesar the way Rhett spoils Bonnie (which one might say plays a role in Bonnie's death), but Caesar will be allowed to pursue her passions without pressure from her mother to change them to something more appropriate.

Mo closes her story of Kitty Duncan Benedict Roberts Duncan:

> But whatever else you count as her failures, count this to her credit: Kitty recognized the distinction, respected the separation, between herself and her daughter; she knew, had known always, where one ended and the other began.
>
> No small achievement, that.
>
> Ask any mother if you don't believe me.
>
> Better yet, interrogate your own. (*KD* 277–78)

It is not easy (and very rare) to allow one's child to be herself, make her own mistakes, follow her own path. As shown in the previous chapters (as well as in real life), unconditional love is an ideal that even mothers have difficulty with. Phyllis is not a happy woman herself, and yet she tries to make Kitty over in her own image—as Ellen O'Hara, also unhappy, tries to do with Scarlett. They seem to have determined that the unhappily familiar is safer than the untried different path, and thus trying to squelch the rebellious natures of these unruly daughters is their way of loving their children.

What Mo has been watching for all along is whether Kitty's rejection of her mother's way of life will lead to disaster. What Kitty has known all along (that Scarlett never realized) is that her mother's life *is* the tragedy. Consider the description of Phyllis after she finally gets her daughter onto the school bus each morning: "Flushed and frazzled, Phyllis closed the door on the outside world, her mother tasks complete for now. She could have relaxed, thrown her feet up, drunk a pot of tea, shaped her nails, let her mind drift. The house was empty of company and quiet, if one discounted the refrigerator's hum. But Phyllis was not a relaxer. Should she throw up her feet, she'd notice dust bunnies underfoot and cobwebs overhead. If she made herself a pot of tea, she'd spy brown stains imbedded in the porcelain. A mother/wife's work was never done. After Phyllis sent her daughter off to school and turned to face her domain, sad to say, she did not see order. She bore witness to barely controlled chaos" (*KD* 18). This passage calls to mind "flushed and frazzled" Mrs. Oakley telling Dorinda in *Barren Ground*, "Wherever I turn, I see dirt gathering" (*BG* 53), as well as Ellen O'Hara, who worked herself into an early grave. For Phyllis, the housekeeping keeps her going, fends off depression. Back during Kitty's first marriage, concerned about what she detects when talking with Dale about Kitty's odd postpartum behavior, Phyllis ruminates about her own periods of feeling "blue. Aimless. Worthless. Almost but not quite desperate enough to take drastic action, behave irrationally, do something she might not live to regret. Only by cleaning, cooking or reorganizing closets with a frenzy that allowed no meditation could she keep those twinges of hopelessness from maturing into full-blown cases of despair" (*KD* 98–99). From Phyllis's frenetic housecleaning to Kitty's wild partying, the reader sees that the daughter is not entirely different from the mother after all. Kitty determines, however, that *her* daughter will be. And unlike her mother, Kitty recognizes the source of the depression is in the conformity that Phyllis embraces to pull herself off the ledge—hence the cycle of depression.

As noted earlier about Ellen O'Hara and Eudora Oakley, Phyllis is not a healthy role model for her daughter. Kitty was certainly right to resist her mother's attitude toward life. Bored by order, Kitty revels in chaos, and her comfort with the untraditional allows *her* daughter to pursue an untraditional lifestyle without worry about her mother's disapproval. It is significant that the one time that Kitty lashes out at her mother, she employs imagery alluding to Phyllis's housekeeping. Usually more inclined to just ignore Phyllis and do what she wanted without explanation, Kitty is piqued to a response on this occasion by Phyllis's criticism of how she is raising Caesar: "You see cobwebs, stained carpets, unmade beds and dirty dishes. And what do you do about it? Hustle your buns off to clean and tidy before the next tornado blows through and makes a mess all over again. We live in a messy, *filthy* world, Mo-ther. You break your neck fighting it; I do my damnedest not to notice. Caesar has to pick her own line of defense. On her own. In her own way. Before you bring in the disinfectant" (*KD* 161). Caesar is still a baby when Kitty says this to Phyllis. As we have seen, Kitty does indeed allow her daughter to find her own way, "*in her own way.*" *The Invented Life of Kitty Duncan* ends with Kitty's laughter—so different from Scarlett and Nel's regret and loss. Mo's closing lines direct us to the source of such enjoyment. Though Kitty may not have received unconditional love, she can give it. She may refuse to regret the consequences of rejecting any "conditioning" others seek to impose with their "love," but she does understand and experience consequences. Kitty has survived these consequences, relatively unscathed; Caesar, accepted for who she is by her mother, is going to thrive.

From hearing about Ashley's engagement and finding her mother not at home to comfort her, to escaping the burning Atlanta only to find that her mother has died, with Ellen's criticism of her daughter's unladylike behavior in between, Scarlett has been disappointed by her mother's love and has pushed away the others who might similarly disappoint her—Rhett (who fell in love but then out of love with her for the same reason: who she is) and Melanie (who did love her but then died, thus leaving her as all others had). Kitty too has suffered bouts of depression that reflect her disappointments in love, but now that she is giving such love to Caesar, the reader feels that both she and Caesar will be all the more empowered for it. And if Mo can learn from the story she tells that the consequences of being false to herself are much more dire than any consequences one suffers for being herself, then she too may be able to give and receive such love.

Afterword

"People have funny ideas. They think the great romance of the book is between Scarlett and Rhett. Now it's a love story, no question, and Margaret Mitchell does a masterful job keeping us in suspense the whole one thousand-plus pages, wondering if Scarlett and Rhett will get back together—something some twenty-eight million readers have been wondering since the book came out in 1936. The Scarlett and Rhett story, however, turns pale as powdered milk when compared with the creamier romance at hand: the one between book and reader, between reader and Scarlett, between a young girl and her own fantasies."

Beverly Lowry, "A Book of Our Own" (87)

"What matters is that lives do not serve as models; only stories do that. And it is a hard thing to make up stories to live by. We can only retell and live by the stories we have read or heard. We live our lives through texts. They may be read, or changed, or experienced electronically, or come to us, like the murmurings of our mothers, telling us what conventions demand. Whatever their form or medium, these stories have formed us all; they are what we must use to make new fictions, new narratives."

Carolyn G. Heilbrun, *Writing a Woman's Life* (37)

During the years that I worked on this book, when I would mention my subject to colleagues, they would recommend a "Scarlett" for my study, but more often than not, the suggested characters were more comparable to the typical misperception of the character type, an unfairly critical view of Scarlett that is probably based largely on her depiction in the movie. It is my hope that this study will bring readers back to the book with a view toward recognizing not only Margaret Mitchell's character's heroic resistance of the limitations her society tried to place upon her but also society's tendency to be discomforted by and judgmental toward that resistance. I am still disappointed in myself for not liking Kat Meads's character Kitty Duncan from the start, for reaching the end of her novel before realizing that this fictional biography was presenting Kitty entirely from the perspective of others—characters who were discomforted by Kitty's refusal to conform. Elizabeth Wurtzel's observation in her book *Bitch: In Praise of Difficult Women,* "how nice it must be to just decide I will not be nice, I am never sorry, I have no regrets: what is before me belongs to me," reminds me of Kitty Duncan. Wurtzel believes that "for men this attitude is second nature" (30), but the perception of such an attitude in a woman results in her being labeled a bitch.

Wurtzel complains on behalf of women who would be so labeled, "All my life, one person or another has been telling me to behave. . . . I have a tough time feeling that feminism has done a damn bit of good if I can't be the way I am and have the world accommodate it on some level" (28, 33). Kat Meads sets her novel in the middle of the twentieth century, but she wrote it in the twenty-first century, knowing that attitudes toward women who resist or even rebel against status quo (still considered "bad girls") are not changing fast enough—just as Margaret Mitchell knew that opportunities for women of her day, in the first half of the twentieth century, had not changed very much since the Civil War that gave her heroine the chance to live a different life than she had been raised to expect.

There are still, in real life, in the twenty-first century, Scarletts all over the world—women who cannot—either because of their circumstances or their own ambitions—accept the limitations set for their gender. I chose for my examination of this character type in literature to focus on southern Scarletts (including Sula, whose community is as influenced by southern history as the others) because the South is an example of a culture particularly oppressive to women, including both women who have been idealized historically, the white southern lady, and women who suffer the double oppression of also being African Americans. The (false) ideals of equality within the American dream and, for all but Sula, the privileged social position of the white southerner place protagonists of the novels covered in this study in the position of a tragic hero, who traditionally comes from nobility and thus falls from a high place. Sula's inclusion, a black character who suffers similarly, reminds the reader of the false privilege of these other women. The effect of idealizing the southern lady is that the higher plane from which these women may fall is the proverbial pedestal, and these women would rather kick that pedestal out from under themselves and see what happens after they fall than live such a confined life. Like the peasant audience of Shakespeare's tragedies, the reader can appreciate the significance of these women's stories: if such tribulations can happen to a woman in the so-called democratic United States, what does that say about the suffering of a young woman growing up in a country that does not even pretend to value equal rights for women? Recent headlines in the months during which I revised this book answer that question: in the fall of 2012, a fourteen-year-old Pakistani girl, Malala Yousufzai, was attacked, shot, and continues to be threatened by the Taliban for asserting that women have the right to be educated too.

Young Malala lives in a world even more oppressive to women than the Old South, but the brutal attack on her has inspired worldwide support for her efforts to resist the limitations set for girls. In the works of fiction covered in this study, which reflect the less violent, more subtle oppression of women in a country that claims to believe in equal rights for all (but significantly articulates this assertion as "all *men* are created equal"), the punishment for resistance is condemning and ostracizing rather than trying to assassinate the female rebel. Ironically the less extreme methods are more effective in that they inspire less public outrage and the unconventional woman is isolated by her different values—unless she finds someone who shares her values or who loves her in spite of her difference.

From her mother's love, which seemed to be given on the condition that Scarlett behave herself as a proper southern lady; to Ashley's cowardly declarations of love, which keep her from giving her heart to another man; to Melanie's love, the value of which Scarlett does not realize until Melanie is gone; to Rhett's false admiration, which merely reflects his own ego, Scarlett is repeatedly disappointed in love. Is it any wonder that she seeks fulfillment in less romantic pursuits? If the protagonist of Ellen Glasgow's 1925 novel *Barren Ground* is the prototype from which Margaret Mitchell drew her heroine, it is not surprising that Mitchell's novel ends with Scarlett alone, like Glasgow's Dorinda Oakley, and, indeed, the characters' similarity to each other helps the reader to recognize the triumphant ending implicit in Scarlett's impending return to Tara, the place where she previously discovered her inner strength, just as Dorinda finds her fulfillment in the dairy farm she created. Both novelists reveal that, albeit untraditional to leave their heroines alone in the end, it is still a happier ending than matching them up with men who cannot really love them. We may feel sorry for what is missing from these women's lives (in my opinion it is a Melanie more than a Rhett), but we are still assured that both Scarlett and Dorinda will live fulfilling lives.

Scarlett O'Hara is to be admired rather than criticized. This young woman, who is only twenty-eight by novel's end, loses almost everyone she loves and yet has the energy to go back to Tara and start over. Start over, indeed: with the knowledge she has gained regarding Melanie's superior love—the value of someone who loves her as she is—when Scarlett determines to return to Tara, she thinks of Mammy, who loves her in the way Melanie loved her, more than Ellen ever could, and Scarlett can now appreciate such love in a way she could not until she lost Melanie. In the unwritten sequel, the one the reader is compelled to imagine to follow the untraditional ending of the novel, more important than whether Scarlett wins Rhett back is the possibility that with Mammy's nurturing love, Scarlett will be able to give her son and surviving daughter a future in which, like Kitty Duncan's daughter, they may be themselves.

Besides giving his novel an untraditional, unromantic ending, Charles Frazier distinguishes *Cold Mountain* in his characterization of Ada as not self-loathing about her failure to fit in with Charleston society; she simply lacks any desire to conform to social expectations. She may be introduced wondering how she is going to survive since her upbringing has not prepared her to fill an empty larder, but she does not question her self-worth. Indeed, at one point in the novel, she recalls a moment when she unconsciously admired her own reflection in a mirror, envying the "the sense of assurance" evident in the straight back of the woman whose image she spied and, "realiz[ing] that it was herself she was admiring . . . she thought how odd it had felt to win her own endorsement" (*CM* 111). Considering the pieces of her past that Ada reflects upon in the course of the novel, the reader recognizes that Ada's self-confidence and self-approval at this moment reflect her father's acceptance of her, even though she did not conform to social expectations. Ada, in spite of her unconventionality, did not grow up with the constant message that something was wrong or unlovable about her. In turn, although Ada finds Ruby's behavior completely foreign to her own experiences, she does not judge Ruby—rather, she marvels at Ruby's untraditional knowledge of the natural world around them. And under Ada's admiration, prickly Ruby can forgive and perhaps even learn to love her own father, who cannot even recall the year of his daughter's birth. Ruby is married in the novel's epigraph, happily, it seems, which suggests that she has allowed at least this man into her heart—quite a change for this woman who, through most of the novel, distrusts men.

As the epilogue—and with it Ada's story— comes to a close, Ada is reading what appears to be a romantic novel, which ends when "the old lovers after long years together in peace and harmony had turned to oak and linden." Ada does not seem wistful; still there is no pining for Inman. Her thoughts are of practical matters: "The night was growing cool, and Ada put the book away. The children were sleepy, and morning would dawn as early and demanding as always. Time to go inside and cover up the coals and pull in the latch string" (*CM* 356). She is at peace with her life, and such contentment is what her nature has sought all along. Contentment may not be the typical goal of romance novels, but to my surprise, given its unconventional ending, *Cold Mountain* is ultimately one of the most satisfying novels I've read.

The unromantic ending to Mitchell's novel may have been unexpected to the first readers of *Gone with the Wind*, but the themes and conflicts developed within the novel's pages have since been played out by other female characters who are in one way or another in Scarlett's position: put simply, seeking to be loved for themselves, like Toni Morrison's Sula Peace and Kat Meads's Kitty Duncan, and, when romantic love fails, seeking some other source of happiness and fulfillment, as Scarlett will when, still not finding what she is looking for at her home in Atlanta, with Rhett, she plans to go home to Tara, where she relies upon herself to achieve a fulfilling life, like Ellen Glasgow's Dorinda Oakley and Charles Frazier's Ada Monroe do. Perhaps there is at least evidence in her determination to "think of it all tomorrow" that Scarlett has gotten past her mother's harsh judgment of her and can eventually learn to love herself as Melanie loved her, a first step that will allow her then to recognize love from another the next time it is offered—"After all, tomorrow is another day" (*GW* 1037).

In the conclusion to her seminal study of southern women writers, *Tomorrow Is Another Day: The Woman Writer in the South, 1859–1936,* Anne Goodwyn Jones proposes three interpretations of Scarlett's final assertion of the motto that she comforts herself with throughout the novel. The first two meanings combine Scarlett's previous use of the phrase to put off facing reality with a recognition of her own strength, which one might suggest comes from her ability not to dwell on the negative: "She has lost Rhett, Bonnie Blue, [we can add Melanie here,] and most of her illusions about money, love, and her own power. Hence, when she says that 'tomorrow is another day,' while thinking of her imminent and final return to Tara, it expresses not only a desire to evade the present but also a sense of faith in the future, a faith strained by experience but also taught by it. Her return to Tara will be not solely to the dream of the secure world of her childhood, but also to a reality that, during and after the war, she shaped as she would and could" (*Tomorrow* 351–52). One can imagine a fulfilling future for Scarlett O'Hara as well as for Charles Frazier's Ada and Ruby and Ellen Glasgow's Dorinda. These women's self-sufficiency and fortitude will serve them well into old age, one imagines, and their passion for their work is at least as, if not more satisfying than the happily-ever-after endings of traditional romances.

Anne Jones offers another reading of the ending, however, that reminds us that, even as these women's ability to adapt to their changing worlds allows them to endure and thrive while others (Rhett and Melanie, for example) are defeated, the world itself is not changing fast enough for women. Jones adds, "a third possible meaning to the phrase, that tomorrow is just another day like the last, [is] that the future admits of no change" (*Tomorrow* 352). Many in Scarlett's community (Melanie included) reject the changes brought about by the Civil War as effectively as Scarlett has evaded reality for so many years, and the consequence of this resistance to change is that Scarlett, the one among them who adapts most readily to the changes, continues to be judged harshly by those around her—including Rhett—for her unconventionality. As the authors who have created other Scarlett-like characters set their novels in later periods, we see communities still slow to change, so that Sula Peace, growing up after World War I, and Kitty Duncan, growing up after World War II, receive the same kind of social censure that Scarlett O'Hara suffers. But like Dorinda Oakley, who never allows herself to dwell on the shame of the child she conceived out of wedlock, these women do not spend a lot of time dwelling on the past or even worrying what their mothers would say, as Scarlett does. There is progress in that.

And yet one should note that Toni Morrison kills off her Scarlett-like character—perhaps recognizing that the world was still not ready for Sula: an African American woman living by her own morality was no more acceptable in the first half of the twentieth century than was a southern white woman in the second half of the nineteenth. As Victoria Middleton says of Sula, "In Sula, Toni Morrison celebrates a character whom she might say, as Jane Austen did of Emma, 'no one would like but myself.' To be liked in Sula's world would be a sign of failure" (369). The hope Morrison leaves us with is in Nel's insight, gained as painfully as Scarlett's, of what she has lost, and in the reader's realization of the value of such an affirming, nurturing friendship as these women had, in contrast to their less fulfilling relationships with lovers.

Even the 1960s might not have been ready for Kitty Duncan, but Kitty doesn't care. She will be herself, and she will love her daughter for herself. She will most likely continue to seek a satisfying romantic love, but she seems to recognize that the fun, the *story,* is in the quest itself. As Carolyn G. Heilbrun concludes in her book on *Writing a Woman's Life,* "When the hope for closure is abandoned, when there is an end to fantasy, adventure for women will begin. Endings . . . are for romance or for daydreams, but not for life" (130). The characters who continue to live beyond the page, like Scarlett O'Hara and her literary daughters, are the ones who inspire us to wonder what they're up to next, not the ones with a nicely tied up happy ending.

Bibliography

"*AppalJ* Roundtable Discussion: *Cold Mountain,* the Film." *Appalachian Journal* 31 (2004): 316–53.

Apter, Terri, and Ruthellen Josselyn. *Best Friends: The Pleasures and Perils of Girls' and Women's Friendships.* 1998. New York: Three Rivers, 1999.

Ashdown, Paul. "'Savage Satori': Fact and Fiction in Charles Frazier's *Cold Mountain.*" *Memory and Myth: The Civil War in Fiction and Film from* Uncle Tom's Cabin *to* Cold Mountain. Ed. David B. Sachsman, S. Kittrell Rushing, and Roy Morris Jr. West Lafayette, Ind.: Purdue University Press, 2007. 207–20.

Bakerman, Jane S. "Failures of Love: Female Initiation in the Novels of Toni Morrison." *American Literature* 52 (1981): 541–63.

Bauer, Margaret D. "Genre Conventions with a Half-Twist: An Interview with Charles Frazier." *North Carolina Literary Review* 22 (2013): 21–41.

Bauer, Margaret D., and Liza Wieland. "'I am not Kitty Duncan': Two Interviews with Kat Meads." *North Carolina Literary Review* 18 (2009): 194–205.

Bernikow, Louise. *Among Women.* 1980. New York: Harper Colophon, 1981.

Beye, Charles Rowan. "*Gone with the Wind,* and Good Riddance." *Southwest Review* 78.3 (1993): 366–80.

Bleich, David. *Subjective Criticism:* Baltimore: Johns Hopkins University Press, 1978.

Bond, Tonette L. "Pastoral Transformations in *Barren Ground.*" *Mississippi Quarterly* 32 (1979): 565–76.

Brock, H. I. "Southern Romance Is Dead." Rev. of *Barren Ground. New York Times Book Review* April 12, 1925, sec. 3: 2.

Buma, Pascal P. "Black Female Bildungsroman: Complementary Selfhood in Toni Morrison's *Sula.*" *Literary Griot* 11.2 (1999): 70–96.

Cardon, Lauren S. "'Good Breeding': Margaret Mitchell's Multi-Ethnic South." *Southern Quarterly* 44.4 (2007): 61–82.

Christian, Barbara. "Community and Nature: The Novels of Toni Morrison." *Journal of Ethnic Studies* 7.4 (1980): 65–78.

———. "The Contemporary Fables of Toni Morrison." *Toni Morrison's Sula*. Ed. Harold Bloom. Philadelphia: Chelsea, 1999. 25–49. Modern Critical Interpretations series.

Coleman, Alisha R. "One and One Make One: A Metacritical and Psychoanalytical Reading of Friendship in Toni Morrison's *Sula*." *College Language Association Journal* 37.2 (1993): 145–55.

Commager, Henry Steele. "The Civil War in Georgia's Red Clay Hills." Rev. of *Gone with the Wind*, by Margaret Mitchell. *New York Herald Tribune Books* July 5, 1936: 1–2. Rpt. in Pyron, *Southern Daughter* 11–16.

Crawford, Martin. "*Cold Mountain* Fictions: Appalachian Half-truths." *Appalachian Journal* 30.2–3 (2003): 182–95.

Deer, Harriet A., and Irving Deer. "Women as Outsiders in the Movies and Television." *The Aching Hearth: Family Violence in Life and Literature*. Ed. Sara Munson Deats and Lagretta Tallent Lenker. New York: Plenum, 1991. 269–81.

Denard, Carolyn C., ed. *Toni Morrison: Conversations*. Jackson: University Press of Mississippi, 2008.

Edwards, Anne. *Road to Tara: The Life of Margaret Mitchell*. New York: Ticknor, 1983.

Egenriether, Ann E. "Scarlett O'Hara: A Paradox in Pantalettes." *Heroines of Popular Culture*. Ed. Pat Browne. Bowling Green, Ohio: Bowling Green State University Popular Press, 1987. 120–27.

Eichenbaum, Luise, and Susie Orbach. *Between Women: Love, Envy, and Competition in Women's Friendships*. 1987. New York: Penguin, 1989.

Farca, Paula Anca. "And You, Miss, Are No Lady: Feminist and Postfeminist Scarlett O'Hara Rethinks the Southern Lady." *Southern Studies* 14.1 (2007): 73–90.

Faust, Drew Gilpin. "Clutching the Chains That Bind: Margaret Mitchell and *Gone with the Wind*." *Southern Cultures* 5.1 (1999): 5–20.

Fox-Genovese, Elizabeth. *Within the Plantation Household: Black and White Women of the Old South*. Chapel Hill: University of North Carolina Press, 1988.

———. "Scarlett O'Hara: The Southern Lady as New Woman." *American Quarterly* 33 (1981): 391–411.

Frazier, Charles. *Cold Mountain*. New York: Atlantic Monthly Press, 1997.

Fultz, Lucille P. "To Make Herself: Mother-Daughter Conflicts in Toni Morrison's *Sula* and *Tar Baby*." *Women of Color: Mother-Daughter Relationships in 20th Century Literature*. Ed. Elizabeth Brown-Guillory. Austin: University of Texas Press, 1996. 228–43.

Gaillard, Dawson. "*Gone with the Wind* as Bildungsroman: Or, Why Did Rhett Butler Really Leave Scarlett O'Hara?" *Georgia Review* 28 (1974): 9–18.

Galehouse, Maggie. "'New World Woman': Toni Morrison's *Sula*." *Papers on Languages and Literature* 35 (1999): 339–62.

Gelfant, Blanche H. "*Gone with the Wind* and the Impossibilities of Fiction." *Southern Literary Journal* 13.1 (1980): 3–31.

Gibson, Brent. "*Cold Mountain* as Spiritual Quest: Inman's Redemptive Journey." *Christianity and Literature* 55.3 (2006): 415–33.

Gillespie, Diane, and Missy Dehn Kubitschek. "Who Cares? Women-Centered Psychology in *Sula*." *Toni Morrison's Fiction: Contemporary Criticism*. Ed. David L. Middleton. New York: Garland, 1997. 61–91. Garland Reference Library of the Humanities 1602; Critical Studies in Black Life and Culture 30.

Gingher, Marianne. *"Teen Angel" and Other Stories of Wayward Love*. New York: Atheneum, 1988.

Glasgow, Ellen. *Barren Ground*. Garden City, N.Y.: Doubleday, 1925.

———. *A Certain Measure: An Interpretation of Prose Fiction*. New York: Harcourt, Brace, 1938.

———. *The Woman Within: An Autobiography*. 1954. Ed. Pamela R. Mathews. Charlottesville: University of Virginia Press, 1994.

———. *The Miller of Old Church*. Garden City, N.Y.: Doubleday, Page, 1911.

Godbold, E. Stanley, Jr. *Ellen Glasgow and the Woman Within*. Baton Rouge: Louisiana State University Press, 1972.

Grauke, Kevin. "Vietnam, Survivalism, and the Civil War: The Use of History in Michael Shaara's *The Killer Angels* and Charles Frazier's *Cold Mountain*." *War, Literature, and the Arts* 14.1–2: (2002): 45–58.

Guth, Deborah. "A Blessing and Burden: The Relation to the Past in *Sula, Song of Solomon,* and *Beloved*." *Modern Fiction Studies* 39 (1993): 575–95.

Hardy, John Edward. "Ellen Glasgow." *Southern Renascence: The Literature of the Modern South*. Ed. Louis D. Rubin Jr. and Robert D. Jacobs. Baltimore: Johns Hopkins University Press, 1953. 236–50.

Harrison, Elizabeth Jane. *Female Pastoral: Women Writers Re-visioning the American South*. Knoxville: University of Tennessee Press, 1991.

Harwell, Richard, ed. Gone with the Wind *as Book and Film*. 1983. New York: Paragon House, 1987.

———. *Margaret Mitchell's* Gone with the Wind *Letters, 1936–1949*. New York: Macmillan, 1986.

Haskell, Molly. *Frankly, My Dear:* Gone with the Wind *Revisited*. New Haven: Yale University Press, 2009.

Hawkins, Harriet. "Shared Dreams: Reproducing *Gone with the Wind*." *Novel Images: Literature in Performance*. Ed. Peter Reynolds. London: Routledge, 1993. 122–38.

———. "The Sins of Scarlett." *Textual Practice* 6.3 (1992): 491–96.

Heberlein, L. A. "Grace, Myth, and Invention: A Review of Three Novels." *North Carolina Literary Review* 17 (2008): 187–91.

Heilbrun, Carolyn G. *Writing a Woman's Life.* 1988. New York: Ballantine, 1989.

Hopkins, Jessie. Rev. of *Barren Ground. Atlanta Journal Magazine* May 3, 1925: 20.

Houston, Pam. "A Conversation with Toni Morrison." *O, The Oprah Magazine* July 2009.

Hunter, Brenda. *In the Company of Women.* 1984. Sisters, Ore.: Multnomah, 1994.

Inge, M. Thomas. "Charles Frazier—*Cold Mountain.*" *Still in Print: The Southern Novel Today.* Ed. Jan Nordby Gretlund. Columbia: University of South Carolina Press, 2010. 19–28.

Inscoe, John C. *Race, War, and Remembrance in the Appalachian South.* Lexington: University Press of Kentucky, 2008.

Jones, Anne Goodwyn. "*Gone with the Wind* and Others: Popular Fiction, 1920–1950." *The History of Southern Literature.* Ed. Louis D. Rubin Jr. et al. Baton Rouge: Louisiana State University Press, 1985. 363–74.

———. "'I was tellin it': Race, Gender, and the Puzzle of the Storyteller." *Southern Cultures* 5.1 (1999): 29–43.

———. *Tomorrow Is Another Day: The Woman Writer in the South, 1859–1936.* Baton Rouge: Louisiana State University Press, 1981.

Jones, Carolyn M. "*Sula* and *Beloved:* Images of Cain in the Novels of Toni Morrison." *African American Review* 27.4 (1993): 615–26.

Levin, Amy. "Matters of Canon: Reappraising *Gone with the Wind.*" *Proteus* 6.1 (1989): 32–36.

Lewis, Desiree. "Myths of Motherhood and Power: The Construction of 'Black Woman' in Literature." *English in Africa* 19.1 (1992): 35–51.

Lounsberry, Barbara, and Grace Ann Hovet. "Principles of Perception in Toni Morrison's *Sula.*" *Black American Literature Forum* 31.4 (1979): 126–29.

Lowry, Beverly. "A Book of Our Own." *Oxford American* January–February 1997: 86–90.

Maginnis, Hayden B. J. "The Trouble with Scarlett." *Queen's Quarterly* 102.3 (1995): 641–53.

Matthews, Pamela R. *Ellen Glasgow and a Woman's Traditions.* Charlottesville: University Press of Virginia, 1994.

Matza, Diane. "Zora Neale Hurston's *Their Eyes Were Watching God* and Toni Morrison's *Sula:* A Comparison." *MELUS* 12.3 (1985): 43–54.

Mayberry, Susan Neal. "Something Other Than a Family Quarrel: The Beautiful Boys in Morrison's *Sula.*" *African American Review* 37 (2003): 517–33.

McDowell, Frederick P. W. *Ellen Glasgow and the Ironic Art of Fiction.* Madison: University of Wisconsin Press, 1960.

Meads, Kat. *The Invented Life of Kitty Duncan (Benedict Roberts Duncan).* Portland, Ore.: Chiasmus, 2006.

Meindl, Dieter. "A Reappraisal of Margaret Mitchell's *Gone with the Wind.*" *Mississippi Quarterly* 34 (1981): 414–34.

Merola, Nicole M. "Reading (in) the Blue Ridge Mountains: The Bioregional Imperative of *Cold Mountain.*" *Reader* 53 (2005): 45–75.

Messud, Claire. "Tried in the Fire." Rev. of *Cold Mountain,* by Charles Frazier. *Washington Post Book World* July 6, 1997: 6.

Middleton, Victoria. "Sula: An Experimental Life." *CLAJ* 28.4 (1985): 367–81.

Miller, Danny L. *Wingless Flights: Appalachian Women in Fiction.* Bowling Green, Ohio: Bowling Green State University Popular Press, 1996.

Miner, Madonne M. *Insatiable Appetites: Twentieth-Century American Women's Bestsellers.* Westport, Conn.: Greenwood, 1984. Contributions in Women's Studies 48.

Mitchell, Margaret. *Gone with the Wind.* New York: Macmillan, 1936.

Morrison, Toni. *Sula.* New York: Knopf, 1973.

Munro, C. Lynn. "The Tattooed Heart and the Serpentine Eye: Morrison's Choice of an Epigraph for *Sula.*" *Black American Literature Forum* 18.4 (1984): 150–54.

O'Connor, Flannery. *A Good Man Is Hard to Find.* San Diego: Harcourt, Brace, 1955.

Oleksy, Elzbieta. "The Keepers of the House: Scarlett O'Hara and Abigail Howland." *Louisiana Women Writers: New Essays and a Comprehensive Bibliography.* Ed. Dorothy H. Brown and Barbara C. Ewell. Baton Rouge: Louisiana State University Press, 1992. 169–82.

Pauly, Thomas H. "*Gone with the Wind* and *The Grapes of Wrath* as Hollywood Histories of the Depression." Harwell, Gone with the Wind, 218–28.

Pickrel, Paul. "*Vanity Fair* in America: *The House of Mirth* and *Gone with the Wind.*" *American Literature* 59 (1987): 37–57.

Pierpont, Claudia Roth. "A Critic at Large: A Study in Scarlett." *New Yorker* August 31, 1992: 87–103.

Polk, James. "American Odyssey." Rev. of *Cold Mountain,* by Charles Frazier. *New York Times Book Review* July 13, 1997: 14.

Pyron, Darden Asbury. "*Gone with the Wind* and the Southern Cultural Awakening." *Virginia Quarterly Review* 62 (1986): 565–87.

———. *Southern Daughter: The Life of Margaret Mitchell.* New York: Oxford University Press, 1991.

———, ed. *Recasting:* Gone with the Wind *in American Culture.* Miami: University Presses of Florida, 1983.

Rand, Lizabeth A. "'We all that's left': Identity Formation and the Relationship between Eva and Sula Peace." *CLA Journal* 44 (2001): 341–49.

Raper, Julius Rowan, ed. *Ellen Glasgow's Reasonable Doubts: A Collection of Her Writings.* Baton Rouge: Louisiana State University Press, 1988.

Rubin, Louis D., Jr. *No Place on Earth: Ellen Glasgow, James Branch Cabell, and Richmond-in-Virginia.* Austin: University of Texas Press, 1959.

———. "Scarlett O'Hara and the Two Quentin Compsons." 1977. Rpt. in Pyron, *Recasting*, 81–103.

Schefski, Harold K. "Margaret Mitchell: *Gone with the Wind* and *War and Peace*." Harwell, *Gone with the Wind*. 229–43.

Schmidt, Jan Zlotnik. "Ellen Glasgow's Heroic Legends: A Study of *Life and Gabriella, Barren Ground*, and *Vein of Iron*." *Tennessee Studies in Literature* 26 (1981): 117–41.

Schramm, Margaret. "The Quest for the Perfect Mother in Toni Morrison's *Sula*." *The Anna Book: Searching for Anna in Literary History*. Ed. Mickey Pearlman. New York: Greenwood, 1992. 167–76.

Seidel, Kathryn Lee. *The Southern Belle in the American Novel*. Tampa: University of South Florida Press, 1985.

Shannon, Anna. "'We was girls together': A Study of Toni Morrison's *Sula*." *Midwestern Miscellany* 10 (1982): 9–22.

Smyth, J. E. "Classical Hollywood and the Filmic Writing of Interracial History, 1931–39." *Mixed Race Hollywood*. Ed. Mary Beltrán and Camilla Fojas. New York: New York University Press, 2008. 23–41.

SSSL. "Reading *Gone with the Wind* after 75 Years: An Interview with Margaret D. Bauer." *Society for the Study of Southern Literature Newsletter* 45.2 (2011).

Tate, Allen. "The New Provincialism." *Virginia Quarterly Review* 21.2 (1945): 262–72.

Taylor, Helen. "*Gone with the Wind:* The Mammy of Them All." *The Progress of Romance: The Politics of Popular Fiction*. Ed. Jean Radford. New York: Routledge, 1986. 113–36. History Workshop Series.

———. *Scarlett's Women:* Gone with the Wind *and Its Female Fans*. New Brunswick: Rutgers University Press, 1989.

Taylor-Guthrie, Danille, ed. *Conversations with Toni Morrison*. Jackson: University Press of Mississippi, 1994. Literary Conversations.

Thompson, Carlyle V. "'Circles and Circles of Sorrow': Decapitation in Toni Morrison's *Sula*." *CLA Journal* 47 (2003): 137–74.

Wagner[-Martin], Linda W. "*Barren Ground*'s Vein of Iron: Dorinda Oakley and Some Concepts of the Heroine in 1925." *Mississippi Quarterly* 32 (1979): 553–64.

———. *Ellen Glasgow: Beyond Convention*. Austin: University of Texas Press, 1982.

Wagner-Martin, Linda. "The South as Universe." *South to the Future: An American Region in the Twenty-First Century*. Ed. Fred Hobson. Athens: University of Georgia Press, 2002. 25–55. Mercer University Lamar Memorial Lectures 44.

Walker, Alice. *In Search of Our Mothers' Gardens*. San Diego: Harcourt, Brace, Jovanovich, 1983.

Warren, Craig A. *Scars to Prove It: The Civil War Soldier and American Fiction*. Kent, Ohio: Kent State University Press, 2009.

Weems, Renita. "'Artists without Art Form: A Look at One Black Woman's World of Unrevered Black Women." *Home Girls: A Black Feminist Anthology.* Ed. Barbara Smith. New York: Kitchen Table: Women of Color Press, 1983. 94–105.

Wilson, Michael. "Affirming Characters, Communities, and Change: Dialogism in Toni Morrison's *Sula. Midwestern Miscellany* 24 (1986): 24–36.

Winniford, Lee. "Suppressing the Masculine Metanarrative: The Uncaging of Glasgow's *Barren Ground.*" *Journal of Narrative Theory* 24.2 (1994): 141–52.

Wood, Gerald. "From *The Clansman* and *Birth of a Nation* to *Gone with the Wind:* The Loss of American Innocence." Pyron, *Recasting,* 123–36.

Wurtzel, Elizabeth. *Bitch: In Praise of Difficult Women.* New York: Random House, 1998.

Index

About the Author

Louisiana native MARGARET D. BAUER is the Ralph Hardee Rives Chair of Southern Literature at East Carolina University in Greenville, North Carolina, where she was named one of ECU's ten Women of Distinction in 2007 and received the university's Lifetime Achievement Award for Research and Creative Activity in 2014. She is the author of *The Fiction of Ellen Gilchrist*, *William Faulkner's Legacy: "what shadow, what stain, what mark,"* and *Understanding Tim Gautreaux*.

TAROT HALLOWEEN

Cómo levantar el velo entre los mundos *todas las noches*

STACEY DEMARCO

Grupo Editorial Tomo, S. A. de C. V.
Nicolás San Juan 1043
03100, México, D. F.

1a. edición, noviembre 2015.

Nicolás San Juan 1043, Col. Del Valle
03100 México, D. F.
Tels. 5575-6615, 5575-8701 y 5575-0186 Fax. 5575-6695.
www.grupotomo.com.mx
ISBN-13: 978-607-415-757-4
Miembro de la Cámara Nacional
de la Industria Editorial No. 2961

Traducción: Graciela Frisbie
Formación tipográfica: Armando Hernández
Diseño de portada: Karla Silva
Supervisor de producción: Leonardo Figueroa

Este libro se publicó conforme al contrato establecido entre *Blue Angel Gallery PTY.* y *Grupo Editorial Tomo, S. A. de C. V.*

Impreso en México - *Printed in Mexico*

CONTENIDO

Las cartas

Truco o trato, verdad u osadía: algunos datos sobre la noche más aterradora del año

Cada vez son más las personas alrededor del mundo que están liberando su "monstruo" interior y están celebrando la fiesta de terror, o de Halloween, cada año. Aunque algunos países, como Estados Unidos y México, de hecho tienen esta celebración bien establecida en su calendario anual, otros países apenas están empezando a adoptar la costumbre de hacer lámparas de calabaza y de salir a pedir regalos con "truco o trato".

Yo vivo en Australia, donde Halloween se está popularizando cada vez más cada año, algo que personalmente me fascina. Yo soy pagano y soy brujo, así que creo que este festival tan antiguo ofrece mucho a las comunidades. En la época de Halloween adorno el porche y la terraza con esqueletos (¡al parecer salen de los armarios!) y los niños vecinos siempre me preguntan qué les voy a regalar. Esta es la época en que la gente parece reírse del miedo a las brujas (que siempre es infundado), y al menos en mi vecindario, a los niños y a los adultos les entusiasma tener una bruja de verdad.

La muerte es, en cierta forma, el último tabú en nuestra sociedad occidental. No experimentamos la muerte como solíamos hacerlo. Tenemos hospitales donde mueren las personas; no "preparamos" ni honramos los cuerpos de nuestros muertos en familia como lo hacíamos antes, y la mayoría de las personas no mueren en casa. Tenemos la tendencia a temer aquello que no conocemos. Halloween es una época en la que podemos hablar del tema de la muerte, podemos reírnos de la muerte e incluso hablar con mayor libertad de las personas que han muerto; también podemos examinar nuestros miedos a cosas más macabras. Esto es positivo.

Aunque creo que la creciente popularidad de Halloween, que se ha considerado ante todo una festividad estadunidense, y que tiene algo que ver con la energía del azúcar que se consume en todas las golosinas que se regalan, en realidad tiene orígenes paganos muy antiguos sobre los que la mayoría de la gente sabe muy poco.

Halloween (o la víspera del Día de Todos los Santos) fue tradicionalmente un festival celta conocido como *Samhain* (se pronuncia so-en) que señalaba el inicio de la época del frío y el proceso a través del cual la tierra empieza a retirarse y a "morir". Por eso, el tema central de esta "fiesta" es en esencia la muerte, pero si la vemos desde una perspectiva más positiva, también podría verse como el inicio silencioso de la vida.

La muerte es parte de la vida y es el paso que damos antes de la renovación. Tener una celebración relacionada con la muerte, abordándola con ligereza y con risa, nos ayuda a ver que no hay mucho que temer. Cuando hacemos lámparas de calabaza ahuyentamos a los espíritus "negativos" y al mismo tiempo reconocemos la presencia de las tinieblas. Al entrar a lo profundo de la noche, podemos ver el amanecer con más claridad.

Otros países, como México, celebran el Día de Muertos, que ahora se ha entretejido con muchas tradiciones de Halloween e incluyen obras de arte espectaculares, calaveras de dulce e incluso días de campo en los cementerios para honrar a los antepasados.

Por tradición, se cree que Halloween también es la época donde los muros que dividen el mundo espiritual y el mundo físico son más delgados. Esto nos da una buena oportunidad para honrar a nuestros amigos y a nuestros ancestros que han pasado a mejor vida, y podemos contar anécdotas y volver a vivir historias maravillosas sobre ellos. Festejamos su vida con risas, con comida y diversión. Ciertamente no es una época de tristeza, sino una época para celebrar la vida con entusiasmo.

El hecho de que los muros que dividen el mundo espiritual y el mundo físico sean más delgados en estas fechas, hace que gente de todo el mundo desee usar una variedad de herramientas para la adivinación, métodos para tener una visión fugaz de su futuro o recibir algunos mensajes llenos de sabiduría del más allá. Muchas personas podrían usar un péndulo, consultar una bola de cristal o usar una baraja. Lo que inspiró esta baraja fue una noche de "truco o trato" y de adivinación profunda en mi hogar. Yo quería crear una baraja que honrara todos los aspectos de la experiencia del *Samhain*, los antiguos y los más modernos, para ofrecer a quienes deseen tener una experiencia de Halloween más profunda, algo hermoso y eficaz con lo cual trabajar.

Ahora, un último dato para aquellos que, como yo, viven en el hemisferio sur: muchos hechiceros y paganos que viven en esta región no celebran Halloween el 31 de octubre. ¿Por qué? ¡Porque no es el momento adecuado en relación con las estaciones! En el hemisferio sur, a finales de octubre nuestro mundo está floreciendo, germinando, y lleno de vida… lo que ciertamente no tiene nada que ver con la muerte; ¡estamos en primavera!

Por su parte, quienes siguen la rueda del año celebran el festival opuesto, el Beltaine, una fiesta primaveral relacionada con la creación y el renacer a finales de octubre. De este modo, para nosotros, Halloween se celebra en el otoño, el 30 de abril, la fecha en que el Beltaine se celebra en el hemisferio norte. Sin embargo, la mayoría de las personas siguen la tradición de "truco o trato" el 31 de octubre.

¿Qué hago yo? ¡Un poco de ambas tradiciones! Los niños de mi calle siempre disfrutan disfrazarse e ir de puerta en puerta con la tradición de "truco o trato", así que no puedo desilusionarlos. Siempre hay adornos aterradores en mi casa ¡y hay dulces para darles a los niños que tocan a la puerta! Pero en privado, yo estoy celebrando el Beltaine.

Sin importar cuándo prefieras celebrar este atrevido festival de la muerte, disfrútalo y date cuenta de que algunos de los rituales y símbolos de esta noche, la más aterradora de todas, son muy antiguos. Miles de personas antes que tú, durante miles de años, han iluminado la noche con antorchas, bajo la luz de la luna; han sentido miedo en el cementerio local; han hecho bromas a sus amigos y les han pedido a los espíritus que les revelen algo de su futuro.

Cómo usar esta baraja

En vista de que el arte de la adivinación es tan común en esta noche, permíteme recomendarte algunas formas de usar esta baraja.

La adivinación con una sola carta, que aparece a continuación, es perfecta cuando necesitas una respuesta rápida a una pregunta o una guía breve para tu día. La tirada de tres cartas de Halloween y la adivinación de la lámpara de calabaza son tiradas que se recomiendan para una adivinación más compleja: proporcionan una visión más profunda y completa de tu situación.

Adivinación con una sola carta

Esta es una forma maravillosa de obtener una respuesta clara y rápida a una pregunta específica o de obtener el elemento de sabiduría más importante que necesitas conocer y seguir. Es inspiración y adivinación en su forma más simple. Respira profundamente, pide orientación mientras barajas las cartas y simplemente elige una carta. Incluso podrías decidir hacer esto todos los días, como lo hacían algunas personas en la antigüedad.

Medita en la imagen o en el concepto de la carta… permite que te hable. Piensa en la acción que puedes llevar a cabo para expresar de manera más profunda este dato de conocimiento a lo largo de tu vida.

También puedes desplegar las cartas en una fila y usar un péndulo para que elija una carta por ti.

El péndulo puede ser de cristal, de metal o simplemente puede hacerse con una piedra pequeña y un cordón. Lo suspendes de tu dedo y permites que gire libremente sobre todas las cartas. Cuando sientas que el péndulo reacciona, podría saltar o girar más rápido sobre una carta, elige esa carta.

Tirada de tres cartas de Halloween

El ciclo triple; nacimiento, muerte y renacimiento, es muy importante cuando uno se conecta con Halloween. Honramos este paradigma con esta tirada. Además, como Halloween está muy relacionado con la luna y la noche, en forma simbólica, tal vez te gustaría intentar consultar esta tirada cuando aparece la luna o a la medianoche.

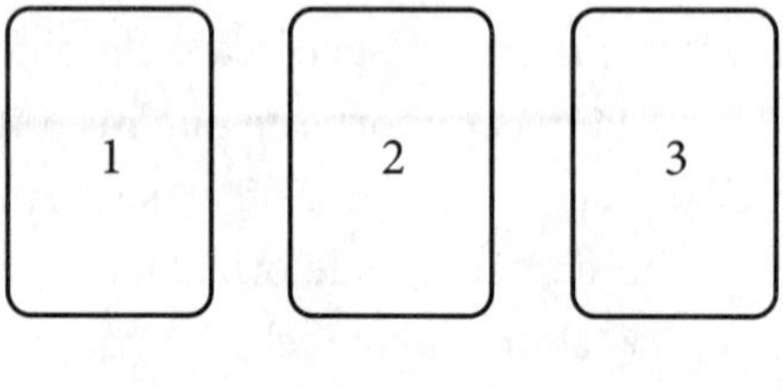

Carta 1: El corazón del tema o cuestión

Carta 2: El desafío

Carta 3: La solución

La adivinación de la lámpara de calabaza

Esta es una tirada que ofrece mucha protección e iluminación. Saca seis cartas.

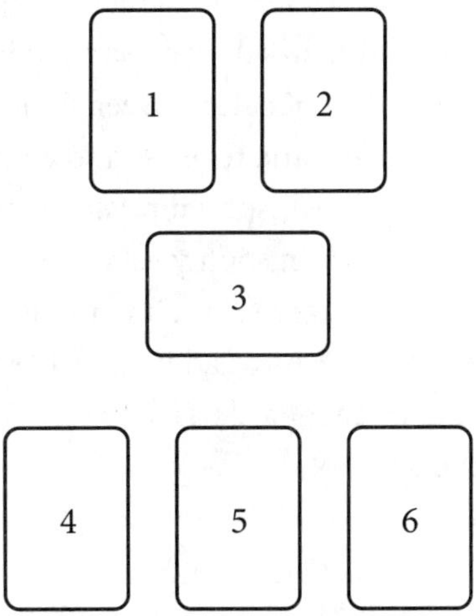

(Se ven como los ojos, la nariz y los dientes de la aterradora lámpara de calabaza).

Carta 1: El corazón del tema o cuestión
Carta 2: El tema oculto
Carta 3: El mayor obstáculo
Carta 4: El miedo principal
Carta 5: La solución
Carta 6: Qué pasará si usas la solución

Recuerda que sin importar qué tirada decidas usar, debes tomar nota de la información que reúnas y recibas poniéndola por escrito. A menudo se trata de mensajes que te llegan del otro lado, ¡así que conviene ponerlos en acción tan pronto como sea posible!

¡Por supuesto, puedes usar la baraja en cualquier época del año que desees! Además de ser una festividad que se celebra en una noche de otoño, Halloween tiene cierta energía espiritual a la que te gustaría tener acceso en diferentes momentos. Esta energía es especialmente poderosa para la transformación y la adivinación y estas cartas pueden ayudarte a ponerte en contacto y recibir mensajes de personas que ya están en el otro lado. ¡Esta baraja te permite captar y cultivar la energía de Halloween cualquier día y cualquier noche del año!

Cómo dedicar las cartas

A muchas personas les gusta dedicar sus cartas y personalizarlas. Permíteme sugerir la siguiente forma de dedicarlas...

Dedicación para tus cartas:

Si puedes, sal de la casa. ¡Esto puede hacerse a la orilla del mar, en la tierra o en el cielo, en las alturas! O puedes elegir un lugar que te guste dentro de tu casa para hacer la dedicación.

Necesitas:

- Hojas de laurel/salvia/incienso para quemarlos
- Sal, de preferencia sal de mar
- Una vela plateada

Quema las hojas de laurel, la salvia o el incienso, o las tres cosas hasta que produzcan un humo fragante.

Echa un poco de sal sobre la baraja.

Di: "Yo limpio, yo renuevo, yo protejo".

Luego enciende la vela plateada y di:

> "Pido al poder de los elementos y
> de las estaciones
> que me bendigan y bendigan estas
> cartas.
> Pido orientación y verdad,
> despertar y claridad,
> y la fuerza y el valor
> para hacer cambios si necesito
> hacerlos".

Ahora pasa la baraja por el humo de las hierbas, diciendo:

> "Dedico estas cartas al mayor bien.
> Que aquí solo entre el bien. Que
> solo hablen a través de estas cartas
> energías benevolentes y verdaderas.
> ¡Que así sea!".

Ahora, si lo deseas, puedes realizar tu primera adivinación, sabiendo que las energías positivas han escuchado tu dedicación y van a responder a ella.

LAS CARTAS

ANCESTROS

El amor y el legado de nuestro ADN

Yo sigo sus huellas
su sabiduría permanece en mi interior
yo soy único, y sin embargo llevo un legado
su sangre corre por mis venas.

Ya sea que conozcamos o no a nuestros ancestros, somos el producto de quienes vivieron antes que nosotros, en lo que concierne al ADN. Externamente, tal vez tengamos el tipo de cuerpo de nuestro padre, los ojos de nuestra madre, la nariz de nuestra abuela, el color de piel de nuestro abuelo.

En el interior, esto se vuelve más interesante. Ahora sabemos que podemos "heredar" la forma en que funciona nuestro cuerpo, el tipo de sangre, los trastornos genéticos, incluso tendencias o propensiones relacionadas con la función cerebral, como la introversión, el talento musical o el talento para las matemáticas.

Muchos senderos paganos relacionados con Halloween creen que nacemos perfectamente imperfectos para ser exactamente lo que se supone que debemos ser. ¿Qué significa esto? Significa que los dones que nos dejaron nuestros ancestros y la sinergia única de la combinación de lo físico y lo mental que se crea en nuestro interior, nos prepara a la perfección para alcanzar nuestro propósito final.

Si sacas la carta de los ancestros debes saber que estás listo para poner en acción tu derecho natural al poder, y eres capaz de hacerlo. Cuentas con el apoyo de quienes te antecedieron. Tal vez haya retos o conflictos, pero tienes todo lo que necesitas para superarlos. ¡Prevalecerás!

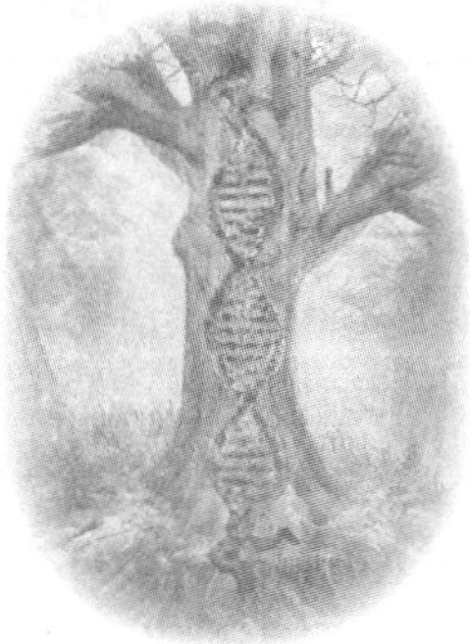

MANZANA

Riesgo y recompensa

El ícono más dulce
deseo de riesgo rojo
veneno y libertad
tentación para los corazones ardientes.

Las manzanas han sido un símbolo de *Samhain*[1] durante mucho tiempo. Una manzana partida por la mitad tiene un patrón de semillas que es similar a un pentagrama, así que los celtas consideraban que era un fruto sagrado. Morder la manzana, una actividad que por tradición se lleva a cabo en Halloween, tiene su origen en el festival *Samhain* y es uno de los juegos más antiguos que se relacionan con esta celebración.

[1] Consultar la Introducción para tener información sobre este festival invernal celta, a partir del cual se originó Halloween.

La forma tradicional de jugarlo consiste en colocar 3 o 13 manzanas en un barril lleno de agua y tratar de morder una de ellas mientras está flotando y se mueve de arriba abajo. No deben usarse las manos y las personas a menudo compiten entre sí para lograr morder una manzana al mismo tiempo. Se cree que los romanos llevaron esta costumbre a Inglaterra y existen muchas imágenes en obras de arte de estas actividades en ambas culturas. Se decía que si una mujer soltera colocaba una manzana que había mordido en este juego bajo su almohada, soñaba con su futuro esposo. En Terranova y en algunas partes de Irlanda, incluso hoy en día, Halloween se conoce como *Snap Apple Night [la noche de la mordida de la manzana]*.

Aunque las manzanas de caramelo (tienen un palillo en el centro y están recubiertas de caramelo), no son tan famosas ahora como lo eran antes en la celebración de Halloween, están volviendo a popularizarse como algo sabroso y divertido que puede prepararse esta noche.

Las manzanas han sido una parte icónica de las creencias culturales de los pueblos desde la antigüedad hasta nuestros días; por ejemplo, la manzana envenenada de Blanca Nieves, el árbol mágico de manzanas de la diosa romana Pomona, y el fruto prohibido en el Jardín del Edén en el cristianismo. Si aparece esta "manzana" en tu tirada ha llegado el momento de ver el papel que juegan los riesgos en tu vida. ¿Estás eludiendo tus riesgos o no estás intentando hacer nada nuevo? ¿Deseas el cambio pero no estás dispuesto a modificar nada? ¿Estás dispuesto a arriesgar para obtener una recompensa mayor? O de lo contrario, ¿estás arriesgando demasiado, o con demasiada frecuencia?

PAN BARMBRACK

Dulzura y sinergia

Un guisante, una tela, una moneda, un anillo
y una vara,
dentro de una hogaza de dulzura moteada,
rebánala y cómetela.
Vislumbrar la totalidad de mi destino.

No es precisamente un pastel y no es precisamente un pan. El *barmbrack* es una hogaza dulce, más grande que una hogaza tradicional de pan; se hornea con harina, azúcar, sal y frutas secas, como las uvas pasas. Hornear el *barmbrack* es una tradición irlandesa durante la época del *Samhain* (Halloween). La persona que hornea este pan debe asegurarse de tener la intención del amor, la verdad y la sinergia mientras lo prepara. Se ocultan en la masa de este pan algunos objetos especiales antes de hornearlo.

Los objetos se usan como una especie de oráculo al azar; cada uno tiene un significado especial, ya que representa el destino de la persona que lo encontró en su rebanada de pan. Los objetos tradicionales son una moneda, un guisante (chícharo), una varita, un anillo y un trocito de tela, por ejemplo, una muselina. En tiempos más modernos se han añadido otros objetos, como medallas religiosas.

Si tu rebanada de este pan tenía una moneda, eso indicaba prosperidad y buena suerte. Por otra parte, el guisante o chícharo significaba que no te casarías ese año, pero si encontrabas un anillo, eso quería decir que seguramente te ibas a casar. La varita, que debía evitarse a toda costa, indicaba disputas y desdicha, mientras que encontrar la tela significaba mala suerte y poco dinero en el futuro.

Sacar la carta del *barmbrack*, revela curiosidad por saber el futuro, pero es importante equilibrar eso con el ahora... después de todo, tenemos las herramientas que necesitamos para cambiar nuestro futuro si queremos hacerlo. La dulce sinergia del *barmbrack* se basa en que todos los ingredientes, incluyendo los objetos, están más completos y son más poderosos estando juntos que en su forma individual, así que esto debería animarte a buscar tu propio “punto dulce”.

GATO NEGRO

La fortuna se encuentra con la oportunidad

Elegante, negro y con ojos de linterna,
se cruza en tu camino bufando.
Buena suerte y fortuna
pasan junto a ti con un beso.

En la tradición popular, se decía que los gatos tenían una pata en este mundo y la otra en el siguiente. Eran un conducto entre el inframundo y este mundo, y entre la fortuna y la oportunidad.

En tiempos de la Inquisición (la Edad Media), se cazaba a los gatos porque se decía que eran aliados de entidades malignas como los demonios y las brujas. Como el negro se relacionaba con los aspectos más oscuros de lo sobrenatural, se señalaba especialmente a los gatos negros. Los historiadores creen que esta matanza sin precedentes de gatos con el fin de erradicar el mal, llevó a un incremento desenfrenado de ratas, y eso a su vez fue la causa de la propagación alarmantemente rápida de la peste bubónica y de la muerte de millones de personas.

Actualmente, por ejemplo, en Alemania, que un gato negro se cruce en tu camino significa mala fortuna inminente. Sin embargo, en la antigua Bretaña se consideraba que los gatos negros eran de buena suerte y se daban como regalo a las novias en el día de su boda. En Japón, incluso hoy en día, se cree que son señal de grandes dichas y que atraen fortunas.

Si un elegante gato negro se cruza en tu camino al usar este oráculo, debes saber que la buena suerte y la fortuna llegarán a ti pronto. También debes saber que tu buena suerte será aún "mejor" si estás preparado para aprovechar cada oportunidad especial que se cruce en tu camino.

CALDERO

Sinergia y sanación

Donde todas las cosas se juntan
bajo presión, fluye la sinergia.
Se crea algo nuevo
un crisol de infinitud.

Una forma tradicional de representar a una bruja es ponerla de pie junto a un caldero hirviendo mientras mueve lentamente su misterioso contenido burbujeante. Cuando ella mueve el enorme caldero de metal que está sobre las flamas, se ríe a carcajadas y lanza encantamientos a todos los elementos, transformando el contenido del caldero en algo mágico.

En la antigüedad y en el medievo, los calderos se usaban comúnmente para preparar todo tipo de cosas, desde cocinar para la cena hasta preparar medicamentos. Este "crisol familiar" por lo general se colocaba en la chimenea de la casa y era parte esencial de las reuniones familiares. Mucha sanación y nutrimento venía de estos calderos.

Sacar la carta del caldero te revela la importancia de combinar una variedad de técnicas o elementos para tener los mejores resultados. No pongas todos tus huevos en la misma canasta. Niégate a elegir un solo camino rígido cuando existe una gran variedad de rutas que pueden disfrutarse y experimentarse. Puedes encontrar tu propia forma de crear algo nuevo. El caldero es una herramienta con la que se logran transformaciones profundas; las cosas cambian cuando se ponen bajo presión. La resistencia se cultiva con el tiempo y esto significa que podrás soportar cualquier presión negativa en forma mucho más sana de adentro hacia fuera.

AMANECER

La luz después de las tinieblas

Después de los momentos más oscuros
siempre saldrá el sol.
La aurora siempre llegará,
no puede ser una sorpresa.

Aunque a menudo se piensa que la medianoche es una hora mágica, a través del tiempo el amanecer también ha conservado algo místico. Todo tipo de seres mágicos tenían que volver a su forma natural al amanecer (por ejemplo, los hombres lobo y los vampiros solo podían estar activos mientras los rayos del sol no cruzaran el firmamento).

El amanecer y las deidades del amanecer eran heraldos de la esperanza y de la vida nueva. Diosas como Ostara y dioses como Helio y Apolo traían vida nueva y traían la luz del amanecer al mundo. El trayecto desde la noche más oscura del alma hacia un amanecer brillante y lleno de esperanza es uno de los caminos más profundos y más poderosos que han seguido los héroes de la mitología una y otra vez.

Si sacas la carta del amanecer, se te está recordando que siempre puedes tener un nuevo comienzo, un nuevo principio. El cambio es imparable y hasta los momentos más difíciles van a pasar, sin importar lo devastadores que puedan parecer. La esperanza es una de las fuerzas motivadoras más poderosas que existen en el universo, y está presente aquí.

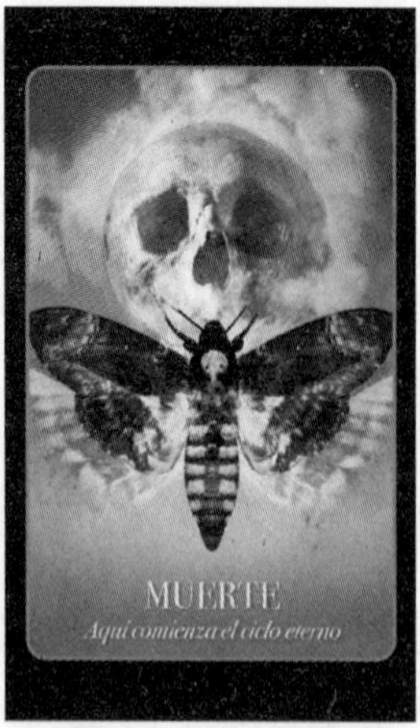

MUERTE

Aquí comienza el ciclo eterno

No es el final,
aunque yo pase en la noche
tengo la oportunidad de volver a vivir
¡aunque eso te cause miedo!

Muchos paganos creían que la muerte era el principio del ciclo de la vida. Cuando piensas en eso, la mayoría de las personas consideran que el hecho de "nacer" es el principio del ciclo de la vida; nacemos, vivimos y morimos, y dependiendo de nuestras creencias podríamos volver a vivir. Por su parte, las culturas paganas ven la muerte como el principio de toda una aventura nueva; el lugar donde el alma puede elegir dónde va a reencarnar, por qué va a hacerlo y qué desea experimentar. Entonces, y solo entonces, nace en un cuerpo que vive y a la larga muere, antes de regresar en un ciclo nuevo.

Halloween es una celebración de la muerte como parte de la vida. Como los seres humanos somos seres conscientes, tenemos conocimiento de la muerte y muchas personas se sienten temerosas e incómodas al respecto. Halloween ilumina la verdad universal de que todos vamos a morir, así como todos nacimos. Por lo tanto, temer ese proceso final no tiene sentido. Halloween nos pide que cultivemos la amistad con la muerte (así como al parecer cultivamos la amistad con el nacimiento) y que no permitamos que nuestros miedos y nuestro dolor nos causen un sufrimiento innecesario.

No tengas miedo si sacas la carta de la muerte, ya que simplemente significa que algo se está alejando, o se va a alejar, de modo que puedas empezar de nuevo con fuerza. Existe un gran poder en esta experiencia. Si sacas esta carta específicamente en Halloween, el mensaje es más fuerte todavía y deberías celebrar este nuevo inicio en forma activa.

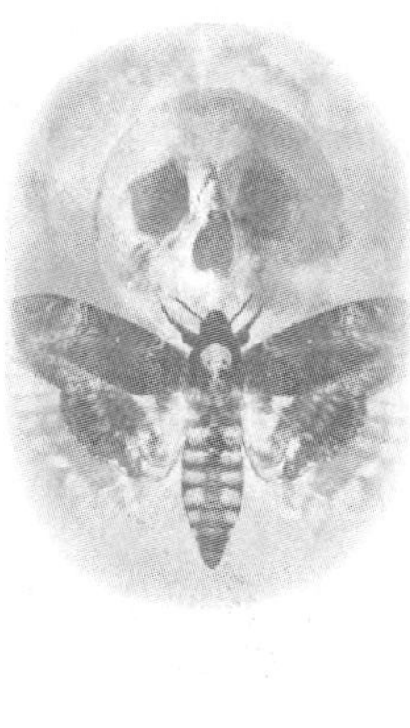

AMOR ETERNO

El amor es amor y trasciende la muerte física

Cuando el cuerpo nos deja
y nuestras almas están arriba
nuestras posesiones ya no están.
Nada permanece
excepto el entrelazarse del amor.

Todos nosotros somos el producto de milenios de amor. Los padres de los padres de nuestros padres; nuestros ancestros por la sangre y por rituales; todos de alguna manera crearon el ADN que está presente en nuestros cuerpos.

El amor, de hecho, da poder a la vida y a la muerte.

Cuando la mayoría de las personas encuentran la muerte por primera vez en su vida, también experimentan dolor y, en cierta forma, ese sentimiento podría describirse como una ausencia de amor y la ausencia de la persona o el ser que se ha ido. Pero la clase de amor que a menudo comparten los miembros de una familia, los amigos y los amantes, al estar separados solo por la muerte física, es la clase de amor que llena a los poetas de lirismo; es un amor eterno y trasciende a la muerte.

Si te toca esta carta, se te está recordando que el amor es la fuerza más poderosa del universo. Es más poderoso que la muerte en sí. El amor permanece. Deja su propio legado y debemos estar conscientes de esto todos los días de nuestra vida. Para aquellos que están listos para tener una pareja y desean tenerla, esta carta también indica que un amor significativo está cerca y que deben estar listos para abrirse a esta nueva experiencia.

PERDÓN

Reducir la carga

Se causa un mal,
hay consecuencias que no puedes negar,
pero estar resentido es como tomar veneno
y pensar que la otra persona
va a morir.

Como Halloween es un festival de una estación fría, es la época perfecta para hacer una pausa y pensar en cómo son las cosas realmente en nuestra vida y en cuáles cargas pesadas no queremos seguir llevando en estos tiempos difíciles y austeros. Parte de este pesar podría tener que ver con relaciones o agravios del pasado, o podría relacionarse con sentimientos negativos hacia otros a los que nos aferramos con fuerza, e incluso con una falta de compasión por "errores" que nosotros mismos hemos cometido.

Se dice que "se necesita ser una gran persona para pedir perdón" pero en muchos aspectos se necesita ser una persona aún más grande para perdonar. Cuando sentimos rencores, la energía negativa es increíblemente tóxica. Es como tomar veneno y esperar que muera la "otra" persona, ¡la que no ha recibido el perdón! Aunque podríamos incluso tener deseos de venganza (y para ser honesto, eso hace que nos sintamos bien durante un rato), es importante que cambiemos esas emociones y seamos capaces de perdonar para poder liberarnos de todo sentimiento de venganza tan pronto como sea posible, lo que es favorable para nuestra salud y bienestar.

Si sacas esta carta, piensa en alguien a quien podrías perdonar... y eso te incluye a ti mismo.

FANTASMA

Arrepentimiento

Como el humo que brota de las cenizas,
como neblina del mar,
los muertos están vigilando,
han venido a acosarme.

La definición tradicional de fantasma es la aparición del espíritu o el alma de un ser que antes era un ser viviente. Los fantasmas pueden tener forma humana, forma animal e incluso en ocasiones forma de objetos inanimados, como los barcos fantasma que se han visto, según los informes recibidos. La creencia en espíritus y fantasmas ha estado ampliamente presente a lo largo del tiempo en diversas culturas, y se han usado diferentes palabras para describirlos; por ejemplo, espíritus, espectros, fantasmas y sombras.

Los fantasmas pueden ser personas que hemos conocido (por ejemplo, nuestros ancestros) que nos visitan para ayudarnos, o presencias que están atadas a un lugar específico porque se les ha dificultado desprenderse de él incluso después de la muerte. El concepto de una casa embrujada o de un lugar "maldito" es el fundamento de muchas historias de fantasmas aterradoras. De hecho, las historias de fantasmas más interesantes a menudo incluyen un espíritu muy iracundo o destructivo que regresa a vengarse después de la muerte. (En el idioma nórdico antiguo, la palabra para "fantasma" tiene la misma raíz que la palabra "furia").

Se dice que los espíritus que no pueden desprenderse de este mundo tienen una razón para ello. En ocasiones es para prevenir a los seres vivos o guiarlos, pero en general es porque no han terminado su "tarea" aquí en el plano de los vivos. Tienen remordimientos que desean resolver.

Si el fantasma se desliza en tu vida durante la adivinación, eso podría indicar que hay cosas que te afligen y de las cuales debes desprenderte. Sentir rencores o lamentar cosas es una carga y a la larga nos agobia. Al llevar a cabo acciones para liberarnos de estas viejas cargas, dejamos libre el camino para acciones más rectas y sabias en el futuro. Podemos empezar a vivir de nuevo con plenitud si nos desprendemos de las cosas del pasado y avanzamos hacia nuevas posibilidades.

CEMENTERIO

Miedo innecesario

Las piedras marcan
el lugar del descanso eterno,
pero los espíritus caminan
¡y están listos para acosar!

Hoy en día, los cementerios modernos son lugares de descanso; normalmente están muy bien arreglados y planificados. Aunque pueden ser lugares profundamente tristes, pocos cementerios son como los antiguos, que eran aterradores y de ambiente gótico; no obstante, conservan un aire tenebroso y son sitios que inspiran miedo.

Debido a las incontables historias sobre cementerios donde se aparecen fantasmas, la idea de caminar por uno de ellos provoca temor en muchos de nosotros; imaginamos que zombis y fantasmas salen de los sepulcros y espíritus malignos se ocultan detrás de las tumbas esperando dañar a un ser viviente ingenuo que pase por ahí. La idea de estar en un cementerio después del anochecer, o lo que es peor, a medianoche, es tema de desafíos y de pesadillas.

Pero esto no es igual en todas las culturas. En el Día de Muertos, en México, familias enteras se reúnen a comer junto a las tumbas de sus seres queridos; la gente toca música, toma vino y comparte alimentos en "compañía de los muertos". El polvo del cementerio se usa como un ingrediente de hechizos protectores, y no para maleficios.

Si sacas esta carta, sabrás que tienes miedos infundados. Las cosas no son lo que parecen y tú podrás vencer los obstáculos que estás enfrentando. Las ansiedades que tienes, aunque son reales, deben hacerse a un lado antes de que lleguen a ser un acoso constante para ti. Lo que debes hacer es confiar en que sabes cuáles son los siguientes pasos que debes dar y que los darás.

CHIMENEA

Felicidad en nuestros corazones y en nuestros hogares

El corazón de cada hogar,
el fuego que une,
el centro de calor durante el invierno,
historias, amor y delicias.

Los romanos de la antigüedad creían que cada hogar tenía un corazón y que ese corazón era la chimenea. La familia se reunía alrededor del fuego para su sustento, para comunicarse y como protección. Este concepto era tan importante para esta cultura que había una hoguera enorme en la ciudad: el Templo Vestal, donde el fuego de Vesta, la diosa del hogar, ardía constantemente y jamás se apagaba. La flama sagrada estaba bajo la protección de soldados que exponían su vida para preservarlo en caso de una invasión.

La hoguera era el lugar donde se honraba a la diosa Vesta en los hogares. En ella las mujeres cocinaban preparando los alimentos. Siempre se ofrecía parte de la comida a Vesta en el fuego, pidiendo sus bendiciones y su protección. A menudo, los esposos tenían asignaciones militares que los mantenían alejados del hogar durante años y años. Sus esposas se quedaban con los hijos y se esperaba que fueran amas de casa, pero a menudo también atendían los negocios familiares y aguardaban fielmente el regreso de sus esposos. Elevaban plegarias a Vesta para que los miembros de su familia regresaran sanos y salvos y para que no se apagara el fuego del amor. Esta práctica inspiró la frase: "Mantener ardiendo los fuegos del hogar".

Si la carta de la chimenea aparece en tu adivinación, se te pide que analices tu idea de lo que el hogar y la familia significan para ti. Dedícate a desarrollar tu fuego del "amor" y a mantenerlo ardiendo y resplandeciente. Haz que tus relaciones sean tu prioridad. Si hay un conflicto en tu hogar y en tu familia, ha llegado el momento de dar pasos concretos para abordar ese tema en forma definitiva. Si tú o un miembro de tu familia están lejos del hogar por un viaje o por razones de trabajo, debes saber que se te está protegiendo.

LÁMPARA DE CALABAZA

Protección

¡Calabaza! ¡Calabaza!
Permíteme darle forma a mi protección,
ilumina el exterior con tu luz,
rechazar el mal y reflexionar.

Halloween no sería lo mismo si no hiciéramos lámparas de calabaza con rostros aterradores. Resplandecen en los porches de las casas, en las mesas del comedor y en todas partes. Las lámparas de calabaza tienen, de hecho, una historia muy rica y un mensaje espiritual.

El término original para la lámpara de calabaza (en inglés *jack-o'-lantern*) era *will-o'-the-wisp* (fuego fatuo), un término inglés antiguo. Se refiere a un manojo de varas que se usaba para encender una flama o se utilizaba como antorcha. Los celtas, los irlandeses y los habitantes de las tierras altas de Escocia tallaban y daban forma a diversas verduras invernales; no solo usaban calabazas, sino también chirivías, zanahorias o betabeles. La época cercana al *Samhain* (Halloween) era, por supuesto, la época en que se decía que las hadas y los duendes vagaban sin rumbo, así que la gente quería que las lámparas fueran aterradoras, pero que al mismo tiempo iluminaran los caminos en la oscuridad.

Hoy en día, tallar calabazas ha llegado a ser un arte en sí y un auténtico ícono de Halloween. Podemos encontrar diseños intrincados, aterradores y graciosos en todas las casas donde se celebra esta fiesta. Actualmente se usa luz eléctrica y también velas para iluminar el interior de las lámparas de calabaza.

Si una lámpara de calabaza te ilumina con su luz, debes saber que estás protegido, que eres capaz de crear la vida que deseas y que el universo te apoya en ese proyecto. Los límites son importantes, pues le enseñan a la gente la forma de relacionarnos, así que si sacas esta carta, eso significa que tal vez desees renovar tus relaciones o establecer relaciones nuevas.

GOZO

Alegría en el presente

Yo estoy aquí,
estoy donde estoy.
Con plenitud de vida y presente,
las tensiones son una farsa.

Además de los "uuuuuuu" de los fantasmas no muy aterradores que salen a pedir dulces en la noche de Halloween, uno de los sonidos más comunes que escuchas es la risa. Hay mucha alegría en Halloween y puede ser una de las noches más divertidas del año si permitimos que sea parte de nuestra vida.

Tenemos vidas muy ocupadas: ya sea que estemos estudiando, que nos encarguemos del hogar, que tengamos un trabajo muy demandante o todas estas cosas a la vez, parece que no tenemos mucho tiempo para detenernos, estar presentes y disfrutar exactamente el momento y el lugar en el que estamos. Se ha dicho que el primer paso de un cambio verdadero es hacer un alto y reconocer que en realidad necesitamos un cambio. Aunque a veces podríamos sentir que hay muy pocas cosas por las cuales alegrarnos y que hay demasiadas cosas que necesitamos cambiar, siempre podemos sentirnos agradecidos por algo que tenemos justo ahora y tener fuerza en esa posición.

Ha llegado el momento de encontrar alegría en el momento presente y de sentirla más a menudo. Si esta carta aparece en tu adivinación, está anunciando la llegada de más felicidad y de un gozo profundo en tu vida. ¡Es un buen augurio!

Busca activamente el placer y desarrolla más cosas que te den alegría personal y risa en tu vida. Después de todo, si hacemos citas con el dentista ¿por qué no hacer citas para nuestro propio placer?

DAMA DE LOS MUERTOS

Aceptación e igualdad

Pálida, sales de la noche
con encajes rojos,
con una corona de flores.
Traes belleza a la muerte,
la igualdad y el gozo
que hay bajo tierra.

La icónica dama de la muerte, con el rostro tan pálido como el de una calavera, con ojos de zombi y ricas flores rojas funerarias adornando su cabello, se ha convertido en uno de los símbolos mejor conocidos de Halloween y del *Día de Muertos* de México.

El modelo original de esta llamativa dama de la muerte se remonta a la antigua diosa azteca Mictecacihuatl. Al paso del tiempo, esta figura conservó el equilibrio entre la belleza y el horror, y llegó a ser la figura gráfica moderna de la "Catrina". También se dice que la identidad de la "Catrina" original se basa en mujeres que eran muy ricas y tenían todo lo que deseaban en la vida. Sin embargo, la muerte se lleva a todos por igual. Por tanto, la "Catrina" le recordaba a la gente que sin importar lo hermosa, rica o popular que sea una persona, al final la muerte nos lleva a todos.

La cultura mexicana tiene una larga historia de "reírse de la muerte" y de verla simplemente como otro aspecto de la vida. En cierta forma, la muerte es el último tabú en muchas culturas occidentales. Tendemos a ocultar todo lo relacionado con la muerte y quizás algunos de nosotros ni siquiera hemos visto el cuerpo de alguien que ha muerto, sin embargo, esto era mucho más común en el pasado.

Solo si reconocemos que la muerte es un proceso natural que llegará a la vida de todos nosotros en algún momento, podremos afirmar la vida. Esta actitud nos libera de gran parte del miedo a la muerte. Si desde el principio se aborda una situación con una actitud ligera, eso podría ayudar mucho. Si te estás aferrando a algo que ya no te es útil, en especial si se trata de cosas materiales, simplifica las cosas y despréndete de ello.

LA LÁMPARA

Remembranza

Enciendo una sola vela
en una lámpara para ti,
una sola flama en las tinieblas
que refleja la autenticidad de mi corazón.

Aunque hacer lámparas de calabaza para ahuyentar a los espíritus es una tradición, existe una tradición más antigua: encender una vela o una lámpara en la noche de Halloween y dejarla en la ventana como una forma de guiar al hogar a las personas que ya han muerto.

Como un símbolo de remembranza y también como la costumbre de "dejar las luces encendidas" para quienes deseen "volver a casa", la lámpara se dejaba encendida para iluminar la noche y tal vez incluso para aliviar la tristeza que la familia sintió por la muerte de sus seres queridos.

Esta carta nos recuerda que es positivo recordar a quienes se han ido celebrando su vida en lugar de llorando su muerte. El hecho es que las personas con quienes no tuvimos una buena relación o incluso aquellas con quienes no simpatizábamos, nos dejan lecciones valiosas. En ocasiones aprendemos más de nuestro némesis que de nuestros amigos, de modo que las tinieblas pueden iluminar nuestros puntos fuertes y nuestros verdaderos valores para que podamos vivirlos con mayor claridad y plenitud.

MEDIANOCHE

La hora más mágica de todas

Las tinieblas me envuelven
la hora del hechizo espera
verdadera magia y encantamiento
y hechizos que cambian el destino.

La mitad de la noche, la medianoche, es la hora en que se cree que los fantasmas, las brujas, los demonios necrófagos y la magia suelen estar activos. Los momentos de transición, como el mediodía, el momento entre los cambios de mareas o incluso la luna nueva, son por tradición instantes poderosos para la transformación mágica.

En algunas tradiciones cristianas, la hora de los hechizos es a las tres de la madrugada porque es la hora opuesta a la hora en que se dice que murió Cristo, las tres de la tarde.

Pero existe un consenso según el cual la medianoche es la hora de mayor magia, en especial en la época de Halloween. Se dice que en cuanto el reloj marca la medianoche en Halloween, los espíritus atraviesan el velo y si son benévolos, traen mensajes positivos. Si no son muy benévolos, son traviesos y en el mejor de los casos juegan bromas; en el peor de los casos causan estragos.

Date la oportunidad de relajarte en la oscuridad apacible de la medianoche. Tal vez sientas que es tu hora más oscura pero debes saber que la luz regresará. La aurora siempre viene después de la noche más negra. También debes saber que es importante reconocer que todos tenemos tinieblas en nuestro interior, del mismo modo en que tenemos luz, y esto no es algo de lo que debamos escondernos.

MOMIA

Cambio

Arena en su boca,
envuelta en vendajes,
celosa de los vivos,
en camino a la vida eterna.

Los egipcios de la antigüedad tomaban la muerte muy en serio. No la veían como muchos de nosotros que sentimos que es un final que nos provoca miedo. Ellos veían la muerte como el inicio de una vida nueva y a menudo como el comienzo de la vida eterna en un lugar mejor, en el "más allá".

La práctica de honrar y preservar el cuerpo mediante un complejo proceso de momificación era un elemento central en la cultura del antiguo Egipto. No solo era un proceso físico de embalsamamiento, sino un ritual que se llevaba a cabo con todo cuidado para garantizar la preservación del cuerpo para el otro mundo. Otras culturas también momificaban a sus muertos; por ejemplo, los incas, los argentinos, los maoríes y muchas otras de las islas del estrecho de Torres en Australia.

En los relatos modernos de terror, la momia se ha convertido en un ícono. Desde las primeras historias de horror a principios del siglo XX hasta las películas que alcanzaron gran popularidad como *La momia* y *La momia regresa*, la trama normalmente se centra en el hecho de que la momia vuelve a la vida y maldice y persigue a los seres vivientes. El descubrimiento de las tumbas del rey Tutankamón y otros tesoros egipcios que estuvieron ocultos durante mucho tiempo, en la década de 1920 en particular, inició una explosión de películas y novelas relacionadas con momias.

Si sacas de la baraja la carta de la momia gimiente sabrás que el cambio es inevitable, y que sin importar cuánto te esfuerces, las cosas no permanecerán exactamente como están. Esta carta también indica que este cambio será ventajoso para ti. ¿Los finales, las puertas cerradas, las barreras? Solo son una pausa saludable y un indicio de que es necesario cambiar de tácticas. No se trata de una maldición, simplemente te señala que has desarrollado un patrón. Puedes tomar el control y cambiarlo.

CANTO DE LA NOCHE

Talentos ocultos

Canta un ave de color rojo rubí
en las tinieblas llenas de sonido,
como un regalo sin abrir,
con los listones todavía atados.

Es poco usual que las aves canten durante la noche; las que lo hacen se conocen como "cantores de las tinieblas" y casi siempre se les considera sagradas… ¡o aterradoras! Desde el ruiseñor que es como un cantante de ópera hasta la lechuza ululante, escuchar a un ave que no puedes ver cómo entreteje su magia en el cielo de la noche es algo que ha cautivado a los seres humanos a lo largo del tiempo.

En el pasado, en la época de Halloween, una noche en la que se dice que el velo entre los mundos llega a su punto más delgado, se consideraba que estas aves eran presagios o mensajeras de los dioses. Dependiendo de la cultura, sus cantos se percibían como de buena suerte y como algo positivo, o por el contrario, se les consideraba una advertencia relacionada con seguir cierto camino. En algunas mitologías, el ave de la noche podía guiar a las personas para que descubrieran sus talentos y su verdadero propósito; estas aves eran una especie de guías en las tinieblas que llevaban a la gente hacia el amanecer.

Si esta hermosa y tímida ave canta para ti y aparece durante tu adivinación, sabrás que debes quitarle la envoltura al regalo que eres tú mismo. No hay tiempo que perder. ¡Basta de excusas!

LECHUZA

Mirar sabiamente, actuar sabiamente

Tú que tienes alas silenciosas y sabiduría,
criatura de la noche que lo ves todo,
muéstrame el camino,
yo seguiré tu vuelo.

Durante miles de años, las lechuzas han sido parte de la tradición popular y se les ha considerado animales especiales o sagrados. Debido a sus enormes ojos de mirada directa y a su apariencia etérea, se cree que tienen sabiduría y que son heraldos de lo sobrenatural.

Existen cientos de especies de lechuzas y casi todas son aves nocturnas y carnívoras. Es interesante que tengan plumas de diseño especial, que hacen posible que vuelen en silencio durante la noche, lo que les da una increíble ventaja al cazar… ¡es como si tuvieran una modalidad de sigilo!

Se decía que numerosas deidades eran capaces de convertirse en lechuzas y tal vez la más famosa de ellas fue la diosa griega Atenea, conocida por su inteligencia y su capacidad estratégica. Incluso en nuestros días, Atenas, la capital de Grecia, tiene a la lechuza de Atenea en su símbolo oficial.

Si la lechuza ululante viene a buscarte en esta noche de Halloween, eso significa la necesidad de recibir consejos sabios o más información antes de tomar una decisión, eso garantizará la seguridad de tus acciones. Piensa antes de actuar emocionalmente y asegúrate de pensar basándote en estrategias, no en forma impulsiva.

VER EN LA ESFERA DE CRISTAL

Intuición

Suaviza tu mirada,
inicia el trance,
se abren mundos enteros,
comienza la danza.

Ver la esfera de cristal es la técnica de adivinación que permite a ver imágenes inconscientes (o imágenes de lo divino o lo sobrenatural) que aparecen en una superficie o al interior de ella. Las personas ven estas imágenes en una esfera de cristal, en un espejo negro, en el agua e incluso en la superficie del hielo. Es una técnica muy antigua que por tradición se lleva a cabo en *Samhain* (Halloween).

La clave para ver la esfera de cristal con éxito es estar tan relajado como sea posible, minimizar las distracciones, suavizar la mirada y permitir que algo se presente.

El enemigo de la capacidad de ver la esfera de cristal con éxito es la distracción... que podría venir del interior y del exterior. Desconecta el teléfono, la luz eléctrica, la música, y si estás viendo la esfera de cristal en el exterior, date el tiempo para sentirte a gusto en el entorno y escucha bien todos los sonidos para que tu mente no necesite interrumpir tu concentración posteriormente. También es de importancia vital que tranquilices a tu mente tanto como sea posible.

Si sueles meditar con regularidad, tal vez desees usar esa técnica, o de lo contrario, puedes simplemente cerrar los ojos y concentrarte para hacer tu respiración más lenta... esto por lo general es muy eficaz. Si tienes una pregunta específica que desees hacerle a un médium que usa la esfera de cristal, exprésala claramente. Luego, cuando te sientas relajado, dirígete al interior. Imagina que estás concentrando tu energía interna y luego enfócate en el punto del tercer ojo (el punto del chacra que se encuentra en el centro de la frente, justo arriba de las cejas) e imagina que se abre. Después mira con suavidad la superficie que vas a observar y simplemente permite que se formen imágenes y mira lo que te presentan. No involucres a tu mente racional; ¡esto tiene que ver con recibir no con pensar!

Si sacas esta carta, sugiero que trates de verla, para empezar. También indica que tal vez desees desarrollar más tu intuición y no confiar solo en la parte lógica de tu mente para encontrar respuestas. La verdadera sabiduría implica un equilibrio entre la lógica, la imaginación y la intuición.

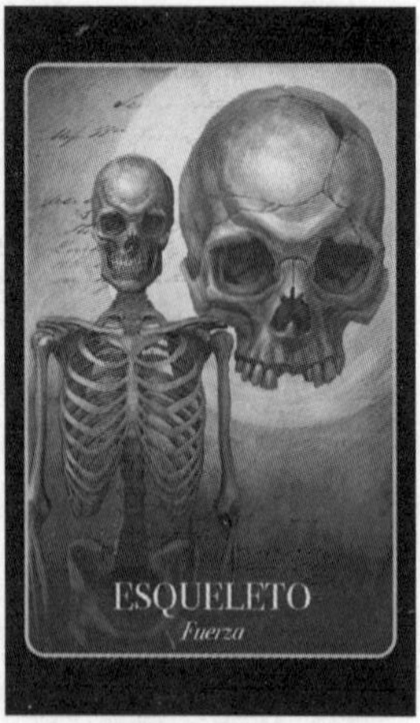

ESQUELETO
Fuerza

En el exterior es carne,
en el interior es hueso,
hay fuerza en la vulnerabilidad,
hemos crecido en el poder.

Halloween es un festival de terror. Se supone que debe asustarnos; se supone que debemos sentirnos agradablemente liberados al experimentar miedo. Salimos a pedir dulces siguiendo la tradición de "truco o trato", aunque sabemos que alguien podría sorprendernos; vemos películas de terror sabiendo que sentiremos temor. ¡Incluso nos disfrazamos de esqueletos, sin carne, y con los huesos a la vista de todos! En pocas palabras, en Halloween mostramos nuestra vulnerabilidad y también nuestra fortaleza para enfrentarnos a nuestros miedos.

Se requiere de una fuerza increíble para mostrar nuestra vulnerabilidad. A menudo podría ser el curso de acción más osado y también el más aterrador. Muchas veces, es un catalizador poderoso para el crecimiento personal, aunque no podamos percibirlo en ese momento.

Al mostrar lo que somos en realidad y al manifestar una vulnerabilidad equilibrada, podemos buscar y recibir mayor comprensión por parte de otras personas. Al admitir que estamos equivocados o que no tenemos la solución cuando se espera que la tengamos, creamos más espacio para resolver las cosas con mayor rapidez. Pedir ayuda y apoyo en lugar de actuar como mártires y sentir resentimiento, muestra fortaleza y sabiduría, no debilidad.

Si la carta del esqueleto capta tu atención, atrévete a mostrar fortaleza y vulnerabilidad si eso es lo que sientes en realidad. La vergüenza, el orgullo, el resentimiento o el remordimiento son cargas pesadas que no es necesario soportar durante la noche más oscura de todas.

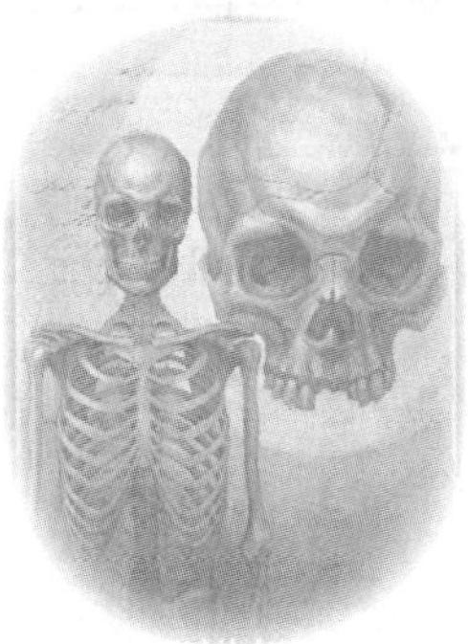

CALAVERA DE TINIEBLAS

Puntos ciegos

Quizás no tengamos deseos de entrar ahí,
a las sombras, a la oscuridad,
a lo desconocido.
Pero cuando buscamos, descubrimos
y nuestro poder crece.

La calavera de tinieblas, hermosa y misteriosa, nos anima a ver la parte de nosotros mismos que normalmente permanece oculta o tan fuera de la vista como sea posible.

Es probable que no mostremos aprecio o agrado por ciertos aspectos de nosotros mismos, y sin embargo a veces nuestros mayores tesoros están en estas áreas. Cuántas veces has escuchado de artistas famosos o personas muy exitosas en su campo que son víctimas de acoso por el hecho de ser diferentes; no obstante, el que sean distintas es lo que hace que sean tan poderosas.

Asimismo, todos nosotros, en cierta etapa de nuestra vida, tenemos ciertos "puntos ciegos" que podrían causarnos dolor y dificultades. Aunque no podamos ver la situación con claridad, los patrones de dolor que se repiten podrían alertarnos de su existencia…, son síntomas, por así decirlo. Por ejemplo, suceden las mismas cosas con frecuencia; a lo mejor la gente nos traiciona repetidamente; tal vez fallemos en algo muy seguido, o tengamos la tendencia a no terminar lo que hacemos. Podemos encontrar la paz y eliminar estos patrones trabajando para descubrir nuestro punto ciego o incluso consultando a nuestras amistades cercanas o a profesionales para que nos ayuden a ver lo que nosotros no podemos ver.

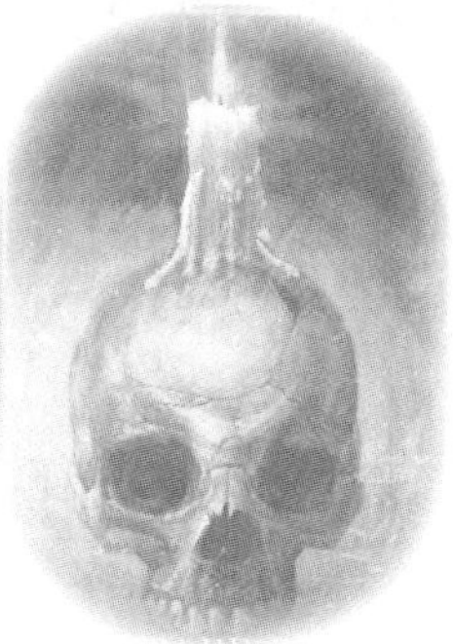

CALAVERA DE FLORES

Crear a través de las cenizas

Florecer y prosperar,
el trabajo debe hacerse,
a través del fuego y la ceniza
llega nuestra fortuna.

Antes de abrirse, las flores son los botones de una planta que brotó de algo muy pequeño, como una semilla o un bulbo. La semilla necesita tierra bien preparada y nutritiva para crecer y desarrollar su potencial. Algunas plantas y árboles solo tienen semillas después de sufrir a causa del fuego o después de un periodo de gran adversidad, como una sequía o una inundación.

A veces deseamos tener una vida diferente a la que llevamos y eso podría requerir de un cambio radical. A veces, para tener esa vida nueva, todo se hace pedazos y eso puede ser incómodo. Es posible que perdamos contacto con nuestras relaciones o que ellas cambien. Quizá perdamos nuestro trabajo; tal vez tengamos que mudarnos de casa o podríamos enfermarnos... todos estos son sucesos importantes que nos llevan a evaluar de nueva cuenta la "manera" en que vivimos.

La calavera de flores ilustra el hecho de que existe una certeza y al mismo tiempo cierto rigor en la realización de una nueva creación, o en volver a empezar. En ocasiones, el universo nos da una página en blanco para comenzar a trabajar; así podemos construir lo que queremos en realidad, y no conformarnos con menos. La calavera de flores no solo celebra una especie de energía de fénix, sino una energía de éxito y de lograr florecer plenamente en medio de la adversidad.

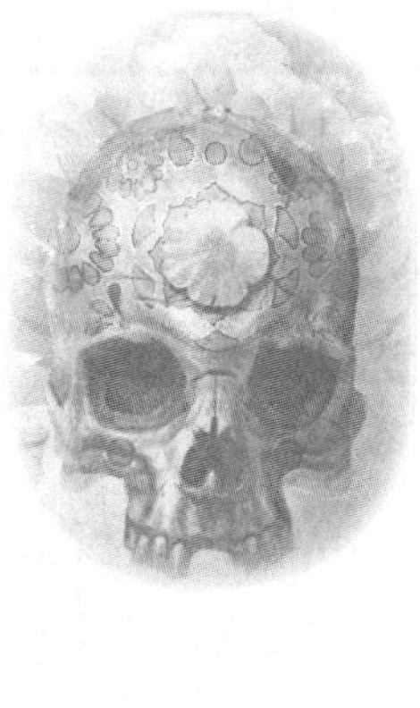

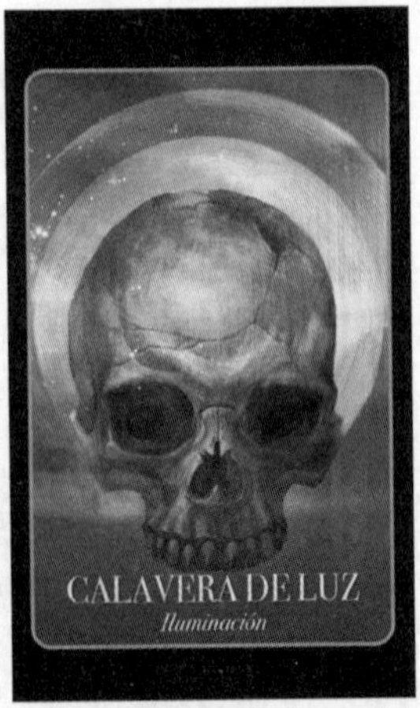

CALAVERA DE LUZ

Iluminación

Podemos permanecer en las tinieblas,
existir solo en las horas de la medianoche,
pero al encender la antorcha
la victoria es nuestra.

Como sugirió Jung, el famoso psicoterapeuta, conocer nuestro lado oscuro nos ayuda a enfrentar el lado oscuro de otros. Dedicar tiempo a "conocernos" y a tratar de entender nuestra naturaleza más destructiva o nuestro aspecto más sombrío puede llevarnos a vivir una felicidad enorme con menos ansiedad.

La idea de que se nos muestre el camino en los momentos más difíciles y el saber siempre que nunca estamos solos en las tinieblas es la clave de este elemento mágico. La luz normalmente es algo reconfortante, ¡pero a veces en realidad no queremos ver al "coco" que está debajo de la cama! Es tan aterrador y tan grande que no sabemos cómo vencerlo. Sin embargo, con solo iluminar esas tinieblas con la antorcha, la victoria es nuestra.

Si la calavera de luz entra en tu vida, sabrás que ha llegado el momento de abrirte por completo a la claridad de una iluminación brillante. Deja que otros te vean; trata de ver y de actuar con base en lo que se te muestra. Ya pasó el tiempo en el que queríamos ocultarnos, en el que queríamos fingir y soportábamos incomodidades aceptando el statu quo cuando en realidad eso no era apropiado para nosotros.

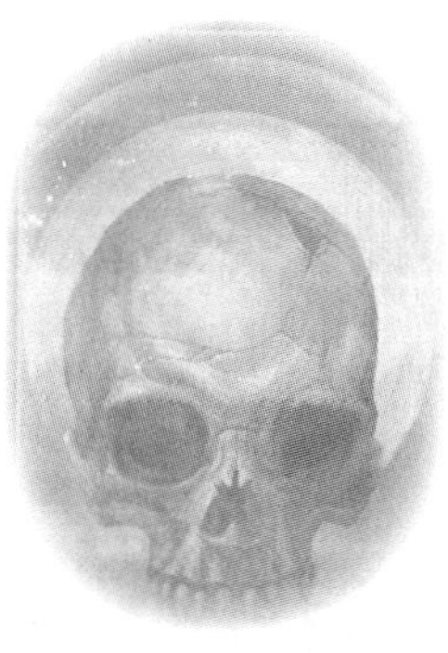

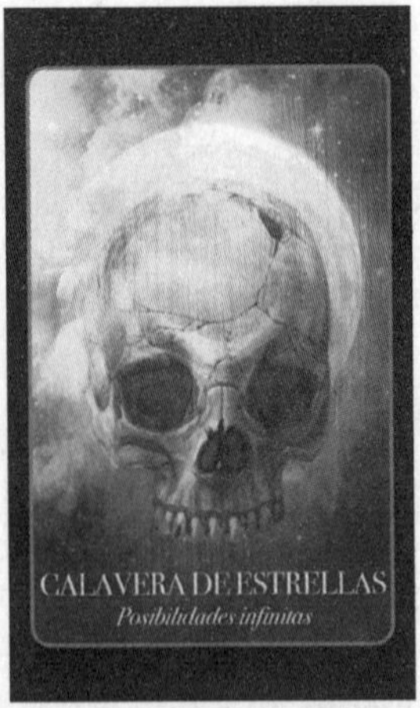

CALAVERA DE ESTRELLAS

Posibilidades infinitas

¿Por qué pensar en pequeña escala
cuando las galaxias giran en nuestro interior?
Date cuenta de que estás hecho
de lo que están hechas las estrellas
y ahí empiezan las posibilidades infinitas.

Esta calavera nos hace regresar a la idea de que todos estamos hechos de lo que están hechas las estrellas, ¡pero muchos de nosotros pensamos a pequeña escala! Todos nacimos con un lienzo en blanco para pintar en él y en realidad somos un cielo abierto de posibilidades.

Es fácil sentirse pequeño en un mundo que está tan ocupado, que es tan impersonal y que al parecer está demasiado absorto en sí mismo. En ocasiones podemos sentirnos perdidos y no ver con claridad la dirección que debemos seguir, perdiendo de vista nuestro lugar en el cosmos. La calavera de estrellas nos recuerda que lo único que nos limita es nuestra imaginación y las fronteras que nos marcamos. Si podemos soñar algo, es posible.

Esta carta indica que necesitas pensar en grande y pensar más ampliamente sobre tu futuro y sobre lo que te gustaría lograr. Tal vez hay creencias falsas, a menudo antiguas, que ya no te sirven cuando estás creciendo y cambiando. A veces estas creencias ni siquiera son tuyas..., tal vez te las transmitieron tus padres o la comunidad en general, pero sientes que no estás de acuerdo con ellas. Necesitas esforzarte, con todo tu corazón y con toda tu alma, para vivir la vida que deseas y para honrar tus propios anhelos y tu verdad.

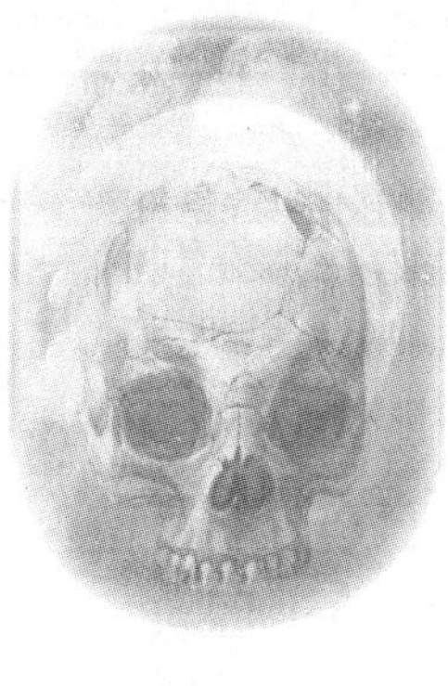

ARAÑA

Comunidad y tejer redes

Teje su seda sola,
en la oscuridad, con la esperanza de captar
sueños que se peguen a ella,
en una enorme red de conexión.

Masas de telarañas pegajosas son el toque final de las decoraciones de Halloween. La idea de una casa embrujada llena de la "obra de arte" de una araña enorme y peluda, es un detalle de horror clásico. Pero hasta los que simpatizamos con nuestras amigas de ocho patas, ¡nos sacudimos de inmediato una telaraña con la que nos topamos en la oscuridad!

Aunque la mayoría de las arañas no son venenosas, los seres humanos sentimos un miedo innato hacia ellas. Tal vez es por sus colmillos o por su veneno. Tal vez es por todas esas patas que se mueven al mismo tiempo. Tal vez es por los lugares donde viven, a menudo oscuros y ocultos…, o tal vez es por la forma en que nuestra cultura occidental popular las ha demonizado haciéndolas parecer gigantescas, feroces ¡y capaces de devorar seres humanos! Sin embargo, algunas culturas ven a las arañas con respeto en formas muy positivas. En muchas tradiciones amerindias, por ejemplo, la araña es la criatura que da vida a otros animales y sostiene la red de la vida. La diosa Abuela Araña (y también hay una Mujer Araña) es una deidad importante que lleva sabiduría, seguridad y comunicación a todas las tribus. Ella ha creado y ha tejido todas las estrellas del cielo y hace telarañas suaves para dar descanso y apoyo a quienes están llenos de problemas.

Las telarañas pueden verse como un símbolo de conexión, no necesariamente como una trampa. A veces existe una línea muy fina entre el apoyo que recibimos de la familia o la comunidad y el control al que estamos sujetos por parte de ellos. Esta carta se relaciona con este discernimiento. También sugiere que revises la forma en que te comunicas con la comunidad, en el trabajo o con las personas en general, y tomes acciones para mejorarla o hacerla en una forma ligeramente distinta. También indica que debe haber un equilibrio entre lo que haces por ti mismo y lo que haces por otros… Si damos demasiado al exterior, nuestra fuerza disminuye y no podemos tejer una red de apoyo para nosotros mismos.

TRUCO O TRATO

Travesura y juego

Acechando y pisando fuerte,
con ojos brillantes y canastas para dulces,
nuestros rostros y cuerpos
ya no nos pertenecen.
Risas, esqueletos y ataúdes de dulce.

Es muy divertido salir a pedir dulces siguiendo la tradición de "truco o trato", ¿pero por qué lo hacemos?

En la antigüedad, la gente creía que en Halloween, al caer la noche, llegaban espíritus traviesos y tal vez también espíritus agresivos o espíritus más alegres, más benévolos. Ellos pensaban que si se vestían como espíritus (o tal vez como criaturas menos aterradoras) no se les reconocería como seres humanos y no serían atacados por los fantasmas. La idea de provocar algo de caos, actuando como uno de ellos era una forma de imitarlos (y de divertirse) en la noche de Halloween. En Inglaterra, durante la Edad Media, se le daba a esta práctica el nombre de *souling* (actuar como almas).

Hoy en día la tradición de "truco o trato" es todo un evento. Dedicamos mucho tiempo, gastamos mucho dinero y nos esforzamos mucho para disfrazarnos de las criaturas más aterradoras e incluso vestirnos como nuestras celebridades favoritas y otros ídolos de la cultura pop. En lugar de las tradicionales manzanas acarameladas y los panes *barmbrack*, repartimos una variedad alucinante de golosinas. Eso no importa, pues la idea de ahuyentar la muerte y la oscuridad sigue en pie.

Yo creo que el "truco o trato" de nuestros días también une a las comunidades, ya que permite que nuestras familias y nuestras amistades conozcan a las personas del área en una forma que no es agresiva y es divertida. Muchos de nosotros no conocemos a nuestros vecinos, ni siquiera a los que viven en la casa da al lado, y Halloween nos da una excusa para no ser tan reservados y ampliar nuestros límites.

Si sacas la carta de truco o trato en tu adivinación, tal vez ha llegado el momento de examinar el papel que tienen el juego y la travesura en tu propia vida. No tienes que ser un niño o una niña para relajarte y darte tiempo para jugar, y puedes compartir ese gozo con otros. A veces tememos cometer errores y el juego es una forma de aliviar la presión que nos causamos para siempre hacer todo a la perfección. Además, vale la pena saber que existe un equilibrio entre la manipulación y la travesura; la manipulación no es agradable y la travesura contiene, en su esencia, un sentido de diversión irrelevante.

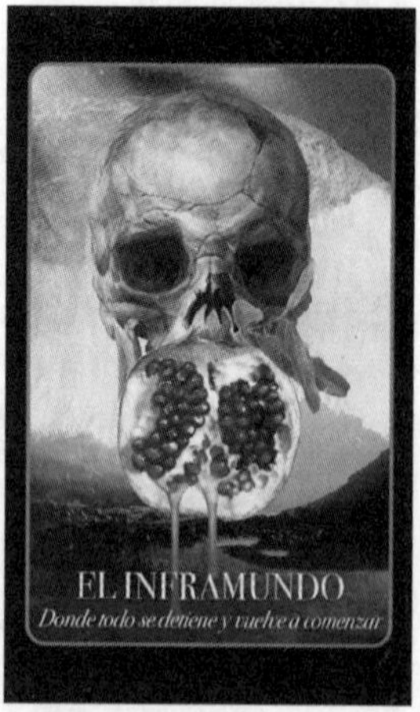

EL INFRAMUNDO

Donde todo se detiene y vuelve a comenzar

Otro mundo, lleno de sombras,
viajar desde el lecho de muerte,
donde nos detenemos y nos transformamos,
en el reino de los muertos.

La idea de un "inframundo", de todo un mundo al que iremos después de la muerte, es un concepto que está presente en una enorme variedad de culturas y épocas. Los sumerios, los turcos, los incas, los griegos y también los siberianos, los maoríes y el pueblo jemer (la etnia predominante en Camboya), todos tenían una palabra especial para referirse al inframundo. Lo que es diferente es la forma en que esas culturas abordan este concepto… El hecho de que lo vean como un lugar de descanso donde uno rejuvenece o como un lugar de horror y de castigo.

El infierno de los cristianos es un lugar de tinieblas, fuego y castigo. El inframundo egipcio es un lugar de juicio, de paz y de renovación. En la cultura maorí es un lugar intermedio de espera, sabiduría y transición. Muchos de los mitos que mencionan al inframundo a menudo incluyen el concepto de un lugar de espera, de pruebas, y a la larga, un lugar donde se llevará a cabo un juicio. También puede ser un lugar de gozo y paz.

Si se presenta la carta del inframundo en tu lectura de cartas, se te pide que consideres exactamente lo que tienes que hacer para transformar tu vida en algo que sea más fácil o más auténtico para ti. Esto podría incluir un cambio de rumbo. Podría incluir dificultades y pruebas. Sigue adelante. Aunque las cosas podrían decaer o desaparecer y sientas que tu vida está vacía por un tiempo, esto es temporal. Se está creando el espacio donde podrás crear algo nuevo.

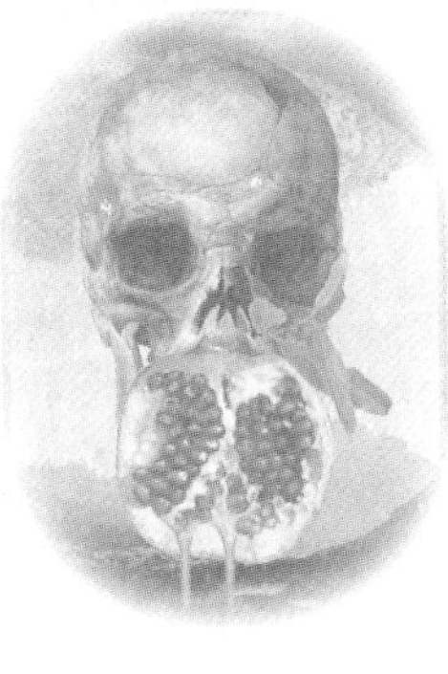

VAMPIRO

Inteligencia emocional

Lo más profundo,
lo más frío,
la sed de sangre,
el hoyo que nunca se llena,
el deseo como una inundación.

Aunque en la literatura, en el cine y en los juegos encontramos incontables ejemplos de vampiros, de alguna manera el arquetipo de la criatura sedienta de sangre, que ronda por las noches y que en cierta forma es elegante, se sigue reinventando para seducir a las nuevas generaciones.

Aunque la forma del vampiro, hermosa y en cierta forma deseable, no empezó a entrar realmente a la conciencia pública sino hasta mediados del siglo XIX, la idea de seres humanos que se alimentaban de sangre, que es la fuente de la vida, es mucho más antigua. Los egipcios, los sumerios, los habitantes de la India y los pueblos de los Balcanes tienen mitos en los que aparecen criaturas similares a los vampiros.

El vampiro es una figura interesante porque es horripilante y al mismo tiempo deseable. El que alguien nos desee tanto que quiera estar totalmente unido a nosotros es reconfortante... hasta que nos damos cuenta de que no queda mucho en nosotros que podamos dar.

La mayoría de nosotros hemos escuchado hablar del concepto del vampirismo emocional; la idea de que la gente se alimenta de nuestra energía, de nuestra buena voluntad y se aproveche de nosotros mediante la manipulación y para satisfacer sus incesantes necesidades.

Si la carta del vampiro aparece en tu lectura de las cartas, podría indicar que alguien te está consumiendo en esta forma y que ha llegado el momento de poner límites más fuertes. Necesitamos estar muy conscientes de aquello que nos da energía en la vida y de aquello que nos quita esa energía. Debemos tener claro que necesitamos que la gente nos necesite y de las razones por las cuales invitamos a esa clase de gente a nuestras casas, a los lugares donde trabajamos y a nuestras vidas, si de hecho están cerca de nosotros. Desarrollar una inteligencia emocional en nuestro interior nos ayudará a defendernos de esta clase de ataques emocionales y psíquicos, y hará posible que cultivemos todo tipo de relaciones saludables y de igualdad.

EL VELO

El futuro

Hay una cortina de niebla
que nos divide a todos,
el velo que esta noche se hace más delgado.
El tejido se vuelve transparente
y el futuro ya no está borroso.

Los celtas de la antigüedad llamaban *Samhain* (que se pronuncia so-en) a la noche más larga del año. Creían que había un velo de niebla que separaba al mundo de los muertos del mundo de los vivos, pero que en dos noches del año, *Samhain* y *Beltaine* (la noche más corta) ese velo se hacía más delgado.

El que el velo se adelgazara significaba que los ancestros estaban más cerca que nunca y que incluso los dioses también lo estaban. Eso podría significar que sería más probable que ocurrieran comunicaciones de parte de los muertos y que la adivinación (cuando la Divinidad nos habla a través de algo) sería más eficaz.

Por lo tanto, si al usar este oráculo se levanta el velo, debes saber que otros mundos están cerca. Escucha especialmente los mensajes que podrían llegarte sobre tu futuro. Mira lo que deseas que suceda; haz planes, determina tus intenciones, ¡piensa en grande!

HOMBRE LOBO

Explorar lo salvaje

La luminosidad le da vida,
se eleva una luna salvaje,
dolor, sangre y colmillos,
pelaje, aullidos y apariencia de lobo.

Después de una lucha dolorosa, intensa, desgarradora, contra el cambio, el hombre se deja vencer por la magia. Aúlla sin control bajo la luna llena; ahora este ser, mitad hombre y mitad lobo, se yergue gruñendo ¡y va en busca de sangre! ¡Sí! ¡Todos conocemos el poder del hombre lobo!

Cuando terminaron los juicios contra brujos y brujas en Europa, se desarrolló un interés intenso en el hombre lobo como parte de los relatos populares; este interés evolucionó tanto que el hombre lobo llegó a ser el tema central de cuentos de terror. Esto ha sido muy constante a partir de entonces y el hombre lobo o "licántropo", ha estado presente con regularidad tanto en relatos orales como escritos. Por supuesto, durante los últimos cien años el hombre lobo ha sido el protagonista de películas de gran popularidad, como *American Werewolf in London (Hombre lobo americano en Londres)*, y de libros como la reciente serie *Twilight Saga (La saga crepúsculo)*.

El hombre lobo es una especie de ser metamórfico, pero es un ser que por tradición tiene muy poco control sobre su salvajismo. En cierta forma, se libra dentro de su cuerpo una batalla entre la "civilización" y la naturaleza de un animal salvaje. La vitalidad, la fuerza y la libertad del animal contra la razón, el control y el intelecto del hombre… ¿pero cuál es la fuerza dominante? ¿Dónde está el equilibrio sano entre nuestra naturaleza animal, que es salvaje, libre y conectada a la naturaleza, y nuestro carácter humano radicalmente "civilizado" que está separado de la naturaleza o la domina?

El hombre lobo nos pide que tomemos en cuenta este equilibrio y que lleguemos a lo profundo de nuestras propias ideas sobre lo salvaje, la independencia y la tarea de ser custodios del planeta. ¿Cuándo fue la última vez que pasaste todo un día al aire libre? ¿Cuándo fue la última vez que echaste la cabeza hacia atrás y le aullaste a la luna? ¿Sofocas la vitalidad y la curiosidad de tu cuerpo y de tu mente sentándote todo el día frente a una computadora? El hombre lobo te reta a crear un equilibrio entre la naturaleza y tu propia naturaleza.

INVIERNO

Lo sagrado de hacer una pausa

Camino suavemente,
ya que la tierra se está quedando dormida.
Una canción de cuna para descansar y detenerse,
para guardar los secretos del alma.

La muerte es aterradora a pesar de que no podemos escapar de ella (o tal vez debido a eso). Sin embargo, cuando llega el invierno, sabemos que muestra una muerte literal y metafísica. En algunos lugares del planeta, los climas extremosos hacen que la nieve y el hielo cubran todo lo que nos habla de la vida y el terreno queda improductivo e inmóvil.

En el invierno la tierra se desacelera, hay menos luz y en ocasiones el clima es más húmedo. Muchas plantas se secan, muchos animales son menos activos y a lo largo de los siglos el invierno ha sido una época menos activa y más difícil para aquellos que trabajan la tierra para su sustento. El invierno con frecuencia trae consigo el final de un ciclo de vida… una muerte literal o en sentido figurado.

Si sacas la carta del invierno, ha llegado el momento de dejar morir lo que ya no te es útil. Aunque parece natural y correcto permitir que se sequen las cosas que te han estado molestando, lo que realmente deberíamos hacer es cambiarlas. Cualquier cosa que sea superflua, adicional y molesta, déjala ir.

LA BRUJA

Tejedora terrenal de los mundos

Tierra, aire, fuego, agua,
una mujer hermosa, una mujer extraña,
tejedora de los mundos, hija de la luna,
bruja: la que cataliza los cambios.

Durante aproximadamente dos milenios se han dicho cosas horribles sobre las brujas. En un principio, fueron las sanadoras o las mujeres ingeniosas de la aldea. La palabra inglesa *witch* (bruja) viene de la palabra celta *wicce* que significa "tejedora" o "sabia". Cuando la nueva religión, el cristianismo, se extendió, se dijo que los custodios de las antiguas tradiciones paganas, entre ellos las brujas, eran malvados y, como ya sabemos, se les persiguió. Se vieron obligados a ocultarse en lugares subterráneos (o bajo el cielo oscuro de la noche) y quedaron a merced de los malentendidos y las tinieblas.

Sin embargo, en el ambiente de Halloween, vemos a las brujas como las tejedoras de magia y de cambio. Mediante hechizos y rituales, e incluso con recetas de hierbas (¡que, por supuesto, a menudo se preparaban en calderos!), las brujas tejen en sinergia los poderes de este mundo y del otro para resolver problemas y para sanar.

Tener en tus manos la carta de la bruja, significa que puedes tejer tus propios cambios a lo largo de tu vida ¡y que la magia realmente está en movimiento! Debes entender que tienes poder y que es real. Esta carta también podría indicar que otros pueden sentirse amenazados por el hecho de que desarrolles tu poder personal y que posiblemente no aprecien ni les agraden los cambios que puedas lograr a medida que creces. Debes prepararte para esto y no desanimarte. Llegarán a ti nuevas amistades y mejores oportunidades.

ZOMBI

Control

Los muertos se levantan,
balbuceo de voces,
en busca de nuestro cerebro,
nuestros gritos resuenan.

Recientemente, los zombis se han puesto de moda, casi al igual que los vampiros. Si enciendes la televisión, no puedes escapar de los gemidos y gruñidos de estos muertos vivientes. (¡Y de hecho parecen tener la intención de apoderarse de tu cerebro!) Incluso, hay marchas públicas de zombis, en las que las personas se disfrazan de zombis y "aparecen" en masa en las calles de las ciudades.

Pero los zombis no solo son un ícono divertido de la cultura popular. Por tradición, se les relaciona ante todo con la religión del vudú que ha florecido en África y en Haití. Se dice que los zombis son cuerpos muertos animados mediante los encantamientos que entona un hechicero, conocido como *bokor*, que por lo general les da vida con un propósito determinado.

Se dice que el hechicero capta una parte del alma viviente para animar al cuerpo y que esta siempre es una acción temporal, porque el alma no puede estar en ese cuerpo en descomposición durante mucho tiempo o porque Dios va a recuperar esa alma.

Uno de los aspectos más aterradores de la idea de los zombis, es que nuestras almas y nuestro ser consciente están atrapados dentro de un cuerpo que no hace lo que nosotros deseamos, sino lo que desea otra persona. Otro de estos aspectos aterradores es la idea de ser enterrados vivos... Se dice que ese ha sido el destino de algunas personas que quedan atrapadas en cuerpos que ya están muertos.

Si el zombi llega vacilante a tu vida, ha llegado el momento de analizar el concepto del control. ¿Quieres controlarlo todo dejando muy poco a la expresión libre? ¿Eliges parejas que no son iguales a ti para poder manipularlas con mayor facilidad y cambiarlas de modo que sean como a ti te gusta? ¿O permites que otros te hagan eso? Si no estás viviendo tu vida más auténtica, ha llegado el momento de encontrar la razón y hacer cambios.

INVISIBILIDAD

Autenticidad

El corazón late, sentimos,
pero no vemos.
Ellos nos tocan, nos estremecemos,
llegan sin ser vistos.

¿Recuerdas esa sensación que a veces se tiene de que alguien te está observando? No puedes verlo, pero tienes la sensación clara de que "hay alguien ahí". Se te eriza la piel de la nuca. Crees que ves algo con el rabillo del ojo, pero cuando volteas, no hay nada… solo el aire vacío. Este es el poder de la invisibilidad; el miedo indirecto y la amenaza encubierta de tener que luchar contra algo que no puedes ver.

Los seres humanos tenemos un sentido de la vista muy agudo, así que no es sorprendente que nos sintamos intranquilos cuando hay cosas que no vemos. En la antigüedad, la gente creía que todo tipo de criaturas, míticas y físicas, y por supuesto las deidades, podían volverse invisibles a voluntad. Cuando consideramos que hay animales que tienen un camuflaje tan maravilloso, por el color de su piel o por la forma en que se comportan, que a veces aunque los tengamos frente a nuestros ojos no podemos distinguirlos en el entorno, nos damos cuenta de que la invisibilidad no es un concepto tan lejano a la realidad.

En muchas culturas, la idea de seres que pueden observarnos sin ser detectados era, y sigue siendo, común. Se dice que los genios, los ángeles, los espíritus de la naturaleza, las hadas e incluso quienes practican la magia, como los hechiceros o hechiceras, tienen el poder de aparecer y desaparecer a voluntad. Posteriormente, en la literatura y después en el cine, la invisibilidad llegó a ser un poder común y ahora tenemos súper héroes ficticios que son invisibles e incluso tenemos mantos de invisibilidad.

El concepto de la invisibilidad es una espada de dos filos. Aunque es una herramienta poderosa para obtener información o para ayudar a alguien sin ser vistos, las personas que la usan podrían enterarse de información que tal vez no es para ellas y podrían sacarla de contexto o utilizarla en forma no ética. Es un poder de manipulación y es fácil abusar de él.

La idea de ocultarse y no ser visto es también un aspecto importante del lado oscuro de este concepto. Todos hemos nacido para iluminar al mundo con nuestra luz y para desempeñar el rol que nos corresponde. Ocultar nuestros talentos, no expresar lo que somos en realidad, robarnos las ideas de otros o trabajar siendo "otra persona" en lugar de ser lo que somos en realidad, son aspectos que debes considerar si sacas esta carta en una tirada.

SOBRE LA AUTORA

Stacey Demarco es la bruja moderna; le apasiona llevar la magia práctica a toda la gente e inspirarla para que tenga una conexión más profunda con la naturaleza. Es autora de los *bestsellers Witch in the Boardroom (Bruja en la sala de juntas), Witch in the Bedroom (Bruja en la recámara)*, y posteriormente escribió, *The Coffee Oracle (El oráculo del café)*. Es coautora, con la médium Jade-Sky, de *The No Excuses Guide to Soulmates (La guía sin excusas para las almas gemelas)* y *The No Excuses Guide to Work and Purpose (La guía sin excusas para el trabajo y el propósito)*. Las cartas de sus oráculos, *Gods & Titans (Dioses y titanes)* y *Goddesses & Sirens (Diosas y sirenas)*, con obras de arte de Jimmy Manton, que honran a las deidades masculinas y femeninas, ya están en la segunda edición, y la baraja de sitios sagrados y llenos de energía, *Earth Power Oracle (Oráculo del poder de la tierra)*, que se publicó en 2014, fue muy bien recibido y ampliamente elogiado. El *Ocean Guardians Diary (Diario de los guardianes del océano)* en el que presenta al Capitán Paul Watson, un activista legendario, apoya a la Organización Pastores del Mar (Sea Shepherd Organisation) cada año.

Stacey es una vegetariana comprometida, es activista a favor de los animales y disfruta las aventuras y los viajes;

vive en Sidney, Australia, cerca de la orilla del mar, con su esposo y sus mascotas. Stacey tiene consultas privadas, imparte seminarios y dirige retiros centrados en la naturaleza para guiar a las "Almas Indómitas", a nivel nacional e internacional.

Para mayor información visitar: www.themodernwitch.com.

TÍTULOS DE ESTA COLECCIÓN

El verdadero tarot de Marsella. *Kris Hadar*

Tarot animales divinos. *Lisa Hunt*

Tarot Babilonia. *Sandra Tabatha*

Tarot místico del gato. *Lunaea Weatherstone*

Tarot Halloween. *Stacey Demarco*

Tarot de los Orishas. *Fernando Silva Tonche*

Tarot Oro. *Ciro Marchetti / Barbara Moore*

Tarot revelaciones. *Zach Wong*

Tarot Steampunk. *Barbara Moore*